God's Witnesses in the Heart of the World

God's Witnesses in the Heart of the World

Leonardo Boff, O.F.M.

Translated and Edited by
ROBERT FATH, C.M.F.

Claret Center for Resources
in Spirituality

RELIGIOUS LIFE SERIES
Volume Three

Chicago Los Angeles Manila
1981

Printed in the United States of America
Library of Congress Catalog Card Number: 81-65303

Originally written in Portuguese by Leonardo Boff, O.F.M., and translated into Spanish by M. Díez Presa, C.M.F., in 1977. Spanish title was *Testigos de Dios en el Corazón del Mundo,* published by Publicaciones Claretianas in Madrid.

Contents

Preface

Renewal in religious life does not arise simply from the elaboration of new ideas, from a more incisive interpretation of a founder's rule, or from the adapting of a community's lifestyle to the demands of a changed world. All authentic renewal is rooted in a strengthened and deepened experience of God. Only in relation to such an experience can, and should, new theoretical constructs be articulated and those of the past reinterpreted, and only thus can a more suitable presence of religious life in the Church and in society be sought.

The texts collected here—born of events and without any prior systematic intention—are meant only to translate into a reflection of faith what is already being sought for, and concretely lived out, in many Latin American religious communities. The human problems created by underdevelopment on the one hand, and aspirations to liberation on the other, turn out to be theological metaphors revealing God and, at the same time, placing inescapable demands on the Christian conscience. Religious have placed themselves in a position of listening and obedience (*ob-audire*) to this concrete word of

God. Committed to the wretched masses of our people, they have felt themselves evangelized by them and asked for explanations. These religious have had an extremely profound religious experience, which is even now bearing its fruit in religious life after being duly elaborated. These fruits are not the exclusive property of Latin American religious life, but belong to the Church in general, incarnated and concretized in this region in a special and specific way. Thus we believe the reflections that follow can benefit anyone seeking the face of God—the face discerned and discovered by all great religious in every time and place.

Even without a thoroughgoing systematization, the present texts still have an Ariadne's thread that unifies them and makes them a whole: the concern to detect the living presence of the Risen One in a concrete, historical setting; and to hear the voices and demands which he causes to be raised in this setting so that it may at last be freed from anything that enslaves and alienates it, thus making that world's climate more conducive to real and authentic love.

Despite their limitations and fragmentariness, these pages are meant to help the religious life not only to understand and love more deeply, but to make it enter into a conversion process, conversion to the living God who appears today with a more demanding and challenging face. Through such a conversion, religious life will be doing no more than realizing its irrevocable vocation: to reveal God's presence in the heart of the world.

Petrópolis
June, 1976

1

The Foundation

Like all life, religious life is nurtured by some substance that gives it life and makes it grow in accord with its essence. What is the concrete nature of the foundation of religious life? This should not be sought either in an idea or in the more noticeable institutional aspects of religious life. Religious life, as institution and as dynamic process, is no more than the translation and the historical consequence of its foundation and of the substance which continually nourishes it.

To investigate the foundation of religious life is to seek something which transcends religious life, to delve into the mystery of which religious life claims to be no more than an articulation, and one of its most significant manifestations. The more securely religious life rests on its foundation, the more authentic it will be, and the better it will preserve its perennial meaning for all people.

This foundation has been perhaps most visibly revealed in Christian religious life. But it does not exhaust its revelation there nor in any particular moment of history; rather it fills all history, always breathing in the midst of humanity. Such a consideration, far from relativizing religious life, opens a wider gateway to universal fellowship.

1

Religious Life as a Universal Phenomenon of Religion

Religious Life as a Sign of God's Love for Humanity in the World to Come

If marriage can, and should, be seen as a sign of God's love for people in this world, religious life can be considered the sacrament of God's love for humanity in the world to come. Religious life is centered in God, making of him, "inasmuch as he is God," the fundamental concern of human existence. It is a radical love patterned on the Absolute. Thus one claims to live that life which constitutes the eschatological Kingdom of God, when He will be all in all. The historical sign of that Kingdom is virginity or celibacy, although this is not exclusively confined to religious life nor necessary for religious life. Virginity and celibacy represent the definitive condition of men and women in the Kingdom—a situation lived here and now within that tentative and ambivalent incarnation which is the Kingdom in its earthly phase.

As an eschatological sign, virginity and celibacy undertaken for the sake of the Kingdom of God are more expressive than marriage. The statement of the Council of Trent, according to which virginity is "something better and more blessed" than marriage (DZ 1810), should be understood in that light. It does not affirm that the celibate as an individual is a more perfect or more blessed person—this depends on the individual call to celibacy or marriage. Only by realizing one's own vocation does one come to be a happier or more blessed person. Even so, as a sign of the world to come, virginity expresses, more radically and directly than does marriage, the future life in which neither flesh, nor blood, nor marriage, nor parental relationships any longer have a place (Mt. 22:30).

Nevertheless, what constitutes the foundation of religious life does not reside in virginity or in any other vow. The vows are only expressions of something deeper and more essential: the experience of God. From this viewpoint, religious life reveals an anthropological dimension much more extensive than, and transcendent of, the various forms it has assumed in different cultures and religions of the world.

Perhaps a rapid survey of religious life as a universal phenomenon can highlight some important dimensions of the real crisis in the understanding of religious life in the Church. We will begin with religious life as a phenomenon in the Catholic Church and then present other, perhaps more comprehensive, perspectives.

Religious Life as a Phenomenon in the Catholic Church

Religious life arose very rapidly in the Church as an exclusive search for God. Consider the anchorites of the desert, the rise of cenobitism, and the great contemplative, active, or mixed orders that endure to this day. The history of both the Eastern and Western Church is largely the history of religious life. While the origin of this phenomenon can be debated in the light of sociological research, one cannot doubt the existence of its determinative factor: love of God and neighbor.[1] There are countless men and women who, in order to live that love exclusively and with total dedication, left everything in order to embark on a life of consecration, and who continue to do so today.

Consecration in religious life, "which is rooted intimately in the consecration of baptism and incarnates it more completely,"[2] implies a reservation, or a person's being set aside, not in order to live apart from humanity but in order to be more available to serve humanity. Consecration, in this understanding, implies mission.[3] We will return to this implication later. For the moment we limit ourselves simply to considering that, despite the present crisis, there are thousands of religious in the world: orders, congregations, and secular institutes with their various works and ministries of contemplation, evangelization, human development, and fostering of religious values in general. These give powerful testimony to that "consecrated" and "missionary" character which religious life implies.

But is it possible for religious life to have any future in a world which defines itself as secular, a world where reason and technique dominate reality? What is the radical, original experience from which religious life sprang? How do we recapture that experience today and articulate it in our world? The answers to these questions place religious life in relation to its deeper meaning and elicit principles that enable us to deal with the real crisis.

Religious Life as a Phenomenon in Christianity

Religious life is not an exclusively Roman Catholic phenomenon, but also exists in other Christian denominations. Here we present only a few examples. The Eastern Orthodox Church is profoundly imprinted with the cenobitical experience in the monasteries of Mt. Athos and Metteron, as also by others in Yugoslavia and Russia.[4] The same can also be said of the dissident Christian churches of Ethiopia, Egypt, and Eastern Syria, among them the Maronites and the Armenians.[5] Religious life was not extinguished in Anglicanism, as can be seen in the Anglican Franciscans, Poor Clares, and Benedictines.[6] Even when the Protestant tradition turned a wary and critical eye on monasticism and religious life (one can look at Luther's short work *De votis monasticis judicium*), it did not prevent the rise, in our own day, in a clearly charismatic way, of the Protestant and ecumenical community of Taizé with Roger Schürz and Max Thurian, nor of the Sisters of Mary in Darmstadt, Germany.[7] The list could be extended.

Religious Life as a Phenomenon in the Religion of Biblical Monotheism

In the ninth century, Islam saw a major flourishing of religious life in Thebes, Syria, Arabia, and Egypt. Parallel with the Christian development came anchorites, and later cenobites, dedicated to both mysticism and study. Even in biblical prophetism we can discern certain elements of religious life. There were schools of prophets in Gibeah, Ramah, Jericho, and Gilgal. The prophets and the "sons of the prophets" wore special clothing and even practiced a certain kind of tonsure.[8] Better known in Judaism are the Essenes and the Qumran communities near the Dead Sea. The manuscripts discovered in 1947 reveal the austerity practiced by the different communities, involving a strict, regular observance, sharing of goods, and celibacy.[9]

Religious Life as a Phenomenon of World Religions

The study of world religions reveals many elements which later came to be embodied in religious life. Consider, for example, various initiation rites, communal recitation of set prayers, and the virginity of the Vestals.

A significant example occurred in the cultivation of monasticism in India and within Buddhism. In the sixth century B.C., a new religious experience swept India under the influence of the Upanishads. The strongly earthly perspective in the *Rig-Veda* had, as its foundation, nothing less than the experience of the illusory nature of the world and the emptiness of existence. Its ideal was nothing less than the absorption of the individual personality into the universal personality (Atman-Brahma). Thus many men and women abandoned the world and lived a solitary, celibate life of complete poverty and asceticism, seeking self-knowledge through introspection. At first there were the *Bahiskshu* (mendicants), with an itinerant lifestyle; later they joined together in great monasteries (*ashrams*). Even today there are thousands of *sadhus, gurus,* and *sanyassis*—ascetics and itinerant religious. In the *ashram*-monasteries absolute celibacy, extreme poverty, and deep meditation were actively cultivated. There are also religious congregations such as the *Remarkrishna,* dedicated to hospital work, and the *Siri Vinoba Bhave,* founded in 1959, totally dedicated to the contemplative life.[10]

Buddhism is essentially monastic, oriented toward meditation and self-transformation (*Zen*). In Hinayana Buddhism (the Small Vehicle), found especially in India, Ceylon, Burma, Thailand, Laos, and Cambodia, the monastery plays a central role in society, with its community life, meditation, chapter of faults, and also its work of helping people. In Mahayana Buddhism (the Great Vehicle), practiced especially in China, Hong Kong, and Vietnam, the monastery maintains a much more rigid structure, in the style of our great abbeys, including divine offices to Buddha, extended meditation, vigils, and rigid conventual discipline. Even the vocabulary is similar to that used in our ecclesiastical expressions. One speaks of entering and leaving the congregation, of novitiate, faith, heresy, mortal sin, confession, pardon, and absolution of sins.[11]

It would take too long to reflect on religious life in all the world's religions. But throughout this brief survey, one thing is sufficiently clear: religious life is a phenomenon common to all the world's religions,[12] not only Christianity. Christianity found it already established and structured. Christianity merely gave it a specific form and a new motivation. But the question can be raised. Is there a basic common structure, perhaps unrecognized, found in all forms of religious life both in Christianity and outside it?

Evidently each instance of religious life will incarnate a more or less provisional form or type of this fundamental structure. Yet there is something that unites them all, rooted in the same basic, original experience. Can we not apply to religious life in general what St. Augustine said of Christianity: "What is called Christian religion existed from the beginning of the human race, up to the time Christ became incarnate"?[13] Religious life would then be a universal phenomenon, a sign of the fullness that found its truest expression in Christianity. To develop this idea, it is appropriate to make some observations of an anthropological and structural nature.

The Anthropological Structure of Religious Life

It seems that, despite the diversity of its forms in different religions, religious experience is the original structural element, which, without equating all such experiences, unifies all the historical manifestations of religious life.

But what is religious experience? We are aware of the many theories formulated to present an answer.[14] Yet the following observation is helpful: every person is an openness to the totality of the real. In fact, the person questions not only the particulars which he or she immediately experiences and lives, but also can formulate a basic question about the real as a totality. To ask such a question is already to define oneself religiously. Later we will discover a better reason.

Vatican II in its "Decree on the Church and Non-Christian Religions" (*Nostra aetate,* 1) could very well say:

> People look to the various religions for answers to those profound mysteries of human life which today, even as in the past, deeply concern the human heart: What is a human being? What is the meaning and purpose of life? What is sin and what is goodness? What causes our sorrows and why? What is the path to true happiness? What is the truth about death, judgment, and retribution after death? What, finally, is the ultimate and ineffable mystery which enfolds our existence, from which we came forth, and toward which we direct ourselves?

To raise such questions is, in itself—we repeat—to formulate a religious question. In the answer, in which religions refer to the ultimate meaning a person experiences already through a basic, unconscious trust in the goodness of life, God always appears. We will analyze this in greater detail in the next chapter. God is truly that "ultimate and ineffable mystery which enfolds our existence," and which we experience as the ultimate depth of everything, as the absolute and unconditioned reality which everything shares.

All people, sooner or later in their lives, ask about the meaning of their lives, as well as the meaning of the world, and reach some kind of answer. Therefore, in this particular way, all men and women are called to express themselves religiously. The religious dimension belongs to the deepest level of our human personality, as has clearly been seen by the Jungian school of psychology: the most hidden layers of the human psyche, in either the individual or collective unconscious, are of a religious nature.

Through symbols, rites, institutionalized religious life, and through religions themselves, those contents of the unconscious are manifested in conscious life, concretized and objectified in a socio-cultural framework.[15] The basic experience is the same in all religions. Only its interpretation and its cultural and historical forms of expression vary, taking on specific forms in each case.

The Reason for Determining the Source of Religious Life

Religious life, according to the above description, is then the radicalization, greater intensification, and centralization that some divinely inspired people come to within that religious experience found as a basic experience in all people. Religious life is the full, conscious concretization of the human religious experience.

All people have a basic, inescapable religious disposition, yet all do not make their religious experience the fundamental goal and motivation of their lives, the experience that determines and qualifies their own existence. Specifically, some people receive a special charism from God, which makes them feel the demands of the religious calling more deeply and intimately than any other calling. They make it the center, the orientation or cynosure of their lives. Thus they discover the full meaning of their existence, as well as the specific tasks they are called upon to do to serve humanity. Cultivation of this sensitivity has a meaning in itself, like love, friendship, and self-denial in behalf of others. It is not, of itself, ordered toward something that gives it its meaning or value. The religious, as Paul VI said, is a specialist in God and the affairs of religion.[16] Thus it is a matter of a value in itself.

Thomas Aquinas expressed the same thought differently,

saying that religious life is the perfection of the virtue of religion.[17] Living more intensely what everyone experiences, i.e., religious experience, religious are changed into a sign in the midst of humanity, set apart and witnessing to that vertical dimension, or depth, which is the center of human reality. Each person, as the image and likeness of God, is a deeply expressive revelation of that God in history and in the world.

The Theological Transcendence of the Universal Phenomenon of Religious Life

True believers, those who consider themselves Christian and interpret all history in Christian terms, cannot fail to see in the universal phenomenon of religious life the benevolent, salvific work of God who loves and gives himself to all and who wants all to be saved.

Religions represent the response people have given, and continue to give, to the saving will of God. It has been possible to fall into errors and false interpretations about the divine reality and the mystery of human existence, but all religions affirm categorically the communion of the person with the absolute mystery, called God, and they decipher, in the light of that mystery, the meaning of human and earthly reality. Thus theologically, all religions are experiential expressions of transcendence. According to Vatican II, the Church is present in them because there is an *Ecclesia del Abel justo,* which is always made real wherever love is being lived, wherever fellowship with others is being sought, and wherever brothers and sisters are united and kneel in prayer and adoration of the true God, hidden under many names.

In this understanding, and also following Vatican II, the Church is the universal sacrament of salvation which is realized in increasingly complete stages, from the atheist of good will who follows his or her conscience to the fullness of the person who possesses the Holy Spirit.[18]

Thus a true, hidden Church exists which is more than sociological Christianity, one which is realized when a person is open to the Absolute through religion, and which is preeminently realized when one leaves the world for religious life and renounces everything with the intention of being completely dedicated to the task of seeking God in oneself and in others.

From this perspective, religious life appears as a sacrament of the existential destiny of humanity, as a sign of the transcendent dimension of human life, and as a witness to the existence of a supreme reality—God—experienced as present within the person (the Augustinian *intimior intimo meo*) and, at the same time, as the totally other (the *superior summo meo*) for which it is well worth the pain of sacrificing all the good things of the present life. In these universal terms, religious life is an incarnate symbol of the love of God in human terms, which in turn symbolizes the world to come.

The Source of the Christian Religious Vocation

Christian religious life, like all religious life, is the articulation of human religious experience. What all Christians experience through baptism reaches greater fullness in religious life through the living of the evangelical counsels (*LG,* 44; *PC,* 5). Religious are as those called, able to be changed into a sign of the presence of God among human beings—a prophetic sign. Christianity incarnates and lives out the experience of God in a particular way. The following are some of the basic characteristics of the Christian religious experience.

The Experience of God in the Person

Christian religious life springs not only from the experience of a transcendent God as the ultimate meaning which fulfills our life, but also and above all from the earthly and temporal, even when manifested in a human context. Christianity professes that the flesh is the locus of salvation (*caro cardo salutis,* in Tertullian's phrase). God does not reject the material, nor does he despise the human condition. In Jesus of Nazareth God became visible and palpable. The *Logos* which permeated all reality, and which was interpreted as the meaning of life and human history, was certainly not an abstract idea. It was truly an invisible reality, but one which desired to become visible, "became flesh and pitched his tent among us" (Jn. 1:14).

What specifies the Christian religious experience, then, is the experience of God in the man Jesus, Son of the living God (Mt. 16:16). Christ Jesus, as taught by the believing Church, "is perfect in his divinity, and perfect in his humanity, truly God and truly human." To take this affirmation seriously is to believe that God, through the incarnate Word, has really become human.[19]

Contemplating Jesus, we can say that it is not possible to speak of God without speaking of humanity, nor to speak of humanity without having to speak of God. The human person has a divine depth, just as God has a human dimension. In Jesus "the goodness and loving kindness of God appeared" (Tt. 3:4). The Christian lives because of this faith and lives this faith. The religious radicalizes and deepens that faith in both understandings. The special meaning of the vows is found in light of that radicalizing and deepening. This radicalizing is expressed in different ways according to the three dimensions of the human person or, if you prefer, according to the threefold relationship which defines the person in relation to the world, other people, and oneself. The relationship with God, as a totality, radicalizes them all. The vows of poverty (in relation to earthly goods), of celibacy (in relation to others), and of obedience (in relation to God, the great other, and oneself) do not destroy this threefold relational character of the person, but direct it according to a special modality and specific motivations, which both arise from and are subordinated to the special experience of God in Jesus Christ.

Since God has revealed himself in humanity, it is necessary for the Christian (and even more so for religious) to see God in other people and to aid others to encounter and understand him. Thus religious—as Christians—should be, at one and the same time, defenders and promoters of divine values in humanity and untiring defenders of humanness, which actually means the ability to receive divinity.

"History Pregnant with Christ"

In order to be the personal center of the highest form of religious experience, as well as the one who, as the God-Man, lived that experience in a unique way, Jesus Christ constitutes the true Alpha-and-Omega Point, the key to interpreting all reality and all experience. What had previously been applied to God was valid now also for the God-Man. All is through him, for him and in him (Col. 1:16). The person is not only the image and likeness of God (Gn. 1:26), but also the image of Christ (Rm. 8:29, Col. 1:15) or, if one prefers, the image of God in Christ and through Christ, truly "the firstborn of many brothers and sisters" (Rm. 8:29). Already in Adam grace was the grace of Christ, who is all in all (Col. 3:11). Thus history is, according to the beautiful phrase of St. Augustine, "pregnant with Christ." He has a plenary, cosmic dimension: first as *Logos* (Word); then as *Logos* incarnate in our human weakness; finally as *Logos* risen, with our human condition totally transfigured.[20]

Religious are called to live this Christianization of reality more radically than ordinary Christians are, so that, through faith, they may succeed in discovering the ultimate depth of the human person and of all reality as one where the human is touched by the divine.

Christianity as Experience of a Person

It can easily be appreciated that Christianity, before being a set of doctrines about God, humanity, or the world, seeks to be the concrete experience of a person (Jesus of Nazareth) and the celebration of his real presence in human history. Christ did not come to construct a way, reveal a truth, or light a light. He presented himself as the Way, the Truth, the Life, the Light of the world. He presented himself not as a way to salvation, but as salvation itself. He is the definitive "yes," the Amen, of God to humanity (cf. 2 Co. 1:20). With him the "new man" breaks into the world (cf. 2 Co. 5:17; Ep. 2:15, 4:24; Rv. 21:5), the person whose future fulfillment in Christ we all await. Through faith, charity, and fraternal love—and as members of the Church—Christians already share here and now in that newness of life. It is true we know ourselves to be pilgrims and sinners, and yet, in hope, we know we are already freed and in the Father's house (cf. Rm. 7:24) by having "tasted of the wonders of the world to come" (Hb. 6:5) here in this world.

Religious try to enhance this taste of the world to come by making it the basic orientation and undertaking of their lives. They live that newness of life above all other personal or social concerns, letting no other potential pattern for integrating the world, no matter how attractive, compete with their special life-project. One can be, and must be, a scholar, an administrator, a teacher, or a nurse, for instance. But before all this (if one wants to be a religious-Christian) one must live one's religious identity. One must be a religious-professor, not a professor-religious; the difference is crucial and abundantly clear.

Specific Principles and Motivations of Christian Religious Life

Christian religious life is a particular instance within the general anthropological structure which defines the other forms of religious life already mentioned. It will travel the same or similar paths we discovered in the others: profession of vows, cultivation of ethical values, community prayer, liturgy, meditation, asceticism. Christian religious will have the same structures the others do, but with a profoundly different understanding and for radically new reasons. Christian religious will be poor, celibate, and obedient like religious of other religions, but they will join their poverty, virginity, and obedience to the poverty, virginity, and obedience of Christ. Thus these common phenomena of religious life take on a different meaning and assume a greater depth and importance—not because they are different in themselves, but because their motivations are different.

The most important and distinctive motivations of Christian religious life are discussed below.

The Eschatological Context

Christians, and even more, religious, live with the certitude that Christ gave the ultimate, definitive, and complete opportunity for salvation. We must not wait for another savior of humanity. The Reign of God is already made fully real here and now in the person of Jesus, and will have its human and cosmic fulfillment at the end of time. Since the coming of

Christ the new world is growing and maturing within the old one. The harbinger of the new world which will one day come to fulfillment is the resurrection of Christ himself. The certainty that the end of the present world is approaching (cf. 1 Pt. 6:1; 1 Co. 7:29–34) creates two typically Christian attitudes, as we have already seen: the relativizing of the present situation, and maintaining a critical distance from the realities of the world.

Hope as the Starting-Point

With the resurrection of Christ a new hope[21] entered history: the certitude that life, not death, is the final, definitive judgment God pronounces on human destiny (1 Co. 15:22–25). Christ is the firstborn of the dead (1 Co. 15:20). He is our hope (1 Co. 15:19; 1 Tm. 1:1). Religious life in itself is a testimony to that eschatological value. The asceticism and the various practices of spirituality demanded by religious life are permeated by this certainty: the completion of our history is guaranteed by Christ; in hope we are already saved (Rm. 8:24). Religious are the opponents of the absurd, testifying by their lives to the fullness of life's meaning, as shown in the destiny and in the life of the Risen Christ.

The Primacy of *Agape*

Christianity is defined as the religion of love.[22] God's relationship to the world is motivated by love. Humanity's relationship with God is also one of love. Relationships among human beings should likewise be, and are, ones based on love. The person who has love has everything (cf. Rm. 13:10) since God is love (1 Jn. 4:7). Love never ends (1 Co. 13:8). It is the constitutive principle within society, since love builds up (1 Co. 8:1) and perfectly binds the community together (Col. 3:14).

The novel insight of Christianity is the affirmation of an identity between love of God and love of neighbor. In the "Gospel of the anonymous Christians" (Mt. 25:31–46), the Son of Man is identified with the least of his brothers and sisters. Those who do not love their brothers and sisters cannot love God (1 Jn. 4:20). The way to God passes through the ways of men and women. Religious life, even while being experienced in an eschatological perspective, to be Christian in the full Gospel sense, must be directed to serving humanity, providing an apostolic witness for the tasks of people within the secular city. Christian religious life, as the expression of God become human and present now as risen, cannot be made real, nor proven true, without articulating, in its essential content, the love of neighbor.

The Body of Christ

The actions of religious life take on a deeper meaning by being understood in the perspective of the body of Christ.[23] All the grace-filled people of the world and those who believe in Christ Jesus form a living organism and a *Milieu divin vital:* the body of Christ. Within this body a real interchange of blessings occurs among the members: if one suffers, all suffer; if one is honored, all are honored. Each action has, beyond its individual dimension, social repercussions.

Sociologically the Church is the manifestation and the visible structure of the body of Christ; but as the mystery of communion with Christ, and with God through Christ, it is a reality which transcends sociological limits. The meaning of Church is not fully explained by the phenomenological. It is par excellence the body of Christ (Ep. 1:23). Whoever is in the body of Christ is in Christ. The expression "in Christ" appears 196 times in the New Testament. Whoever is in Christ is a new creature (2 Co. 5:17); the old has passed away, the new world has been created. Humanity already lives in a new situation of salvation and is part of a saving organism in which each gesture and action takes on its full importance.

Such actions thus become dynamic elements of communion with God and all the just. Within this great vision, the slave is also a beloved brother; parents and children are equally members of Christ (Ep. 6:1).

Religious, living with complete fidelity their religious experience in their particular congregations or communities, are brothers and sisters *in Christ,* united by the same bond of *agape*. It is certain that this reality has not yet been manifested here in all its fullness, but when Christ appears our communion will be fulfilled in him (1 Jn. 3:3) since we all reflect the same face of Christ and the unity of his body, although in different ways.

The Following and Imitation of Christ

If we are really situated in Christ, it is logical for us to search in his life and actions for the model for our conduct and the motivation for our attitudes.[24] Peter says that Christ left us an example that we should follow in his footsteps (1 Pt. 2:21). Paul recommends that we be imitators of him as he is of Christ (1 Th. 1:6, 2:14; 1 Co. 11:1). John has Jesus say, I have given you an example, that you should do as I have done to you (Jn. 13:15). The meaning of this imitation of Christ is evident: the Christian should behave in his or her own existential situation the way Christ behaved in his.

We find abundant examples in the New Testament. Peter urges the slave unjustly treated to suffer as Christ did, who, although abused, did not reply with curses, and, afflicted, did not respond with threats (1 Pt. 2:23). Paul urges the headstrong Corinthians to imitate the meekness and gentleness of Christ (2 Co. 10:1). When seeking help for the needy community in Jerusalem, Paul recalls for the same Corinthians the generosity of Christ, who was rich but became poor (2 Co. 8:9). To the Philippians he recommends having and fostering the same attitudes that Christ had: although he was divine he stripped himself of glory and took the form of a slave, humbling himself and becoming obedient even to death on a cross (Ph. 2:5–8).

Right here it is not the divinity that provides the meaning for imitation, but the humanity, and not humanity in its power and glory but in its humility and in the cross, as expressions of supreme love and supreme self-giving.

> "Whoever wants to come after me, let him or her deny self, take up his or her cross every day and follow me" (Mk. 8:34). Followers of Christ are the martyr giving his or her life, the monk or nun abandoning the world, the humble, the poor and the obedient adopting the humility, poverty and obedience of Christ as models.[25]

These are virtues of Gentiles as well as Christians; it is only that the Christian has a new motivation for practicing them:

because Christ the God-Man also practiced them. To imitate God means for the Christian to imitate Christ, in whom God humbled himself unto death.

A yet more radical form of imitation of Christ exists, which is realized in the *following*. In the most ancient Synoptic tradition, to follow Jesus meant to live life in communion with him, in proclaiming his message and sharing his destiny. Jesus proclaims the Reign of God, which means, and demands, proclaiming and realizing a real *metanoia,* a complete and radical change that affects oneself and the structures and conditions of the present world. *Metanoia* deals with the conquest of sin, which makes us enemies of God, and with the overcoming of our entire sin-filled situation in its various manifestations—sorrow, suffering, exploitation of one person by another—until the final conquest of the ultimate enemy, death itself. In order to proclaim that Reign of God (the Good News, the Gospel; cf. Mk. 1:17, 3:4–15 and par.) which is going to break into the world, and in order to prepare people to accept it (Mk. 6:7–13 and par.; Lk. 9:1–6 and par.; Lk. 10:1–30), Christ began calling disciples and followers. The extraordinary thing is that he asked them for the most difficult sacrifices. He asked them:

To Sever All Human Ties. Only one who renounces all ties is fit to be a disciple and Jesus' co-worker in proclaiming the Reign of God. The disciple is called by Christ (and only he, with his messianic awareness, could impose such conditions) and must leave father, mother, wife, or children, must not linger to bury parents. (Lk. 14:26; Lk. 9:59–62). Christ's demands do not admit to, nor allow, any compromise.

To Sacrifice One's Own Life. The words of Christ recorded by Luke (14:27) and Matthew (14:38) and in the Markan tradition (Mk. 8:34; Mt. 16:24; Lk. 9:23; cf. Jn. 12:26) speak of renouncing oneself, taking up the cross, and following Jesus. The modes of expression in these passages should certainly be understood as forms proper to their age, taken from the Roman custom of obliging the condemned to carry the transverse crossbeam on the way to the place of execution.[26] But this does not weaken the spiritual and mystical sense of such Gospel passages. Thus one who wants to be a disciple of Jesus must be willing to offer one's life for the Gospel message and to live in such a way that one carries the cross of contradiction to the surrounding world, even to the point of accepting violent death: those who want to save their lives will lose them, but those who lose their lives for Jesus' sake will save them (Lk. 17:33). One who decides to follow Jesus and live his message can count on meeting the same fate as Jesus (Mk. 9:35, 10:35–40) because the disciple is not above his master (Mt. 10:24).

To Renounce Worldly Goods. Jesus' disciples, incorporated into the mission of proclaiming the Reign of God, are asked also to renounce the security that can be provided by one's social group or professional associates or by the environment in which one lives (Mk. 1:18–20 and par.; Lk. 5:11), surrendering to a life of insecurity, of poverty, as Christ himself did who had no place to lay his head (Lk. 6:8–11 and par.). It is held that Jesus did not demand any vow of poverty, but only total self-giving to the Reign of God (Mk. 10:12), and that Luke (with his tendency to radicalize the theme of poverty) is the only one who places on Jesus' lips the words, "No one can be my disciple unless he or she leaves everything" (Lk. 14:33). It is certain that Luke describes the vocation of the disciples as a call to abandon everything, while the other evangelists affirm merely that they left father, nets, boats. (Mk. 1:18 and par.). But there is no doubt that total self-giving to God's Reign demanded no small renunciations or privations from Christ's disciples.

Such demands in the following of Christ were proposed by Jesus in his own life and in the lives of his immediate coworkers. After the resurrection, the theme is translated into a different context. To follow Christ is to imitate his life; to be in him; to bind oneself to him in faith, hope, and love, through the Spirit (1 Co. 6:17) and the sacraments (Rm. 6:3ff.; 1 Co. 11:17–30). A disciple is, from this standpoint, a soteriological category and a synonym for Christian (Hb. 11:26). In the final editing of the Gospels the call to follow is directed not only to the Twelve but to everyone without discrimination (Lk. 9:23, 14:26).

That traditional process of interpreting the meaning of calling by Jesus, already begun in the early Church, must be continued today. Thus we must ask what the full meaning of following Jesus is. Basically it means to be identified with him, proclaiming what he proclaimed: the Reign of God, which constitutes the absolute meaning of our world and which is manifested in all its fullness in the resurrection of Christ. He is, in Origen's words, the *autobasileia* (the "kingdom-in-himself"), and the Church is nothing other than "the sacrament of the Kingdom of heaven."

Thus, to follow Christ is to be a witness to the absolute meaning of history, because the future will be the Kingdom fulfilled by God where there will no longer be death, nor mourning, nor weeping, nor pain because the former things have passed away (Rv. 21:4). In the name of that absolute and transcendent reality, any forms of the old world which refuse to be open to that future must be condemned. The Christian cannot be complacent or content with results already obtained. Believing in the Reign of God, the Christian must engage in a perpetual struggle, humanizing, unifying, transforming the world more and more into the image of the future.

The following of Christ is a life ordered not by the established canons of the old world and its image of the person, but by the history and destiny of Jesus and by his life of total and universal love for everyone, friend or enemy. In the name of that love he began to question, and to maintain a critical distance from, the social and religious forms of his time, such as the Sabbath observance, the purification laws, the social institution of marriage. His superior attitude toward these things ("You have heard it said . . . , but I say to you . . . .") and his "new teaching" (Mk. 1:27) were unpopular with the authorities of his day, civil and religious, domestic and foreign. But Jesus tore down the walls that separated people from one another and put a new world in their place. Thus he set us free, not to serve the flesh, but to serve each other in love (Ga. 5:1, 13).

Each believer is invited to live this newness of life. Religious, in particular, promise to live publicly and explicitly a life according to the Gospel and to set up for themselves a concrete lifestyle according to Christ. Only thus can they become a sign of the promised world, since between the "now" of faith and the revelation of glory at the Parousia religious have chosen the goods and values of the heavenly community.

The Concrete Realization of the Christian Religious Vocation

All that has been said here constitutes the source and grounding of the Christian religious vocation. But without the concrete experience of God and Jesus Christ, no Christian religious life can be maintained or justified. It would really be nothing more than martyrdom without glory. It would dictate an external framework of formulas, gestures, and behaviors. Instead of a permanent reminder or remembrance for people, it would be a countersign to the radical meaning of life. Still, this root can blossom into many varied expressions of religious life.

First of all, religious (and anyone who wants to be human) must realize the fundamental birthright of each human person: they must strive to be fully human—overlord in relation to evolving reality, brother or sister in relation to other people with whom they live, son or daughter in their experience of God and Jesus Christ. They must not consent (as usually happens in human history) to any kind of alienation within these relationships, nor in their relationship with worldly goods. There always has been, and there continues to be today, the enduring temptation, for religious, of an escapist mentality in relation to earthly tasks. They live their relationship to God and their religious identity in such a way that they actually ignore the inescapable relationship with the affairs and things of this world.

Vatican II has strongly reminded us that

> they are mistaken who, knowing we have here no abiding city but seek one which is to come, think that they may shirk their earthly responsibilities. For they are forgetting that by the faith itself they are more than ever obliged to measure up to these duties, each according to his proper vocation (*GS,* 43).

Out of their real experience of God religious must incarnate themselves in a concrete work or task. From this arise the many diverse charisms of the founders and foundresses of orders, congregations, and institutes. These charisms, as well as the many ways in which religious experience can be lived out, give witness to the concrete incarnation and the possible forms the vocation can assume. First and foremost, being religious should be emphasized, and only then expressed within an order or congregation. Each is distinguished by a particular charism, which generally is a concrete mission or work within the Church and in the midst of the world. There is the charism of contemplation and celebration of the mysteries of God. Religious life, which is always contemplative at its root, expresses this particular aspect in a concrete way—and abbeys and monasteries of contemplatives come into being. There is also a charism to serve the poor. Thus there comes into being a congregation dedicated specifically, according to the charism of its founder or foundress, to care for the sick, the poor, or others. Thus a multiplicity of ecclesial ministries flourishes in the Church, reflecting the richness of the Spirit's gifts.

The individual religious must be situated in that context, fairly evaluating his or her talents and aptitudes. One must try to fulfill one's earthly vocation in accordance with the personal gifts (both of nature and of grace) with which God has enriched one. Thus that individual will succeed in incarnating his or her religious vocation in a form most in accord with his or her nature, formation, and aptitudes. This will lead to one's religious experience reaching greater depths and better expression. The religious will experience himself or herself as a whole person insofar as this is achieved, thus reducing the possibility of becoming neurotic, which happens when one's personal religious experience is lived out in an historical situation (an order or congregation) which does not lead to radical fulfillment and which is not in accord with one's talents and abilities.

Generally orders and congregations, within the charism of their founders and foundresses, present such a wide range of ministerial tasks and opportunities that most religious can express themselves in them and find an outlet for their human gifts and talents. Thus it is possible to fulfill human, earthly vocations within the context of a transcendent, eschatological vocation. Even though they are relative, the concrete realizations of the religious vocation always are important, since in and through them we actually gain or lose our transcendent, eschatological vocation.

In fidelity to a concrete vocation, to a mission, to the charism of an order or congregation, we reveal our fidelity to the absolute vocation. Still one cannot absolutize the relative with the conviction that outside of that particular incarnation or historical form the absolute vocation cannot be fulfilled (or that heaven cannot be attained). There are many and varied roads. But each and every one is serious and important, since they are taken up and understood as the historical forms by which the Absolute and Transcendent makes himself present and operative in the world.

2

Religious Life and the Experience of God

The Return to the Primary Experience of God Through the Destruction of His Images

Even to speak of the experience of God today is to assume a critical stance in the midst of the prevailing crisis over our depictions of the mystery of God. There were times in the past when a real experience of God was attained simply through living contact with the theological doctrines transmitted by the Church and accepted by society. In that way one could live the immediacy of the mystery of God and fulfill the purpose of life. Our age, though, is characterized by a systematic distrust of all discourse which claims to translate what is definitively important or radically decisive in human life into simple concepts. This criticism was embodied in demythologization, secularization of religious themes, the "Death of God" theology, and (in Latin America) the ideological function assumed by religion to maintain social injustice and discrimination in the face of demands for revolution. Such criticism ended in desiccating all our ideas and depictions of God.

In the face of so widespread a crisis, many voices are already beginning to shout a warning:

> Enough! Let us stop and ponder a little. . . . In the world of thought let us use the word "God" no more. Let us keep silent. Let us look for the experience of that mystery which encompasses and permeates our life. . . . And only then let us attempt to babble a Name which is not a name but the name of our love for That which has no name, because it is Ineffable. . . .

We propose to investigate in this chapter the primary meaning of the word "God" which is hidden behind the many names we call him and the many doctrines concerning him. In trying to pinpoint the mode of our experience of God, we must not reject the damage done to the whole idea of God in our civilization. The crisis in depictions of God will not be resolved merely by creating new ones more suited to our times. In the final analysis this would do nothing more than prolong the crisis, assuming uncritically the same generative structure of depictions or images of God, which is precisely what the crisis calls into question. But neither will the crisis be resolved by fleeing back into the peaceful world which preceded it. Rather we must enter into the crisis and get to its roots. It is not a matter of combating some images of God with other images. But neither is it a matter of verifying the experience of God by systematically denying every depiction of God. The primary meaning of the word "God" is found not through affirming or denying every image of God, but through considering the most original and deepest dimension of each of these depictions.

This dimension is the one we are looking for now. But prior to this search we must describe the dimensions of the crisis itself in the depictions of God.

God, the Totally Transcendent Other: Transcendentalism

People who have had a real experience of God have ended up confessing that he is *superior summo meo,* the totally other who dwells in unapproachable light (1 Tm. 6:16). God is that which the intellect cannot totally comprehend: a mystery which, the more it is known, the more it reveals to us the impossibility of ever fully knowing it. It is God-always-greater, in the words of St. Augustine:

> However high the flights of thought may go, he is even farther beyond. If you have comprehended him, it is not God but an image of God. If you believe you have almost comprehended him, then your reflection deluded you.[1]

God absolutely transcends all that exists or can exist. His transcendence means that he permeates everything and is present in everything, without being limited by anything, since he is always beyond. We never reach him because we are always in him. But he is beyond everything. So far there is no special problem.

The problem arises when a person begins to depict the God of Mystery and the Mystery of God. God the Transcendent is depicted as God-over-the-world, and, what is worse, as God-outside-the-world. He is a God without the world. The mystery becomes represented by an enigma.

For the mystic the mystery is that which is opposed to the intelligible. It is proper to the mystery to be comprehended, though it is also its property that it remains mystery within its intelligibility to be the boundlessness of comprehensibility. It always can be known more. The mystery as *represented* by an enigma comes to mean that which is not attainable by reason. It is not that which is unlimited by reason, but it is its limit. Everything not within the limits of reason can be declared mystery. This is how God ended up being banished by reason.

A God foreign to the world is inexpressible. It is simply an object of revelation, understood as a mere in-breaking into the world of him who is outside it: an in-breaking and revelation of a God which would not go beyond some truths and objective representations of himself. To believe would be only to assent to some truths about God without perceiving anything of him himself, forgetting, or being ignorant of, the fact that to cleave to God demands rather a total abandonment—as far as possible—of our ideas and depictions of him.

Such a God would be very close to the God of deism. "The deist is a person who has not yet had time to turn into an atheist."[2] But the deist has already begun to separate the world from God and God from the world. God is a projection of human beings before the name of the Mystery which permeates everything. Before a God depicted as distant, above and outside the world, one does not kneel, clasp one's hands in prayer, or open one's heart in loving intimacy.

Furthermore, such a depiction does not permit valuing the Incarnation of God in Jesus Christ. It is not a God who comes to humanity out of deep sympathy for us. He takes on nothing human, but preserves his majesty and transcendent divinity. No longer is the *kenosis* of God of which St. Paul speaks (Ph. 2:6–7) understood. As a consequence we believe ourselves obliged to depict Jesus Christ, in his capacity as God Incarnate, as one who already knew everything from his mother's womb, who knew about his death from the beginning of his life, and who knew completely about his course and the minutest details of his return to the Father. With such a depiction the Incarnation which the Gospels present to us is robbed of its profoundly human character. One no longer can understand how Christ could be tempted in the desert, for instance. In short, such a depiction ignores how "though he was Son of God, he learned to obey through suffering" (Hb. 5:8).

Such a representation of divine transcendence as distance from the world must have disastrous consequences for the life of faith: on one hand, the experience of life and the world; on the other, adherence to some abstract truths about God, but without any possible correlation between the two. Faith, instead of springing from the heart, seems superimposed on it. The Church appears then as a mere institution, concentrating on defending a deposit of revealed truths and on proclaiming some moral principles divorced from the concrete reality of life. Thus it is not strange that such truths and principles come to awaken in the faithful an attitude of fear and anxiety instead of liberating life and opening it to a generous and complete self-giving of the person to the Mystery of God.

Moreover, the proclamation of God without the world has eventually been replaced by a world without God. The person could not stand up to the dualism which was doing violence to life. The result was to break with transcendentalism, proclaiming that God had died. In truth we ourselves had made God die. Yet what we were basically proclaiming was not the death of God or of the Mystery of God, but of one of the images of God. From this viewpoint, atheism, denying the images of

God, offers the opportunity of a true experience of the living and true God who is in the world and in our images, but who is at the same time always much more than all of them.

God Radically Near: Immanentism

The true faith always lived and depicted God as the One who is nearer to us than we are to ourselves, in the phrase of St. Augustine. God is so situated in the very heart of things that in everything we think about, see, or touch, we think about, see, and touch God subconsciously. Nothing, not even hell itself, is an obstacle to his ineffable presence. No special problem exists in this.

The problem arises when one tries to depict the immanence of God, identifying the depiction with his presence. God is really present in everything, but without denying or taking the place of the world and its realities. There is a way of depicting the actions of God as secondary causes, as if he were no more than one of the causes immanent in the world. Thus we conceive God's Word as we do human words, the divine will as we do human will, the Love and Justice of God as we do the love and justice of human beings. It is a conception of God through which we think we see God *directly* in everything. In such a depiction the world is no longer allowed to be the world, nor is there any place for a properly human history, since everything is directly subsumed into God. God is no more than a phenomenon of the world. He really is depicted as the Supreme Being, infinite, creator of heaven and earth, but as a being alongside of, among, and within other entities, even when this is qualified by calling him infinite and omnipotent. Since he is no more than another entity he can express himself in visions, voices, and interior consolation.

This concept or anthropomorphic image of God has ecclesiological, and even political, repercussions. Divine law is placed in the same category as human law, and revealed doctrines and divine institutions are interpreted as sanctioning human doctrines and institutions. Such a concept lends itself to the manipulative efforts of those in power and to the power of orthodox interpretation to bolster the established order. The one, indivisible Mystery of God unfolds itself in many mysteries of faith. The one Word of God is divided into the many words of Scripture. Some theological current represents the will of God split into innumerable laws, dogmas, explanations, canons, ordinances, and precepts, more and more minuscule as the needs of the situation demand.

The person at once begins to ask, "Are God and his salvation so complicated? Isn't all this purely human language trying to translate the one Mystery of God which cannot be identified with the anthropomorphisms of our language?"

The answer is yes. God is really everywhere. But he is not a phenomenon capable of being apprehended like other worldly phenomena. God is a Mystery which always gives Itself but which also remains aloof, always revealed and always veiled, communicating itself but without becoming jumbled up in the world.

For the concept that depicts God as a phenomenon of the world should be substituted a theological conception: God is in the world but always more than it. The reason (*Logos*) sees God through the world and not directly in himself. Hence the need arises for serious reflection and for serious affirmation of the world seen as the journey of the mind toward God.

In this case also the depiction of God in worldly categories brings about a new denial of God. God is seen as a category of human power, justice, and love which can be manipulated to maintain the privileged position of a few. Religion can actually be turned into an "opiate of the people" when God and divine things become confused with religious institutions and truths. "O God, you are naught but love, but you are the Other Love; you are naught but justice, but you are the Other Justice!"[3] The destruction of the anthropomorphic God is an essential condition for the possibility of an experience of the living and true God who is in the world but not exhausted by the world.

The Transparency of the World as the Way of Experiencing the Living God

We can sum up the preceding by saying that transcendentalism affirms God and denies the world, while immanentism affirms the world and denies God. We must ask whether it is possible to affirm both.

Transcendence and immanence have been considered opposed and exclusive categories. To avoid an impasse we must say that God is not only immanent or only transcendent, but that he is also transparent. St. Paul (Ep. 4:6) says there is one God and Father of all who is above all (transcendent) and in all (immanent) and through all (transparent). Between immanence and transcendence there is an intermediate category, transparency, which does not exclude either of the others but implies both. Transparency indicates the presence of transcendence in immanence. In other words, transparency indicates the presence of transcendence in the world.[4] This presence makes the world of the merely immanent transparent to the transcendent in it. Thus it does not deny the world, but affirms it more deeply, not only as the world but also as the realm and the special manifestation of something or someone who is more than the world: the Transcendent, God. In the words of Teilhard de Chardin:

> The great mystery of Christianity is not exactly the appearance, but the transparence, of God in the universe. "Yes, Lord, not only the ray that strikes the surface, but the ray that penetrates, not only your Epiphany, Jesus, but your *diaphany*."[5]

God emerges and is manifested in the human person and the world. These, then, restore the transparency of God. God is real and concrete, not because he lives above or outside the world, but because he lives in the heart of the world and beyond it—within, but not fully contained therein, and not as a phenomenon of the world. Failing to be alive in the world, God became fossilized in a depiction which placed him outside the world.

How does the transparency of everything in relation to God appear? How is the union of God and the world verified without either confusing the two or denying one or the other? What is the basic dimension which does not give us warrant for objectifications which deny either God or the world?

The answer to these questions lies in the human person, specifically in the dimension of its historicity. The person lives in a concrete historical situation in which one is obliged to take a position, make decisions, and affirm oneself as human. By assuming one's historical situation in a radical way, one comes to experience effectively that one is a being-in-the-world, but at the same time is capable of raising oneself infinitely above the world and every concrete situation, reasoning and making choices which define one decisively and which signify or express one's salvation or damnation. Immanence which is discovered here and transcendence which is proclaimed here are not extrapolated perspectives which have no bearing on one's concrete situation. They are dimensions of one's concrete reality as a human being, not realities merely superimposed on it.

God also possesses a real significance for the person when he emerges from one's earthly, historical situation, when he manifests himself as the radical meaning of a person's life—as the light by which one sees light. God who speaks in the Bible is the God who breaks into history. It is not possible to create a science about him as if he were an object that could be described. The most important function of science consists in predicting the future behavior of the objects of study. When hypotheses are not corroborated in accordance with scientific theory, we say the theory was erroneous; there was no science. The intervention of God is totally unforeseeable. Thus it is not possible to imprison God in the molds of our sciences. If we use theology—which claims to be a treatise about God—we do so knowing that it is only possible within a specific epoch and within the history in which we are living and in which we come to perceive the historical summonses God gives us, as well as the answers which, on our part, we should make to God. The God whom Scripture testifies to is, then, an historical God: the God who accompanies his chosen people in their wanderings and who goes before them as the Way, the Rock, the Light, the Power, the Traveling Companion, the Absolute Future.[6] In light of this interpretation of God as revealing himself in history it is easy to understand the ancient texts of faith, written by a people who tried to find God hidden beneath all the events they lived. Only thus do life and history become transparent.

Thus a God who is experienced is not an abstract idea which floats over history, or the end-point of a theoretical line of reasoning which would be intelligible apart from the concrete life of human beings. To think that way is to fall once more into the pitfall of static representations—either of transcendence or immanence—which we have criticized before. God is the Absolute who appears when people dig deeply and get to the very root of the history which they live. History in this context is not a narrative of past events. It is the dimension in which we live, struggling, making decisions, traveling a road, realizing ourselves. It is in the roots of history where God is discovered as the Way of life, the Power for the daily struggle. This God manifests himself when we are open to him and dare to experience him.

For this to be not just a beautiful theory among other theories, God must be discerned in the precise area in which he lives: experience. In experience, theory and practice are joined, forming a basic unity. Theory is no longer an abstraction, an empty idea to explain practice and to communicate it. Practice is no longer an irrational movement or behavior, but a search for, and realization of, the meaning of life. In the radical experience of our reality, God appears to the human awareness. By the experience of God, sought and found in the heart of our experience of reality, reality becomes transparent and is transformed into a great sacrament which communicates God.

How can we define and, above all, express this experience?[7]

What Is Experience?

The concept "experience" is one of the most discussed and most difficult in our Western tradition. We cannot possibly explain all the rich and varied meanings here.[8] Thus we will limit ourselves to that essential perspective which makes it possible to explain God as historically experienced.

Perhaps the etymology of the word provides the first clue to understanding the concept of experience. *Ex-peri-ence* is the knowledge a person acquires when one goes forth from oneself (*ex*) and studies from every angle and perspective (*peri*) the world of things or realities (*ence*) around one. Experience is knowledge which is not theoretical or obtained from books, but acquired in working contact with reality; by mastering reality, so to speak, one learns and comes to understand. The result of this encounter with the world—in those areas where the encounter takes place—is the destruction of images one had of the world, the acquisition of new data, and the elaboration of new images more in keeping with reality. Experience is incommunicable wealth, which confers authority on the person who has acquired it: a verifiable knowledge—a "tasting"—which has made truth concrete and alive.

Opening ourselves, giving up prejudices and predetermined patterns, are indispensable conditions for experience. To be closed is to deny all questioning and all opportunity to be enriched, revealing an authoritarian and doctrinaire attitude: the characteristic of "knowledge" which is inconsistent and unverifiable, which cannot withstand the impact of experienced reality.

Knowledge born of experience is not mere apprehension or sensing of an object. It is the synthesis of a whole series of encounters with an object, an empirical science of all that is found around us. Aristotle correctly observed that experience or empirical science is not born of an isolated perception, but of an apperception or synthesis of many perceptions and perspectives, unified by what they have in common, within a model or determined schema (*Meta.* 980b). By virtue of our experience of an object, and to the extent we open to it more and more and study it from different angles, the object becomes increasingly more present within us. Thus, an experienced doctor is one who has encountered an illness on repeated occasions and in different forms and diverse circumstances, and who thus does not allow himself to be taken by surprise or to be mistaken. He knows not so much from what he has learned in books but from what he has learned from following the course of the illness and his analysis of the symptoms. His diagnosis of the disease is tested and verified; the knowledge is an experience.

In studying experience from the perspective of the etymology of the word, one must do more than study *peri.* One must also study the Latin prefix *ex,* whose meaning expresses, among other things, an orientation outward, an openness or exposure to something, as in, for example, *ex-position, ex-clamation, ex-istence.* In this sense *ex* indicates a basic characteristic of the human person as *ex-istence.* The person is a being who exists turned outward, in dialog or communion with others and with the world. This results in experience being not only knowledge but communal knowledge. The object is manifested in the human consciousness according to the structural laws of our consciousness. Experience never takes place without some presuppositions. The consciousness already has some *pre-sub-positions,* which are no more than stances historically adopted. The consciousness is not empty, thanks to models of interpretation inherited from the past, from contemporary society, and from personal experience, which are always present in the consciousness. In order to go out of oneself (*ex*) and to encounter objects, a person assumes total control of the things involved.

Experience thus contains a subjective element (existence) and an objective element (things). In the encounter between the two, in the modifications which take place in both the consciousness and the objects, the structure of experience lies. The models already present in the consciousness are confronted, tested, and checked against reality. They can be confirmed, but they can also be destroyed, corrected, or enriched. Experience implies this whole painful, creative process.

In summary, experience is the way we interiorize reality, the way we situate ourselves in the world and the world in us. Still, we must say that experience is not properly a particular experience. A particular experience is a psychic event involving the dispositions and feelings which produce experience in the human person, or emotions, or antecedent evaluations, in accordance with the experience of objects which are made present in the interior of the human person. A particular experience is, rather than a synonym, a consequence of experience by which the particular experience becomes part of the total phenomenon. Experience is thus a broader and deeper concept than any particular event.

As a way of situating ourselves in the world and the world in us, it is clear that experience changes the characteristics of our horizon or context. The horizon is a perspective which allows us to view objects; a focus which illumines reality, allowing us to discover certain aspects of it, to define them and order them systematically. A concrete example can be found in Latin America, where we are accustomed to view everything from the perspective of liberation or oppression: the educational system, theology, preaching, the sacraments, political systems, economic options—everything. Almost instinctively we come to ask the questions: to what extent is a doctrine liberating us or keeping us enslaved? to what extent does this economic option reinforce a situation of dependence or oppression, or to which extent does it break with such a situation and free us? Liberation is thus an horizon, a viewpoint, an experience which allows us to describe objects in their liberating or oppressive dimensions.

The Experience Typical of Our Modern World

The way people have made themselves present to the world has varied greatly throughout history, just as the way they make the world present to themselves has. The mythic individual interpreted the world in categories totally different from ours because that person had a different experience. In turn, the individual of classical metaphysics experienced the world as a hierarchy of beings within an order presided over, and crowned with, the supreme and eternal Being.[9]

What characterizes people today is knowledge which is more and more detailed and definite (although not necessarily truer). Everything is objective, that is, everything becomes the object of human knowing. Knowledge makes people secure since knowledge is power, and power is the subjection of everything to human categories. Such knowledge objectifies God who becomes the object of theological knowledge, the human person who is made the object of a multifaceted scientific investigation, and the world which becomes the object of many different empirical investigations. From this knowledge arise the sciences and their concrete application, technology, which is considered preeminently objective and verifiable. Our world is, and is defined as, a technico-scientific world, the creation of humanity. No numinous or mysterious Power is posited. One wants to decipher everything, know the functional laws of everything, critically control experience, until it becomes possible to establish a sure and exact science.

The naive claim of certain scientific currents of thought has already been abandoned. These defined the sciences as purely objective or, better, as pure objectivity. Thought and science—it is said—are no more than the reflection of reality experienced in the human consciousness. Science suddenly became aware of its own hermeneutical principle. Knowledge is not reduplication. Experience is always woven into a prior model and from previously formulated questions. The answers are in keeping with the questions. The prior scientific model already chooses what it claims to know. We only test what we look for. Thus it is said that scientific data are not rigorously scientific, but are constructed and elaborated through our unavoidable schemas. Thus it can and must be affirmed that scientific objectivity implies human subjectivity, societal choices, and group interests. Lastly, it is always people who create science, creating it out of everything they themselves are, with clear-cut interests and a particular understanding they confer on their enterprise. These presuppositions determine the questions, indicate the models of analysis, and orient scientific interest.

Be that as it may, our experience of the world is marked by a technico-scientific character, distinguishing our age from other periods in history. Among other things, this fact has an important contribution to make to the incarnation of our experience of God within the experience we have of the world today. Objective science involves people who enter into selecting the data to be analyzed or investigated, the research taking on the meaning these investigators attach to it. At an early stage the people are called upon to explain the phenomena they are analyzing by referring to immanent, verifiable causes of these phenomena. They thus form a scientific construct and raise the possibility of its being used to transform the world by technological means.

At a second and more crucial stage, the investigators are asked for the meaning of these human components. Science and technology are a way of situating the person in the world and the world in the human person. What do these things mean or claim to be? What are the people looking for or following in their endeavors? Their basic meaning is being sought, and this requires more than a scientific explanation. The question of meaning embraces the totality of scientific phenomena. As one of the people most attentive to the hermeneutical structure of science, Ludwig Wittgenstein asserted that "even when we have responded to all possible scientific questions, we become aware that our most vital problems have not even been touched."[10]

The question about the meaning of life is unavoidable. It is discovered as we aim higher, yet it is already implicit in science and technology. In fact, if people investigate and try to transform the world, it is because they see a meaning in it, because the world, as well as the human person, continues realizing itself historically.

How God Appears in the Technico-Scientific World

As we have already said, God does not appear as a phenomenon alongside the world or as an object of analysis and science. A God of nature would be an idol, not a God of Mystery. Since he is not a phenomenon of the world, science prescinds from the God hypothesis as an explanation of empirical reality.

To seek God on the phenomenal level is certainly equivalent to looking for nothing, or to meeting an idol. God is not explainable or explicable in the technico-scientific world; rather he is totally absent from it. He is banished. Yet his banishment provides the opportunity for learning what God is, what people can do in their spheres of knowledge and power, and how people can manipulate what is in their purview, to be revealed.

A disquieting problem arises for scientific thought: from where does the impulse or force of spirit come which motivates science's quest for knowledge, conquest, and control? To respond that it comes from Nature is to give a scientific answer, but one that is insufficient since it does not fully answer the question. In fact, one could follow this up by asking where Nature gets it from. Undoubtedly the evasive answers could be multiplied. But finally the scientist would have to confess, "I don't know!" if he or she were to be honest.

Our knowledge and power are thus fundamentally sustained by "un-knowing" and "un-power." Science arises out of radical mystery. It arises thanks to a life-giving force which moves faster and faster, stimulating the desire to know and control everything. Yet science can never control or contain in its categories the answer to the question of the origin of such power and knowledge.

Language can speak of everything except the force which gives rise to speech. The eye can see everything, but can never succeed in seeing itself; the mirror may be broken without breaking the eye. What eye is there that sees everything including itself? Who or What is that Mystery without a name? What is that knowing-not-known, or that un-knowing that "transcends all knowledge and leaves it babbling," as the mystic-poet John of the Cross said.

In fact, have not all religion and all mystics invoked the Ineffable, which is revealed and hidden at the same time, in our conception of the existence of God? Is not God the Word which expresses the Non-Word? The Psalmist says,

> In your light, Lord, I see light. Not without reason the wise man said, "To name the Tao is to name the no-thing. . . . "Tao" is a name which means "without definition." The Tao is beyond words and objects. It is not expressed either in words or silence. Where neither words nor silence exists the Tao is apprehended.[11]

The God of Mystery is, therefore, in the technico-scientific world, but reserved, silenced, in oblivion. Not to speak of him does not mean that he is not present or that he may be denied. There is the virtue of silence. Analogies can be valuable. God is like the root of a tree. We see the tree, look at its leaves, eat its fruit until we discover its nature. What does not appear on the face of the earth—its root—is what gives life and growth to the tree. The root is unseen, cloistered in the silence of the earth. To eat the fruit of the tree or to rest in its shade we need not think of the root, but it is the root that drives the sap and, within the sap, the life. God is like the sun which burns beyond the earth. In the room lit by the sun we do not see the sun. When we look at things, move around, and work in the sunlight in the room we rarely think of the sun itself; it remains in oblivion and silence. But it does not cease to shine on those who forget it any more than it does on the people who study its nature. This is how God appears in the technico-scientific world: veiled, forgotten, silenced. But like the root or the sun, God is always present as the force or life of our will, knowledge, and power.

Whoever pursues such reflections quickly notices how the world begins to be transformed for him or her into a great sign which—despite all technical apparatus—refers to a fundamental reality sustaining it. Not only do the specific things in the technico-scientific world direct us toward God, but everything becomes a pathway, beckoning us to journey toward God. This is true not only of the positive things, but of the negative ones as well, not only of the benefits of technology, but also of its most inhuman manipulations; all are sustained by the same basic principle. We do not want to say God is responsible for evil in the technological world. As we have said, God is not present in the world as a secondary cause or as a mere phenomenon. People are the only cause of evil. Still the force which drives humanity is not our own, but something given to us. The responsibility for misusing this force falls totally on us. Instead of feeling commissioned by God—not being absolute in ourselves—we tend to absolutize our works. We do not perceive that we are at the mercy of something—of someone—that is not us and that continually transcends us. Thus none of our works conforms to the call that comes from the Mystery of God through our consciousness, our reasoning, or our fellowship, but to the call that rather obeys its own voice and its insatiable drive for self-affirmation. Nevertheless, anything which succeeds in overcoming the temptation, which represents the evil in the technological world (that opaque world, centered in humanity where only humanity and its works appear) comes to be transformed, becomes transparent to the root which secretly gives it life or to the sun which indirectly illuminates it.

But let us return to the question that was left unanswered before: what meaning do we look for to realize or live out in our technico-scientific relations with reality? First, technico-scientific activity reveals who we are: principally beings open to the world. Through our works we succeed not only in rising above the biological level, but also in transforming the world and creating a culture. Science and technology constitute the most refined forms of relationship between us and our world. Technological and scientific developments are a concretization of our openness to the world.

But what is the nature of that openness? The human being is open not to specific things but to the world as a totality, differing from animals who have specialized organs for meeting their concrete needs. Still, the new element in human openness is that neither technology nor the technico-scientific culture succeeds in satisfying the force behind our openness. There always remains in us a superabundance or surplus of impulses or drives, which remain radically unfulfilled, drives toward new worlds we keep on creating, new interpretations we go on conceiving, new social schemas we keep on formulating. This means fundamentally that we are more than the world. We have an infinite longing in us. A principle of hope burns in us, which unceasingly impels us to create and resituate ourselves in the world, dreaming or daydreaming of a world which is increasingly more human, more fraternal, until we project a utopia of greatest happiness and greatest fulfillment.

What mechanism impels us in our total openness, as infinite openness going beyond our world and our culture? What gives our works their value? There is no answer except the Infinite. Only the Infinite is capable of satisfying an infinite longing. The word "God" articulated by human beings still expresses the infinite strength of the infinite openness of the person.

The technico-scientific world, when analyzed in its internal dynamic, leads us to pose the problem of God. Openness to the world, incarnated in technological transformation, is no more than a concrete (and thus partial) manifestation of the total openness of the human person. Besides having a meaning for humanity itself, science and technology, through their taking possession of the world, have a deeper meaning. They signify the hidden, unconscious, insatiable search for an Absolute beyond our mastery of the world. But only people who radically involve themselves in the world perceive it. In other words, only those who do not fear the worldliness of the world, only those who try to investigate the radical, basic meaning hidden in the technico-scientific enterprise can find it. Accepting and affirming our temporality, we begin to understand the basic meaning of God as it springs forth from the innermost part of our temporality. God is then neither confused with the world nor does he appear outside it, but he arises as its radical meaning. He is a real and living God who is at our side and on our path. He appears as the unavoidable point of convergence toward which our infinite strivings tend.

In our transforming of the world, our longing, no matter how infinite, only encounters and creates finite realities. No matter how far we exercise our wisdom and our creative power, we still perceive the infinity of our longing, which is unrealizable and which is not the result of our efforts. This keeps on revealing how much more the Infinite toward which we strive cannot be limited to ourselves or to human categories. It also keeps on revealing more clearly that which is not human, but which is more—infinitely more—than we are. Thus the dimension of mystery as total openness of comprehensibility and futurity arises. Religions, especially Christianity, have used the word "God" to designate that supreme and ineffable mystery which impels our life (cf. *Nostra Aetate,* 2).

The meaning present and implied in the scientific character of our world (insofar as science and technology imply a concrete meaning for us) is that Meaning par excellence is present, i.e., the hidden, silent presence of God. Therein lies the impossibility of speaking of the basic absurdity of existence. To speak of reality as absurd is contradictory, since it would have to prove the non-reality of the absurd itself. In doing so a meaning would already be affirmed.[12] God can never be excluded from the world or language. He is present in the very seeking or the very attempt to exclude him.

In asking ourselves, as we did before, for the meaning of the technico-scientific world, we were not simply looking for something we had not yet encountered. At these heights of thought the reflection we make shows that we are already within the Meaning. We ask because we have already been caught up and involved in the Meaning. Our analysis has been limited to calling forth what is already implicit in it, although hidden and silenced, making us think about how light comes from the sun or how the tree lives because of its root.

From this experience of God in contact with our world, we can see the world from a different perspective: in itself the world is profoundly opaque, but it becomes the revealer of God and the articulator of all Meaning, beginning to present itself to us as the transparency of God himself, veiled and revealed in it, given and held back. To take refuge in God as he comes to us is to be open to the area of faith and belief. With our believing, we give a radical *yes* to the hidden Meaning we encounter in the world in which we live.

How God Appears in the Oppressed World of Latin America

Our age approaches the world scientifically, not mythically or metaphysically. Within the wide range of science another perspective is articulated historically. We wish to analyze that perspective in terms of the concrete social situation of Latin America.

Analysis of the Situation

The great masses of people in Latin America still interpret the world from a mythico-religious perspective. This is undoubtedly invaluable in keeping a constantly human perspective because even the technico-scientific individual is "savage and primitive" in the most basic structures of his or her consciousness. In fact, the mythic, metaphysical, and scientific perspectives must be interpreted not successively but contemporaneously. They are the internal structures of the mind. They are like windows of the soul through which we can contemplate the varied landscape of reality.

Thus in our history in Latin America the technico-scientific spirit also has a place and is experienced dramatically. Here technology and science are not innocent, since they have been used historically as tools of domination and oppression and not merely to achieve sovereignty over matter.

Latin America remains an underdeveloped region, dependent on the rich nations of the Northern Hemisphere. A careful sociological study reveals that this underdevelopment is the by-product of the development of the rich nations that continue to keep us in this state of underdevelopment. We are peripheral to the great decision-making centers situated in New York, London, Paris, and Bonn, not in Buenos Aires, Santiago, or Mexico City.

This, in turn, is the result of a worldwide system of economic and social relationships dictated by the Western, capitalist world. This is not the time to criticize this system of human relationship and of the person's relationship to the means of production and consumer goods.[13] Yet it must be admitted that this system's spirit and predominant motivation are centered in wealth and self-interest (private ownership of property, capital investment, free enterprise, labor as a commodity). With such values capitalism creates a terribly inhuman social structure marked by poverty, weakness, and alienation. The organization of power is such that it increases the power of the rich minority more and more while at the same time increasing the helplessness of the poor majority. The exploitation—people's using one another—often assumes ruthless forms and leads to increased social inequality.

Prescinding for a moment from abstractions, let us present some data as illustrations. More than one-third of the world's population suffers extreme poverty, according to information from the United Nations Commission on Human Rights. According to that source,

> The poorest elements of underdeveloped nations live on an income calculated in terms of North American buying power of 30¢ a day.[14] At the conclusion of a Latin-American regional seminar of skilled and

> unskilled workers, held in Buenos Aires in February, 1974 . . . , the fact that 50,000,000 Latin Americans are undernourished due to a diet composed almost entirely of starches was denounced.[15]

To use a concrete example: the regime that came to power in Brazil in 1964 chose to pursue rapid development, erecting a capitalistic structure of economic dependence that resulted in an economic miracle rivaled only by Japan. Yet, according to the government's own statistics, 43% of the total working population earned no more than the minimum wage; 32% earned double the minimum wage.[16] This restriction of salary finds its counterpart in increased concentration of income in a reduced portion of the population. In 1960, 70% of the population received less than 35% of the income, while the best-paid 10% received 39%. The index of concentration of income increased dramatically between 1960 and 1970, when the lowest 70% of the population received 28% of the income, while the top 10% received 47%.[17] According to the data, 56% of the population finds itself at the level of absolute margination (able to buy only the food they must have to sustain life) and 75% at the level of relative margination (able to buy only basic necessities).[18] The Brazilian system thus provides directly for a small segment of the population an enormous increase in wealth. A share in increased wealth, which is theoretically open to all, is effectively restricted to 5% of the population.

Development is thus defined not in terms of independence and autonomy through one's potential, but in terms of the paradigm provided by the rich nations of the Northern Hemisphere, a paradigm unattainable in the more accelerated time frame chosen for the transformation. As Celso Hurtado observed,

> Experience has shown that if the power to attain the object one pursues increases very quickly, structural deformity is aggravated, since an increase benefiting a particular part of the population widens the chasm that exists between the quality of life of the well-off minority and that of the masses or the majority. This chasm is essentially the same as underdevelopment produced. It is possible to conclude then that the betterment of conditions for the masses of the nations of the

Third World, especially those with large populations, can only be achieved by other means. India will never be a Switzerland of millions of inhabitants, nor Brazil a carbon copy of the United States.[19]

Our purpose in citing these data is not propagandistic, but is merely to show the extent of the injustice in the capitalist system. Something is amiss in the option for a world-wide system so concentrated in the Western world. Such a situation constitutes a terrible challenge to the experience of God. One asks how God can even be revealed in such a situation. We said before that God emerges from our concrete history. There is no a priori knowledge of him applicable to our situation. We must then discover the image of God in this inhuman world.

The capitalist system presents God as the Supreme Being who establishes natural categories, among which rich and poor are always found. It preaches a God who demands observance of the laws of nature. It understands need and hunger as personal preferences, competition and free enterprise as consequences of the natural law. It proclaims a God who prescribes preserving the established order without asking if that order might not be the result of selfishness and special interest. The situation becomes more tragic for belief when we see to what extent, in order to justify its oppressive system, it has adopted basic Christian concepts such as humility, obedience, honesty, patience, carrying the cross of Christ, poverty, renunciation, love without revenge. Freud said Christians were "badly baptized." Why? Marcuse comments, "because they accept the Gospel in its most liberating aspects only in some fanciful forms which leave them as unfree as they were before."[20] J. L. Segundo presents an equally sad proof.

Since the capitalist system manifests throughout its development a terrible burden of inhuman domination, the Christian cannot find in his or her experience of social life anything he or she can use to think about God as he is revealed in Jesus Christ. Moreover, one's judgment on the social system must lead one to criticize the notion of God presented by the false image projected by the ideology of domination. Thus we can say that never before has it been so difficult to conceive the Christian God existentially.[21]

The "Presence" of God Discerned from a Double "Absence"

Let us recognize that we do not come to know who the Christian God is a priori, but by taking up the challenges this condition of slavery presents. In so doing a new face of the God of our Lord Jesus Christ will be revealed. In fact, by something of a paradox, God is made present in Latin America by an extremely serious double absence.

In the first place, the oppressive dependence, the margination of the masses, the abject misery, the unbridled profit of the few, the violent repression exercised by the established powers are awakening in us an insatiable thirst for justice, a hunger for participation, a longing for fraternity, and an ardent desire to create social structures that eliminate the exploitation of one person by another once and for all. Because we perceive justice, we chafe under structural injustice; because we long for solidarity, we suffer under a regime based on discrimination; because we are motivated by love, we struggle against the dehumanization of our social relationships.

Justice, solidarity, love, are present by their absence in the concrete situation. God may be the verbal symbol for speaking about justice, love, participation, communion, solidarity. God only possesses an existential meaning when he is the point of reference for justice, love, and human fellowship. Henri De Lubac expressed this well:

> If I lack love or justice, it unfailingly keeps me away from you, Lord, and my worship is no more than idolatry. In order to believe in you I must believe in love and justice; and it is a thousand times more valuable to believe in these things than to speak your name. Apart from these things it is impossible to encounter you; those who are guided by them are on the path which leads to you.[22]

God is thus revealed as *Deus inversus* (God-turned-upside-down). He arises in contrast. However great the darkness is, the Light will be greater. But this Light judges us, condemns us, and demands explanations. It does not allow us to be passive in the face of injustice, which cries out to heaven, and in the face of misery, which God does not want to exist in any manner.

The second absence—sadder even than the first—also makes God present by contrast: the absence of the concrete, living, and true God in those who always have his name on their lips and who worship in his churches. Christianity is the predominant religion in South America. The continent calls on God and worships him officially and publicly. But faith in God and in Jesus Christ does not achieve its full Christian expression. It is too akin to pagan religiosity. In paganism the gods want people as their servants; indeed, people were created to serve the gods. Christian faith, precisely as it was defined and eschatologically oriented by Christ, affirms that God wants to be served in other people. To serve another (in whom God is present) is the command of Christ and the new element in Christian experience of God. It is easy to serve God directly; in itself this does not require another person. But to serve the neighbor involves us with another person, since the neighbor is not an abstraction but a concrete individual in the world who can be wretched or unjust or selfish. To love the poor, sick neighbor who is humiliated and exploited involves us with that person and forces us to take a stand.

Only the one who loves another loves God; the person involved in liberating another is the person who serves the Lord of History. As St. John said, one who does not love the brother or sister one sees cannot love God whom one does not see (1 Jn. 4:20 ff.). Christianity as commonly practiced in Latin America does not bring about this kind of Christian conversion or, if one prefers, this identity which John established between love of God and love of neighbor. The God invoked and worshipped is more an idol than a living and challenging God. Thus there is the tendency to sacralize an inhuman situation, stifling (by arrogating the most holy name of God which is reserved to the Mystery which permeates all reality) people's awareness, rendering them incapable of perceiving the oppressive situation and of reacting critically toward it.

The result is that theological Christianity cannot be identified with sociological Christianity, the charade which calls itself Christianity. Sociological Christianity attempts to live a lie, even though it uses the words and doctrines of

Christianity. On the other hand, the person who rejects sociological Christianity in Latin America as having been appropriated by the established powers as their ideological legitimation, and instead seeks justice, participation, and freedom is very close to theological Christianity. Indeed such a person is closer to the living and true God than the person who, while confessing God and Jesus Christ and practicing orthodox Catholicism, closes both eyes and heart to the margination of the millions, the systematic exploitation, and the legalized repression.

This affirmation, which scandalizes the religious and social status quo, should not alienate us. It is found in the better Gospel tradition. When Christ wants to explain who the neighbor is, when he marvels at a person's faith, when he wants to make clear what prompt obedience is, he does not use the example of pious individuals or revealed religion, but of people not connected with these official standards of virtue: the Samaritan unbeliever, the Syro-Phoenician woman, the Roman centurion. There is a kind of denial a Christian can make which better restores the original divine meaning of Christianity. Such a practice seems urgent and much needed in the Latin American context, given the ideological manipulation of Christianity to make it serve established regimes.

The Commitment to Liberation

God appears not only in his absence.[23] His presence can be discerned in the human reaction to our underdeveloped condition. God emerges positively and experientially in the powerful and universal movement which seeks to wrench this continent out of its backwardness and inhumanity. In the effective process of liberation—the commitment to destroy unjust structures—one begins with the human mind in attempting to bring about the modification of the practices which give rise to dehumanization and oppression. It is in this process of liberation that the primary meaning of the word "God" must be verified, in accordance with the original meaning of this word, "to make true."

In total and serious commitment to liberation we begin to see a dimension in ourselves which is the force for that commitment, the light for our struggle, the meaning of our sacrifice—something superior to us, which arouses our thirst for justice, our longing for fellowship. This something is the focus of our aspirations. When all these aspirations have been realized, God will stand revealed and we will experience God in our historical transparency. In no other way can God be real for us, since he would have no relationship to us and our world. God would be an empty, alienating word.

To commit ourselves to the task of liberation is not to horizontalize Christianity nor to recast it in purely human terms. To counterpose the horizontal and the vertical is to objectify and to distinguish in the realm of thought between two aspects which always appear as one in concrete experience. By making the distinction, Christianity is rendered abstract and thus ineffective in concrete situations. When life and liberation are radically affirmed and undertaken with total commitment, they reveal at one and the same time their vertical and horizontal dimensions. In other words, only people committed body and soul to service of their neighbor begin to see the dimension which transcends the neighbor and themselves, the force which calls us into being, which grounds and makes possible the task of social love, or commitment, and of liberation. Thus true transcendence and the most correct meaning of the vertical are verified: the great Mystery, called God, is revealed.[24]

We can find a name for that Mystery in the prayers and rituals we use to call upon the Holy, calling it by the name which sums up all our aspirations. Let us call upon him as Liberator. Let us do homage to him as the One who calls us into the future. Let us love him as our hope. Let us unite ourselves with him as the power for our struggle and the consolation in the helplessness of our repression. All these expressions are in our dictionaries, but they try to make present the One whom no dictionary can contain or name: the Mystery of God experienced in our concrete life.

The Revelation of God in the Historical Process of the Individual

After what we have said up to this point, it is clear that God is not an object among others which can be directly experienced. Thinking about God is thinking qualified by the world, since our explanations of the world are not ultimate, but are always refined further and sustained by something or someone revealed in the world but not itself the world. Let us explain further.

The human person is a being-in-relationship. Nevertheless we resist allowing ourselves merely to be introduced into a predetermined world. We have our unique, personal journey, original and unrepeatable. In that journey lies our sacredness and dignity. We have our personal experience of the world and in the heart of the world is where we realize the experience of God as the Mystery of the world.

This experience of God in the transparency of the world[25] is not one experience alongside others, as one would experience a sunset or a physical hurt.[26] We have observed this before. Now we must ask how an experience of God is realized in our personal life-journey. We journey on a road never traveled before. "We travel where there is no road, building the road one step at a time," as Machado said. No one can take another's place. No one can live another's life. Likewise each of us must verify in our life-journey our experience of the source which nourishes our life. One reflects on the course of one's life and discovers the One in whom we already live.

Some may notice that their experience of life's mystery is never expressed in terms of an experience of God. God to them is some other thing, more or less untrue. Despite such possible misinterpretation, it must be affirmed that God can really be experienced when he appears as the Mystery or Meaning of our lives since his name cannot be captured either in the words of our language nor in the creations of our imagination. The following reflections do not pretend to describe an experience of God but simply to point out a possible way toward such an experience.

God as the Experience of Goodness and the Radical Meaning of Life

Certainly we all have experiences even though some of them may be trivial. God can still be revealed, even in them. We have all experienced the basic goodness of life.[27] If we live confidently, it is because we have an unconscious, inexplicit trust in the goodness of existence. Life is beset by evil, disease, lies, hate, and ultimately by death. But in spite of these things we do not give up on life, but get up every morning, beginning again each day. There is a grace-filled dimension of life that cannot be destroyed. It is true we cannot define it, locate it, confine it to a concrete situation. Each time we try to capture it we affirm the evil along with the good, the finite along with the infinite; the dimension which is always present without being located anywhere escapes us. We live because of it; although we are disgraced, we do not kill ourselves.

The affirmation of the totally absurd is not merely empty words or a vain desire of people. In extreme desperation, they even look into suicide for meaning in the face of the absurdity of their lives, believing that in death they will find the end of their problems. The very attempt to affirm the totally absurd implies that a meaning exists, a meaning whose absence is filled by the absurd. The meaning is the goodness of life expressed by the revelation of God in human experience. Even those who deny God do not deny a Supreme Being so much as they deny the possibility of being welcomed and accepted by him who is the consolation and basic meaning of their whole lives.

Thus the basic goodness of life presents itself as the experience of the radical meaning of life. We do not create the meaning ourselves. In asking about the meaning we are already recognizing ourselves to be within it. We are raised up by it to assume for ourselves in all seriousness the great and small things of life, the daily routine, life with others, the responsibility of a profession. Despite all human negativity—frustration, insecurity, infidelity—the meaning triumphs over the absurd, the belief in a basic order of the world over disillusionment, the light over the darkness.

God must be considered the origin of the experience of meaning, since he dwells in every experience. God appears secretly even in the words of the prostitute who says,

> Pray for me, Father, because it will all turn out well. I want to work a little more and sell myself for another year to pay for my apartment.

> Afterwards I want to be a woman committed to one man, to have a husband and children. I will love and suffer, but I will succeed in doing it as a person. God is good and he will help me. He will raise me out of this life of humiliation.

People who speak like this speak out of a sense of deep meaning. Who cannot understand that it is God who thus breaks into the life of such a person? The Brazilian *favelados* are forced to submit to back-breaking jobs to earn a pittance. They are the marginated with large families who live almost like animals, in a condition of extreme poverty. Still they have a sense of dignity, which is apparent even in the way they receive people who are better off. They have not lost religion, the joy of life, sensitivity to the needs of their neighbors, or consciousness of human solidarity. They have a wisdom no school except the school of life can impart. God, they say, made the world very good, and one day he will make it so that everyone is equal. In death all are made equal and of one accord, whether or not they want to be, whether or not they intend it.

Who can say that these people are not already living from the depths of their being? Is it not God who is manifested in their awareness? It is our objectification of God which blinds us to such manifestations in human life of God's appearance or emergence. But how can we situate ourselves so as to experience God, who arises out of human life, even at its most trivial?

God as Experience of the Futility of Life

We continually experience our personal limitations. However strong our will is, however correct our conscience, all we intend to do and actually carry out is extremely fragile. Our inner personality is always being further articulated; thus we never master anything sufficiently. At the heart of our actions an insatiable longing throbs. A radical loneliness touches our heart. There are moments and situations in life when no one is, or can be, at our side. We must take up our own journey and our own destiny radically alone.

But awareness of our finitude can only originate in what is

infinite. Only people who know freedom suffer under slavery. However much we experience and suffer from our limitations, we are already conquering them. The experience of our limitations, our breaking points, our frailties, calls us forth to experience the limitless, the unbounded, the absolute. The infinite or absolute is the name we give to the mystery which our own life proclaims. Thus we experience the transparency of God.

God as the Experience of Love

We also experience love as something which is rightfully ours and yet is superior to us. In fact we feel ourselves freely loved by the other: freedom or gratuitousness expressed in acceptance of the frailties and limitations which would, of themselves, kill love or lessen the reasons for which the other person loves us and keeps on loving us. Despite everything, love survives.

On the other hand, we ourselves also love in a way that reason cannot always justify, accepting the weakness and the risk of the other person, sometimes even values contradictory to our own, because of the sheer fact of his or her having met us on the same road. No one planned for the meeting, yet love arises nonetheless from the encounter.

But what is loved in loving someone else? Something determinable, such as beauty, intelligence, affability, goodness, or sympathy would not make us love the other person but merely something that person possessed. What we really love is the living mystery of that person, manifested in that person's actions and attitudes but transcending any trait that can be catalogued. The language of lovers approaches divine language in their oaths of eternal love, absolute fidelity, and irrevocable self-giving because love partakes of the Mystery of love, which is God himself. Human love serves the greater Love: the person is the locus and the incarnate manifestation of the God of Love and the Love of God, as well as an instance of goodness in human life. Only through sharing in the experience of love can one come to understand who God is at his most intimate. This is what the New Testament declares in saying that God is Love (1 Jn. 4:8).

This is the basic reason why love is always a sorrowful experience. The human "thou" is not the ultimate "Thou," nor does a human being fulfill the heart's yearning for an absolute "Thou." The person who is loved is only a sacrament and a symbolic presence of the Other Love. The human "I" must cherish the beloved "thou" and, joined together, they must place themselves within the absolute "Thou." Only then does love become perfect, because one dies to self and rises to a personal Love, which is God himself.

"If You Have Seen Your Brother, You Have Seen the Lord"

God is also revealed in every experience we have of another person. I am never related to another as to an object to be categorized. In the person of the other I am called toward a Transcendent, but I discover a living transcendence. Moreover, the person is a mystery, not as an unknown quantity not yet investigated by human sciences, but as one who proceeds from complete knowing and resists all human probing. The person is unique, original, and unrepeatable, never to be completely known by science. We each respond in our own way to our own becoming. What is the human person? To the extent the person goes on communicating, the person continues to open himself or herself to the horizon or limits of questioning until the person loses himself or herself in the Mystery we call God.

The ultimate experience of the human being, then, is the experience of Mystery. No one, no matter how sinful or miserable, can prevent the transcendence from revealing itself. We are always greater than our sins, always greater than our ecstasies of mystical love. There is a mysterious wellspring in the human person, a "beyond" which is the permanent transparency of God in the world. The human person is thus the greatest sacrament of God.

From our sacramental character derives the sacredness, dignity, and awesomeness of the human person. From this derives also the identity Jesus himself affirmed between love of God and love of neighbor. This identity is not merely legalistic (it is so because God wants it that way), but an ontological reality: in the depths of our humanity we are nourished by Mystery, the Mystery which is the source of our own Mystery. God unceasingly communicates himself and gives himself to us throughout history, basically through each human individual. Loving another we are radically loving God. As Clement of Alexandria put it, "If you have seen your brother, you have seen the Lord" (*Stromata*, 1. 19).

This experience of God should make us continually resist the temptation to turn a person into an object. Both the temptation and the need for conquering it are abundantly clear. All we need to do is analyze human beings in their existential situation to conclude that God is not something extrinsic to us, revealed only in the privileged moments of our life, but perpetually present in the tapestry of our lives, constantly revealing himself in our comings and goings.

It is true we can have privileged moments, clearly gratuitous, in which we do not question ourselves because we know that God has intervened in our lives. This shows God's transparency: despite the magnitude of the problems, God gives us peace and serenity. There is a place in life for such moments, perhaps after a long period of purification, after an acute crisis, or as an intervention in an alienated and sinful life. God arises not only as question or answer, but also as transparency and proof. In every case we experience a grandeur infinitely greater than that of the created universe; we feel ourselves to be kings and priests of all creation; we experience our power to live and give thanks and praise to God in the name of everyone and everything. Then we can invoke the Mystery we feel in ourselves:

> Lord, despite my sin, I can let you enter me! I can expand to the most remote part of the universe. At any moment whatsoever I can take everything and offer it to you, praise you as Lord, give thanks to you and say: No matter what happens, even from the depths of my nothingness, I will not stop praising and thanking you forever.

When we have this kind of experience, we know God has entered our lives. What is more real to us than our own reality? What more certainly exists for us than our own existence? In short, what has been revealed to us is what surely concerns us and gives meaning to our lives. In such a situation we may have the most liberating experience of our lives. In that moment we feel the need to give thanks and we know to whom to address ourselves: to God.

The Christian Experience of God

Up to now we have tried to examine the experience of God as it takes place in human life. We have not spoken yet of the peculiarly Christian experience of God. We must now ask what makes up that experience or how the God-Mystery revealed himself in Christianity.

In what is perhaps too theoretical a formula we can say that in Christianity the experience of the Mystery is articulated as a history of the mystery. The Meaning of history does not remain diffused or confused with reality, but has pitched his tent in the world with the name Jesus (Jn. 1:14). The mystery is that the Mystery can so radically, without loss of its identity, become non-Mystery, flesh, history, and can subsist in what is different from itself. If it could not do this it would not be absolute Mystery. Thus, living, it can die, and dying, it can live. The impalpable can become palpable, the invisible visible. God can become human:

> What we have heard and seen with our eyes, what we have touched with our hands, concerning the Word of Life—for that life was made visible and we bear witness and announce to you the eternal life which was with the Father and was revealed to us—we announce to you. (1 Jn. 1:13)

Christian faith thus bears witness to the history of God, who, being Infinite and Transcendent, became finite and immanent as part of our world. Celebrating this absolute self-communication of God, Christianity sings of the radical nearness of the Mystery. The kindness of God, which is experienced as limitless love, appeared as total pardon, as a merciful presence among us. The life of Jesus is the life of God. The acceptance and pardon of Jesus is the acceptance and pardon of God himself.

Such an affirmation can be a scandal to philosophy and apophantic theology. It will seem blasphemous to anyone who maintains the total non-objectivity of the Mystery, and idolatrous to one who affirms the absolute transcendence of the Mystery. But do we know what the Mystery is? It gives itself in the rational and the irrational, in the most distant and the most intimate, in history and beyond history. What is proper to the Mystery is the power to become entirely other, to stand outside itself. The otherness of the Mystery is his *kenosis:* his becoming a human being, a slave, a crucified one who descends to the underworld. Such was the journey of Jesus Christ, the journey of the *Deus inversus* (cf. Ph. 2:6–13). Thus new possibilities for religious discourse are opened up, corresponding to what is narrated in the history of this event of divine gentleness and kindness.

How did this history of God incarnate in the world proceed? How does God reveal himself in Jesus of Nazareth?

The Experience of God in Jesus of Nazareth

Only by situating Jesus in his world and his own concrete circumstances can we see what is original in his experience of God.[28] Certainly the God of Jesus is the God of the Jewish people experienced in the Old Testament. But this experience takes on a special character because the Incarnation had as its object not only to prove what we already knew about God, but also to reveal definitively who God really is.

We cannot forget, for example, that the ultimate motive for condemning Jesus was rooted not so much in his disagreement with the Pharisees over interpretation of the Law and Old Testament truths but, as the Gospels clearly point out, in his substituting the God of love and pardon for the God of the Law. Thus he was condemned for his different experience of God. Let us examine this from different perspectives.

A World of External and Internal Oppression

The world in which Jesus lived was politically under a regime of dependency, inherited from a former time.[29] The external dependency manifested itself internally in the presence of occupying troops, tax collectors, the Sadducees playing Roman politics, and the presence of Roman-Hellenistic culture, which made the oppression more hateful, given the religious nature of the Jews. With Herod's death, the kingdom was divided among his sons (Lk. 3:1–2). Later Judea went on to be governed by a Roman procurator.

Socially and economically Galilee, the scene of Jesus' main apostolic efforts, was a well-populated area, primarily agricultural. The occupation of Jesus' family was that of a *teknon,* which signifies either carpentry or roofing. There was work for everyone, but the region still was not well off. It was ignored by the economic system, so great need brought droves of rural people into the towns looking for work. Day laborers thronged the town squares (Mt. 20:1–15) or hired themselves out to large landowners so as to be able to pay off their debts.[30] Mosaic Law, which gave the firstborn double that of the other children, conspired to increase the number of day laborers, who, when they could not find work, easily became a true proletariat composed of beggars, tramps, and thieves. There were also landlords who exploited their tenants through mortgages and expropriation of property in payment of debts. The tax system was indefensible and complex. There were taxes on virtually everything: family members, land, wages, crops, water, meat, salt, and roads. Herod's grandiose building contributed even more to the impoverishment of the people.

Foreign domination was a true test of people's faith in promises. Some movements for liberation, especially those of the Zealots, attempted to pave the way for, or even provoke, the saving intervention of God. As dependency and oppression grew greater, the hope and expectation of the imminent intervention of God burned more brightly, prodded by the dreamy fantasies of the apocalypticists who saw in everything a harbinger of the restoration of the Kingdom of God and the consequent liquidation of all the enemies of the people.

Even so, the true oppression lay not so much in the presence of Roman power as in the legalistic interpretation of religion and the will of God, especially by the Pharisees.[31] The Law, instead of illuminating the encounter of people with God, degenerated—with its minuscule traditions and interpretations—into a bitter slavery imposed in the name of God (Mt. 23:24; Lk. 11:46). Those who lived on the fringes of the Law were lost. They could not hope in God. They were social outcasts. Even the sick considered illness as punishment for the sins of their ancestors. For the Pharisee justification lay in the Law, not in God. Christ himself indicted the Pharisees: "How well you violate the commandment of God in order to follow your traditions!" (Mk. 7:9). Everything was measured by the standard of the Law: who the neighbor was, who was pure or impure, what professions were immoral, along with the social discrimination this led to. The Pharisees, despite believing themselves perfect, are cursed by Christ for ignoring the most important part of the Law: justice, mercy, and faith (Mt. 23:23).

God Experienced as Liberator and Absolute Meaning

Against this depressing and enslaving backdrop Jesus arose, with his special experience of God. God appears fundamentally as Liberator. Jesus' first words were ones of liberation: "The spirit of the Lord is upon me, because he has anointed me to proclaim Good News to the poor, liberty to captives, sight to the blind, freedom to the oppressed, to announce a year of favor from the Lord" (Lk. 4:18–19).[32] He says to everyone, "The time is fulfilled and the Kingdom of God is at hand. Repent and believe in the Good News" (Mk. 1:15).

"The Kingdom of God" is the key phrase which explains his experience. It indicates the radical meaning of the world, freed from sin, hate, suffering, and death. It is the utopia, the goal of history, realized now as the Good News. Thus the sick are cured (Mt. 8:16–17), mourning is transformed into joy (Lk. 7:11–17). Since they are harmful elements of nature (Mt. 8:27), sins are pardoned (Mk. 2:5), demons expelled (Mt. 12:28), and death is destroyed forever (Mk. 5:39).

God is the meaning of the world already transformed and transfigured. This is what is indicated by "the Kingdom of God." Therefore, "Blessed are you poor, for yours is the Kingdom of Heaven; blessed are you who are hungry for you will be filled; blessed are you who weep for you will be consoled" (Lk. 6:20–21).

Jesus does not concern himself with particular instances of liberation, either political or religious. All creation will be liberated. This is not only a prophetic or utopian proclamation—Jewish and pagan prophets of every age proclaimed the coming of a new world, and Jesus is certainly one of them. But this is not where his originality lies. What makes Jesus different is that the utopia is realized in him. He does not say the Kingdom will come, but that the Kingdom has already come and is in our midst (Mk. 1:15; Mt. 3:17; Lk. 17:21). Jesus experiences God as already present, carrying out and fulfilling his final victory through Jesus' own preaching and prophetic action and miracle working: "If I expel demons by the finger of God, it is a sign that the Kingdom of God has already come to you" (Lk. 11:20). He knows he is acting in God's name, since he alone is strong enough to overcome that demonic power (Mk. 3:27). In this rests the novelty of Jesus: with Jesus, God is in our midst.

God Experienced as Father of Infinite Goodness

The presence of the Kingdom demands total dedication on the part of human beings. It is necessary to be open to the God-who-is-present. But what is this God like? Is he still the God of the Law, demanding literal obedience and minute observance as the Pharisees believed?

The Gospels show two facets of Jesus, apparently contradictory—one strict, the other lax.[33] On one side is a Jesus who, in God's name, imposes greater demands than the Pharisees: not only one who kills, but even one who is angry is liable to judgment (Mt 5:21); not only consummated adultery, but even a lustful look makes a person an adulterer (Mt. 5:27–28); if one's eye or hand or foot is a cause of scandal, it must be cut off or plucked out (Mt. 5:29–30). The entire Sermon on the Mount is a radicalization of the demands of the Law, making its observance virtually impossible for human beings.

On the other hand, there is a Jesus superior to the Law, so much so that he can exercise a laxity which scandalizes the pious of his time (Mt. 13:57). He is not too concerned about rigorous observance of the Sabbath, considering people more important (Mk. 2:23–26; Lk. 6:6–10, 13:10–17, 14:1–16; Mk. 1:18). Neither he nor his disciples were ascetics like John and his disciples, so they were accused of being gluttons and drunkards (Mk. 1:18; Lk. 7:34; Mt. 11:19). Jesus criticizes the distinction between neighbor and non-neighbor (Lk. 10:29), and the laws of purification (it is not what goes into a person's body, but what comes out of the person's heart, that makes the person unclean—Mk. 7:19). He accepts everyone, especially those considered public sinners, with whom he eats (Lk. 15:2; Mt. 9:10–11), lepers (Mk. 1:41), and the Samaritan woman (Jn. 4:7). He prefers publicans, prostitutes, and sinners to theologians and the pious (Mt. 21:32).

How can these contrasts be reconciled? They cannot if we take the Law as the criterion. But it is possible if we consider the typical experience Jesus has of God. His strictness is evidently not that of the Law, but strictness which helps abandon the absolutizing of the Law, and emphasizes trust in God who is above and beyond the Law. Jesus experiences God not as a judge or prosecutor concerned only about the Law, but as the Father of infinite goodness. "Abba" is the word Jesus uses to call upon God, and it means "Daddy." It is an intimate term of endearment, which expresses the fullness of Jesus' experience. "He speaks to God like a child to his father, full of trust, secure, yet at the same time respectful and ready to obey."[34]

We enter into a relationship with the Father-God through love and complete self-giving. It is not enough to fulfill the Law to the letter. Love knows no bounds. It is not the object of legislation, and is beyond any Law. Thus let us never be satisfied with our love of God. Let us always stand in his debt.

> Jesus has radically eliminated the complacency of the person who feels he or she has fulfilled one's obligation to God, or is conformed to him, or can demand what he has promised us. He says in addition that we have to consider ourselves worthless servants who have done what they had to do. Jesus eliminates all claim to be justified before God by rejecting the Pharisee and accepting the prayer of the publican (Lk. 18:13).[35]

The Pharisee is rejected because, even though he has done good works, he judges himself just. No one is good or just except God alone (Lk. 18:19). Before God we are all publicans or sinners. To regard ourselves as such makes us just, while considering ourselves just makes us sinners. Jesus' strictness is thus not of the Law, but of a love which admits no limits.

In the light of God seen as a loving Father, we can also understand what would seem to be Jesus' laxity. It is neither disobedience nor moral anarchy, but the kind of love which has overcome the distinctions the Law had introduced between pure and impure, neighbors and non-neighbors, good and bad. Thus he loves God who is kind to both good and bad (Lk. 6:35), who makes the sun shine on good and bad. Everyone is worthy of love because God has made everyone worthy of love. Thus we can understand the admonition of Jesus, "Be merciful as your heavenly Father is merciful" (Lk. 6:36).

By eating with sinners, letting the impure touch him, talking to a sinful woman, Jesus is visibly expressing God's love. Jesus is loving as the Father loves, whose infinite goodness and love Jesus experiences. Jesus' God is the father of the prodigal son (Lk. 15:11–32), the God who searches for the lost sheep (Lk. 15:4–7), who pardons debtors who have no way to pay their debts (Lk. 7:41–43), who pays those who work a shorter time the same as he pays those who work longer (Mt. 20:15). Sinners, prostitutes, the poor (for Jesus, not only the economically poor but also those who suffer oppression and cannot defend themselves, the hopeless, and those who cannot claim salvation[36]) should feel that God is a kind father who pardons and calls everyone to communion with him.

Jesus does not preach a doctrine about the infinite goodness of God. Rather he demonstrates that goodness by being merciful to everyone. This is not simply humanitarianism, but the translation of his experience of God as Father, as Love, as Grace, as Pardon. Because Jesus feels himself completely accepted and loved by God, he himself accepts and loves everyone. He will not turn away anyone who comes to him (Jn. 6:37).

Jesus' Contemplative Vision of the World

Jesus is not a theoretical theologian who comes to God through reasoning and mystagogical initiation. God for him is a God of experience, near but at the same time transcendent to the world. He discovers God's active presence in everything and feels united to the Father's activity: "My Father is always working and I too am working" (Jn. 5:17).

Such immediacy of the divine presence and his experience of God raise Jesus to a contemplative vision of reality. Christ reads and interprets the world not with a profane understanding, but with a divine one. In the lilies of the field, the birds of the air, the seed of the sower, the harvest, the vine—in everything—Jesus discovers the sign and the presence of God. Jesus completely abandons himself to God, knowing that God cares for his life and gives him something to eat and something to wear (Mt. 6:24–34).

Jesus can affirm that every aspect of life, positive and negative, invites him to place himself before God. Let us cite some examples. Jesus hears reports of a steward's dismissal and his machinations for emerging prosperous from the trouble he has made for himself. Jesus uses this as a parable to explain the meaning of conversion (Lk. 16:1–12). A thief enters by surprise, without warning. Such conduct suggests to Jesus the sudden coming of the Son of Man (Lk. 12:39–40; Mk. 3:27). Jesus' parables prove he could draw a divine lesson out of the most ordinary things of life. This is possible only for someone who has a contemplative perspective on life. Life is not something meaningless or profane. It is permeated by the presence of God the Father, who is total love. Jesus lives the immediacy of God's presence.

God Makes Us Discover We Are All Brothers and Sisters

The fatherhood of God becomes real for us when we come to see another person as a son or daughter of God and as our brother or sister. This is the new characteristic of Jesus' experience of God. Jesus does not use the word "God" without linking it to concrete humanity. The Pharisees used God to justify hatred for their enemies (Mt. 5:43) and to separate pure and impure. For Jesus, God is seen precisely in life and in our relationships with other people. God's relationship to us manifests precisely who God is: the Father. According to Jesus each individual is worth more than anything else in the world (Mt. 6:26)—more than the spectacular objectives of the revolutionaries (Mt. 11:12), more than meticulous fulfillment of the Law (Mt. 23:23). The person is more important than the Sabbath, than cultic worship (Lk. 10:30–37), or than sacrifice (Mt. 5:23–24; Mk. 12:33).

God wants to be served in others, not in himself alone. To speak of love of God is always to also speak of love of neighbor (Mk. 12:31–32; Mt. 22:36–39). Love of neighbor is what determines our salvation. When Jesus is asked what one must do to be saved, he answers by quoting the laws of the second table of the Decalogue, which all refer to the neighbor (Mk. 10:17–22). This is the best form of human conduct, since God identified himself with the most needy, marginated, and despised (Mt. 25:31–45; Mk. 6:20–21). These people are proxies for God, the places where we meet God and his salvation.

God Is Always Father, Even in Extreme Abandonment

The goodness of God is not a romantic dream which excuses or justifies everything. His goodness is such that in relation to it we are all bad. But, despite our evil, God accepts and loves us (Lk. 6:35). God's goodness is stronger than hate and injustice, over which he will triumph in the future. He calls all of us to bring that future to fulfillment.

Jesus confirms all this, suffering because people lived imprisoned in their religious securities instead of being open to the message of God incarnate in himself. One must never forget that it was the pious of Jesus' community who condemned him. Jesus came to announce and bring about a total liberation, and we know their reaction. He was accused of blasphemy, of being insane and possessed, of being an impostor (Mk. 2:27, 3:22, 24; Mt. 27:63) and a seditionist (Lk. 23:3, 6; Jn. 5:18, 11:49–50). These accusations foretold his death, which seems so contradictory and absurd (Hb. 5:7) since it signifies the Jewish rejection of the liberator sent by God.

The great trial of Gethsemane shows the profound anguish of Jesus, and, at the same time, his resolve: "Let this cup pass from me, but not my will, but yours, be done" (Mk. 14:36). He was abandoned by everyone to the darkness, yet he knew that the God of all love and goodness was there in the night. His trial was extended even to Calvary: "My God, my God, why have you abandoned me?" (Mk. 15:34).

> A theology which does not fully appreciate that the Son of God became a man, weak and mortal, will end up being scandalized by the anguish and human 'despair' of Jesus, forgetting that without that darkness one cannot fully understand his trust in the Father.[37]

Having emptied himself, Jesus ends by entrusting his spirit to the Father (Lk. 23:46), knowing the Father will confer the absolute meaning on the absurdity of the death of an innocent man whose uniqueness lay in his having loved "unto the end" (Jn. 13:1).

The resurrection shows that to trust in God to such an extent is not meaningless. The triumph of life over death and love over hate ends by revealing completely who the Father is, the Father whose goodness nothing can conquer and whose love can transform the cross into the means of liberation.

Such was Jesus' experience in the most painful moment of his life. In it he revealed not only the Father, but also the absolute mystery of God as Father, Son, and Holy Spirit.

The Revelation of the Trinity in the Experience of Jesus

Jesus Christ is the one who effectively revealed the central mystery of Christianity, the Trinity.[38] Given its importance, we would expect it to have been formally proclaimed: "I teach you the absolute mystery of God, as one divine nature subsisting in three persons: Father, Son, and Holy Spirit. This is not the case. The rare occurrences of the trinitarian formula (as in Mt. 28:19, "Go, make disciples of all nations, baptizing them in the name of the Father and of the Son and of the Holy Spirit") are not intended to teach a formal doctrine about the Trinity. They occur in a missionary context, or a baptismal or charismatic one.

The revelation of the Trinity occurs primarily in the concrete words, action, and sufferings of Christ. The subsequent reflection on the mystery from both biblical and theological perspectives by the great councils of the Church does no more than explicate, in the language of their day, what was already clearly said in the New Testament and the life of Christ, although in different terms.[39]

The Trinity is not revealed to satisfy our intellectual curiosity. Indeed, the intellect can scarcely understand the mystery. It is rather the communication of a mystery of life and salvation. In fact, with the revelation of the Trinity, the mystery of humanity, each one of us, was revealed.

How the Trinity Is Revealed in the Life of Christ

We have already spoken of Jesus' intimacy with the Father. On the one hand Jesus experiences creaturely distance from the Father. Jesus prays, calls upon, and praises the Father (Mt. 11:27); he hopes and trusts in the Father with an intimate tenderness expressed in the word "Abba." He feels separate from the Father even while he remains in the Father always. On the other hand, he experiences his sonship (Mk. 13:32; Mt. 11:27): "Everything has been given me by my Father, and no one knows the Father except the Son and the one to whom the Son chooses to reveal him." He acts as the agent of God, adopting such prerogatives of God as forgiving sins and correcting or reforming the Law. His messianic consciousness is so certain that he knows he is Liberator and bases salvation on adherence to his own person (Lk. 12:8–10). He not only acts in God's place, but makes God himself visible. His intimacy with the Father is so deep that he can say that he and the Father are one (Jn. 10:30). Thus Jesus reveals both his distance from, and his intimacy with, the Father.

The Father, at the same time, reveals the Son through the divine insistence of the Son on faith in his person. It is true this faith is almost always joined to cures or miracles (Mk. 2:5, 5:34–36, 11:23; Lk. 17:6, 19; Mt. 17:20, 21:21). But this reveals the Trinity by revealing the divine dimension of the Son. Those favored with miracles believe in Jesus as one who possesses God's power with which he heals, pardons, and gives life. Jesus, on his part, acts as one possessing divine authority in himself. He does not ask for a miracle; rather he acts miraculously, i.e., with divine powers. What is impossible for a man is possible for Jesus (Mk. 10:27). The revelation that Jesus is Son takes place in the life of Jesus long before it becomes a doctrinal formulation.

In Jesus' activity the Holy Spirit is also revealed. Although there are few references to the Spirit (Jn. 14:16ff, Mk. 3:28–30), Christ in the Gospel is always presented charismatically or as filled with the Spirit from the outset (Lk. 1:15–41, 67). The Spirit descends on him in the form of a dove, consecrating him for his mission (Mk. 1:9–11; Jn. 1:32–33). The Spirit leads him into the desert (Mk. 1:12), and moves him to perform miracles and carry on other works of liberation: "If I expel demons by the Spirit of God, it is a sign that the Kingdom of God has come to you" (Mt. 12:28). The divine power at work in Jesus is called *exousia* (authority) or *dynamis* (power) (Mk. 1:22–27, 2:10, 5:30, 6:2–15, 9:39, 12:24; Lk. 5:17), a force which breaks forth from Jesus and surprises even him (Mk. 5:30). The power at work in Jesus reveals what will be called later, in the New Testament, the Holy Spirit, the Spirit of Jesus. That power and the Spirit have both identity and differences.

The kerygma of the infant Church, in the light of the Paschal experience and the charismatic gifts, explained even further the revelation contained in Jesus' earthly life. John and Paul especially perceived unity and also the rich differences in that unique mystery by which the Father, the source of all salvation, sent his Son with the power of the Spirit to redeem and liberate the whole world. The Father is always with the Son, and the Holy Spirit with them both, as the presence and the reality of the work of salvation in the world.[40]

This affirmation of trinitarian faith is no more than the translation into intellectual concepts of the historical and salvific experience of Jesus as lived by the Christian community. Its basic meaning is that God, the absolute Mystery, communicates himself to humanity. The Mystery of God is thus the Mystery of God-with-us. This one God as the source of everything and himself without a source is called Father; as permanently present in the world and revealing himself in his truth in all the richness of his mystery he is called Word, or

Son; as giving himself as gift, as love, as unity, and as the source of growth, he is called the Holy Spirit. Christian faith has discovered that mysterious process in the very history of salvation. But this Christian awareness corresponds to the divine reality of "one God who exists in three distinct manners of subsistence."[41] Thus the Trinity is as original and real as the divine unity itself.

The Experience of the Trinity in Our Life

The revelation of the trinitarian mystery means something substantially important to us. Without that revelation we could not fully realize our humanness. Karl Rahner asserts

> The Trinity for us is not simply a doctrinal reality. It is a living reality which is fulfilled in our existence and which is given to us independently of the Scripture which teaches us it exists. Moreover, such biblical teachings have been imparted to us because we are of such a nature.[42]

How do we experience the Trinity? It is certainly not a reality which takes its place alongside other realities. It is rather an absolute Mystery which permeates and is able to penetrate all our being, which grounds, and must ground, the mysteriousness of our personhood.

In fact, there are obvious indications of the Trinity in the mystery of human life.[43] Our life seems to arise from a single source within us, constantly revealing itself and opening us to its true nature more and more, communicating itself through words, actions, and a whole universe of symbols and expressions. The person is intellect, but at the same time a striving for communion with another, self-giving, a search for love and unity. Thus it is will. But the expression of oneself as truth and the giving of oneself as love flow ceaselessly from the mysterious font of personhood, always greater than the sum of all its acts of communication and expression.

We say the Father is, by definition, that which has no origin, the invisible source of everything. We find this echoed in the mystery of our personhood as being-in-itself, the source or center from which all our expressions emanate. The Word, or Son, is essentially the revelation of the Father both in his trinitarian and extra-trinitarian processions; he makes the Father visible (Jn. 14:9). The reflection of the Son in the human person is our intellect, which reveals the depth of our personhood. The Holy Spirit is the gift of the Father and the Son, the bond of love and unity both inside and outside the Trinity. That love is reflected in the human will as the gift of love and the striving for unity.

To live the radical experience of personhood is to live the experience of absolute Mystery-without-origin (the Father), which communicates itself through our consciousness (the Son) without losing its fundamental unity, by returning completely to its source (the Holy Spirit).

We must understand that this is not a deduction of the Trinity from the nature of the human person. It is, on the contrary, an attempt to understand the human person from the Trinity and from the self-communication to us of each divine person exactly as that divine person is within the Trinity itself.

Christian faith, more than a religion of mysteries, appears thus as the religion of one mystery: the self-giving of God to the person as mystery, truth, and love. Thus it spurs us on to recapture the original simplicity of Christianity. Around the year 180, the martyr Speratus, questioned by the consul Saturninus about what Christianity was, answered, "If you dispose yourself to meditate on it with a calm and open spirit, I will tell you it is a mystery of simplicity."[44] The deepest and most authentic experience of God demonstrates this simplicity. It also demonstrates how simple our relationship with God should be. Basically it is the radical experience of ourselves, sustained by, and rooted in, God himself.

The Experience of God in Religious Life

After what has been said above, it will not be difficult to discern and define the specific vocation of religious. Paul VI said very precisely that religious must be specialists of God.[45] The specific charism of religious is to explicitate the experience of God in Jesus Christ, lived in fellowship, expressed by public consecration, introduced into the world as a prophetic sign of the future of the world.[46]

The Cantus Firmus: *the* Memoria Dei et Jesu Christi

To explicate the experience of God in the following of Christ means to make that experience one's basic life-project, the orientation for all one's activities and one's main point of reference. The *memoria* of Jesus constitutes, to use the beautiful phrase of Bonhoeffer, which Teilhard repeats, the *cantus firmus* around which the other voices sing.[47]

From their experience of God, religious contemplate, or should contemplate, the world, humanity, their task within the Church or society. The conscious cultivation of one's awareness of God should not lead religious to flee the world but to give a new coloring to their relationship with the world. Their basic attitude must be that of Christ: a contemplative attitude which allows them to see, discover, live, and savor the mysterious presence of the triune God in everything. The works thus carried out, the commitments thus undertaken, the program of action thus outlined are not like other works, commitments, and programs of action. If their religious experience is real and authentic, it will end up making the endeavors of religious persons reveal and communicate their experience of God.[48]

Such experience of God, as Christian and in order to be Christian, must be modeled on that of Jesus, which implies not only an intimate experience of God the Father but also acceptance of that whole complex of graces and sacrifices, which inevitably appears in human life—even the lives of Christians and religious. The cross is the sorrowful form of our encounter with God in total self-abandonment, which is conjoined with an unlimited trust in Him who can transform death into life and the old creation into a new and different one.

The Desert as a Search for Paradise

In order for that *cantus firmus* to resound in their lives, religious must be constantly vigilant, must search with all their hearts for their lost innocence, must long for self-purification so that God will not only have a place in their lives, but also pervade and fill every part of their personality.

Western spirituality has called all this "the desert." It is not a geographical place, but a spiritual one. The desert means interior abandonment, freedom from everything that can extinguish or obscure the experience of God, control over representations or images that can disturb the spirit or compete with the *cantus firmus* and thus destroy the basic life-project of the religious, which consists in maintaining one's entire being in God. Thomas Merton said:

> Paradise is not yet heaven; it is not the final goal of the spiritual life. Really it is only a return to the beginning. It is to begin again, a new opportunity. The monk who has gained purity of heart and has recovered, in a certain way, the lost innocence of Adam, still has not completed the journey. He is only ready to begin then, ready for a new task "which eye has not seen, nor ear heard, nor the heart of man conceived." Purity of heart is only an intermediate goal of the spiritual life. The ultimate goal is the Kingdom of God.[49]

To anticipate this Kingdom, to live out of the riches of the future age which is proclaimed as already within the present, is the characteristic mode of religious life.

The Experience of God in Fellowship

The Christian experience of God, as we have already seen, is inseparable from the experience of the other. Whoever experiences God as Father experiences the other as brother or sister. The characteristic of fellowship in the life of religious is more than living together under the same roof. It arises out of the experience of God given in and through the brother as in Jesus Christ God himself becomes our brother.

All authentically Christian experience is experience of solidarity and communion: by experiencing God we also experience the Church. All experience takes its place within the life of the Church, which lives in its life the experience Jesus of Nazareth had of God the Father and the Holy Spirit.

The experience of religious, no matter how personal, must be confronted by that of Jesus and that of the Church. The concrete way for religious to do this is to adhere to the basic charism, since in and through it a path of experience has been opened, one followed in an exemplary and model way by the founders and foundresses of their respective orders and congregations. By following this concrete path, although it is limited, one discovers, and helps to discover, the grandeur of God and the sublimity of the Mystery of Christ and his presence in the world through the Church.

Experience of God in the Midst of the World

Religious consecration implies more than a reservation of the person to God. God does not need people or things for himself. But he does need agents, people who make him present in the world. Consecration implies, then, besides reservation, mission and being sent in the name of God. If God calls and chooses people, it is in order to send them out. The world is the place for our earthly realization not only as human beings, but also as religious. It is the place where the authentic experience of God is verified, or is to be verified, in order to later project it soteriologically above the world.

Religious serve, in the midst of the world, a prophetic and eschatological function. Their being situated in the Absolute should relativize all that is temporal and earthly. The earthly and temporal can never be the goal ultimately longed for and sought, but only a road or pathway toward the attainment of the ultimate goal. This is in no way to depreciate the relative, but to give it its most authentic value. Religious, taking a special stance oriented toward the Absolute, also assume a special posture toward the relative. In fact, if their eschatological consciousness demands a total relativization of the earthly, it also demands that they embrace the relative with seriousness in order to become a way of prefiguring the Absolute here and now and making it real in terms of human history. Basically the eschatological is no more than a means of elevating history and our human commitments, a way of always keeping up our journey without stopping or establishing fixed positions in regard to anything here below. Only in this way will people be permanently open to the only More, the unique Future, able to still the restless human heart.

People of today, participants in a producer-consumer society, often feel lost in a jungle of sensory stimuli that reach them through an infinite number of channels of communication. They feel a greater and stronger drive in their lives than merely to produce, work, and consume their energy in combatting death. Whether it is by a positive presence or a negative absence, they discover another dimension of human life, not oriented toward pragmatic ends: the dimension of grace, meaning, and the joy of life.

It is in this area where language of the divine and of the mystery becomes significant. People today are too rationalistic and profane in their relations with the world. They do not allow themselves to become aware of the Mystery of Love, the radical meaning of life, nor to recognize what is inaccessible to reason. Religious in the midst of the world should be a prophetic sign, a sacrament of that dimension in which God arises as Meaning and the Hope of humanity always aspiring to a beyond. We often notice that when a religious really appears as a man or woman of God, as a prophet, people come to him or to her as to a fountain from which saving water flows. Religious are valuable not so much for what they do for people as for what they are for people: signs of God and of the Meaning consciously or unconsciously sought by everyone.

What specifically is the place of religious in the world? It is precisely in the place where the world feels itself called into question and experiences scandal, and thus where the world experiences its transcendence. The poor are the ones who occupy this place, and thus religious belong with the poor. The poor are not only those who lack material goods. They are also those manipulated by society because they cannot fit into its structures: the manipulated, the used, the depersonalized. The fact that so many poor people exist in the world is the accusing conscience of society, the byproduct of society's affluence and progress. In the presence of the poor, society senses its limitations and is called to open itself and restructure itself so there is no longer any room for the exploitation of one person by another or for manipulative techniques. Christ directs his message preferentially to the poor. In their questioning and challenging, the poor are par excellence the sacrament of God and the messengers of Christ.

Thus the place of religious is that proper to the poor. Out of the midst of the poor and as poor themselves, they direct themselves to everyone else. Especially in Latin America, where poverty permeates society, a reinterpretation of the religious life is demanded that makes religious a prophetic, accusing sign to a world ensconced in power and wealth:[50]

> Only by condemning poverty and by becoming poor in order to protest against it can the Church [and with even more warrant, religious life] preach something which is special and particular: *spiritual poverty*, i.e., the openness of humanity and history to the future promised by God. Only in this way can it fulfill, honestly and with the prospect of being heard, the prophetic function of denouncing all injustice which conspires against humanity and the liberating proclamation of a real human fellowship. . . . For the Latin-American Church [and for religious life] this witness today is an inescapable and urgent test of the authenticity of its mission.[51]

Thus, given the critical importance of the experience of God for religious, what is the concrete reason religious life exists? Its basic task—more important than its practices, acts of piety, rules and constitutions, and its structures—is to create a favorable climate for an authentic experience of God. Without the experience of God in following and imitating Jesus, the observance of the Rule and the other ascetic practices constitute a martyrdom without glory rather than a concrete expression of the experience of God.

This experience of God must not be considered a gift reserved for the few. It is the indispensable condition for all religious life. Without this experience dogmas are no more than petrified skeletons, morality no more than an oppressive suit of armor, religious practices no more than a monstrous series of predetermined actions, an expression of fear seeking security, a ludicrous charade without an interior spirituality. Mysticism is not located in the extraordinary; it is the transfiguration of the ordinary. Thus the mystic does not have secrets to reveal or keep. The mystic sees God in everything only by continually seeking a God who is always greater than the one the mystic meets in every moment.

The Experience of God in the Process of Life-Death-Resurrection of Language

At the beginning of this long chapter we alluded to the inadequacy of all representations or images of God. Thus those who too precipitately proclaim the death of God have not been unfaithful. Yet it was not a solution either. On the contrary, it only made the problem greater. We have tried to resolve the crisis not by elaborating images more modern or more in keeping with our culture (which would be mere substitution within the crisis), but by delving into something more fundamental than any image: historical life in which mystery or the dimension of immanence and transcendence (i.e., God) appears. At the root of everything is an encounter with God, not apart from, within, or beyond the world, but together with the world. God is only real and significant for humanity when God arises out of our own existence. In order to be real and significant, despite being mystery, God has a name, and our spirit constructs representations and projects images of him. This is how we concretize our experience. In this action the drama of religious terminology begins, and we must be aware of this drama.[52]

The Mountain Is a Mountain: Knowing-Immanence-Identification

The first moment of the experience of God, under the impact of the encounter, is our naming of him: Lord God, Rock, Holy One, Father. These very words are transfigured, assuming such weight as to translate (so we think) what we experience of God. We create an image. We are unaware of its being only a human representation of what cannot be represented.

That God is the kind Father constitutes a very serious truth and is not merely symbolic. But our initial, experiential knowledge of God ends up becoming a sophisticated system of philosophical and theological argumentation, elaborating concepts and a minute logic about the divine. We thus end up identifying God with these concepts and images of him we have constructed; that is, we situate him in our language and intellectual discourse. It goes without saying that this is reflected in our relationship with God. We pray out of these doctrinal formulations. We speak to him, fall on our knees before him, tell him our troubles, hope for his grace and salvation out of these images. Thus, we give life a radical Meaning and we live our closeness to, and experience of, God. The mountain is a mountain; God is God the Father.

The Mountain Is Not a Mountain: Unknowing-Transcendence-Disidentification

In the second moment of the experience of God we realize the insufficiency of all representations of God. Whatever we say about him is symbolic and figurative. He is beyond every name and every concept. God is absolute transcendence.

How have we become aware of this second moment? Perhaps we have passed through a great crisis and the moorings of our religious practices have pulled loose. For example, how do we understand God in the presence of an innocent man or woman who is imprisoned and cruelly tortured? How do we reconcile the goodness of God the Father with the situation of a beloved wife abused in the very presence of her imprisoned husband until she dies?

Yes, God is Father, but another kind of Father. He is not a greater Father than those on earth, but a different Father. With this we begin to question all our representations, to such an extent that a theology of the death of God can arise. This theology decrees the death of all discourse about the divine, saying that such language hides God instead of revealing him. This is how we come to understand the saying of the Zen masters, "If you meet the Buddha, kill him." Because it is not the Buddha, but only his image. This is to say: transcend the image and finally dispose yourself to encounter the true Buddha. We find a similar notion in the great masters of Christian spirituality. Consider, for example, St. John of the Cross, the great enemy of visions and ecstasy and the great opponent of every kind of privileged experience.[53]

God is not encountered among the things of this world. If we thus encounter him, we are encountering an idol and not the living and true God who is always beyond all human knowing. The mountain is not a mountain; God the Father is not a Father-God like our earthly fathers.

The Mountain Is a Mountain: Tasting-Transparency-Identity

In the third moment of the experience of God we rehabilitate our images of him. After having affirmed and denied in the first and second moments, respectively, we return critically to reconcile ourselves with the images. We accept them for what they are, representations, not the reality or identification of God. We understand we can reach God only through images or representations. We begin to savor them because we feel disentangled from them and in a certain way we stand free before them. They are the scaffolding, not the edifice, and we accept them as such. We do not try to know God; we savor the divine wisdom in everything. Everything concrete becomes transparent to God because everything is symbolic and figurative of God, his wisdom, love, goodness, etc.

This rehabilitation is possible only by passing through the first and second moments and having freed ourselves from the simplistic "wisdom of the language," and having passed through the purifying word of the "cross" which "destroys the wisdom of the wise" (1 Co. 1:17–23). Anthropomorphism no longer hinders us, since we know that what we say about God is anthropomorphic. But clearly, if God can be anthropomorphic (in humanity's image), it is only because we are theomorphic (made in the image of God).[54] Everything is simplified. There is no longer any place for speculation. It is sufficient to see, but to see deeply. God, without being confused with other things, is present in them because things, for one who sees deeply, are transparent.

Those who arrive at this third stage exclude nothing and throw nothing away. They assume everything because everything is the revelation of God. "Who is the Tao?" asked a disciple of the Zen master on one occasion. The master responded, "He is the ordinary mind of each person." "And what is the ordinary mind of each person?" asked the disciple. The master replied, "When we are tired, we sleep; when we are hungry, we eat."[55] For those who perceive the presence of God in everything, everything manifests the gift of God and the gratuitousness of his love.

This simplicity leads everything back, whether good or bad, to unity in God. From this point of view, Paul can admonish the Romans:

> Present your bodies as a living sacrifice, holy and acceptable to God, because your true sacrifice consists in this. . . . He who gives, give

with simplicity; he who rules, rule with solicitude; he who does works of mercy, do so with cheerfulness. (Rm. 12:1, 8)

In short, "whether you eat or drink or do any other thing, do it for the glory of God" (Rm. 10:31). Those who experience the mystery of God no longer question; they merely live the transparency of everything and celebrate the appearance of God in every situation.

Do not think, however, that the experience of God happens only in this third stage. It is a total experience which implies knowing, unknowing, and savoring. Thus it is important not to confine it to any one stage. The third stage again becomes the first, and a new dialectical process begins again: affirmation, denial, and reforming the names of God. Thus we go on realizing and deepening our experience of God, our experience of that God who in each moment reveals and hides himself, gives himself and reserves himself, that God who is, and will always be, the Mystery and our eternal Future.

2

The Expression

The experience of God in the following of Christ, which forms the basis of religious life, always has its own special expression. The ways it is expressed can vary, as well as the way we make the journey, according to the nature of the historical epoch and the plan of God. Yet in all these various forms there are certain constants in religious life, namely, the experience of God in Jesus expressed through the vows. We must ask how we are to understand the vows. Must they be seen only juridically (even though there may be juridical elements in them)? Must they be seen in a theological and charismatic perspective? Or must we rather not look at them from that perspective that presents life as a unity even when referring to God, the special characteristic of religious life? On the other hand, as historical expressions, what is the future orientation of the vows?

The pages that follow only highlight some aspects of a total reality. We see these aspects in concrete situations in which we need light so we can walk more securely along the pathways of life, which so often lie in shadows. The dual value of life's concrete forms and expressions is that they put us in touch with the source of that life and manifest and historify that source in our concrete living. Thus such expressions are valuable stepping-stones or bridges so long as they continually transcend themselves and remain inextricably linked to their essential meaning. The essential element here is the basis for Christian religious life.

3

The Vows and the Human Person

The Problem of the Vows

One of the most disputed areas of religious life is that of the vows (poverty, chastity, and obedience). Such disputes may indicate both a lack of knowledge of the vows and a lack of an in-depth experience of them on the part of religious.

For those who live religious life deeply the vows are no problem, even though the vows certainly demand an ongoing sacrifice. The problem with the vows lies not in the vows themselves but in something deeper, in the very meaning of religious life. For many people religious life has been emptied of its human and religious content, and thus of any meaning. It is seen as a heavy load of rules, constitutions, traditions, spiritualities. It lacks any unifying principle or any thread to guide one through the maze. It lacks reasons to give meaning to the rules, forms, and expressions of religious experience.

The real crisis, then, lies in the absence of an Absolute in life, one which can give a meaning to even the most insignificant actions. Without the immediate and dynamic presence of this Absolute in the life and experience of religious, religious life becomes a martyrdom without glory and a monotonous repetition of empty, ritualistic words and actions.

The saints did not question the vows; they lived the Gospel fully. They did not enter religious life with the intention of observing particular vows, but of living for God in every dimension and every concrete moment of their lives.

There is no denying that today religious life in the Church is juridically oriented around the three vows. Canon 487 says the profession of the three vows sets religious off from the laity. In practice the Church recognizes as religious only members of institutes or movements in which vows are made or promises are made to live the evangelical counsels within community life. We must ask, then, how the institution of the vows arose.

Today religious life is experimenting with new forms of expression more in keeping with the modern world. Such experimentation was unknown before, and many saw the vows as an obstacle or an unattainable ideal, arbitrarily invented to define religious life. When investigators examine forms of religious life no longer based on the vows, especially chastity, they say the vows are merely the concrete historical form adopted by religious life in the Latin Church. They go on to say there is no intrinsic connection between religious life and the professing of the three vows. They say they do not want to belittle the value of the vows, but only to note that they are historically relative and not essential to being a religious.

The One Basic Vow: Total Consecration to God

The interpretation of the vows given by these investigators is based on a poor understanding of the content of the vows and disregards the internal dynamic of religious life. The efforts of many to free the vows from juridical conditions really result in a deficient liberation. Almost nothing is achieved, while the true purpose of the vows remains as obscure as ever.

A Look at History

Looking at the history of religious life, it can be demonstrated, perhaps surprisingly, that the vows properly so called arose very late. At the beginning, among the Egyptian anchorites and the Eastern and Western cenobites, an intention (*protesis, propositum, professio, pactum, conventio*) of living a specifically religious or Gospel-oriented lifestyle was made. The holy founders and foundresses proposed a *conversio morum,* a life according to the Gospel, or according to specific aspects of the Gospel, such as a life of poverty, evangelization, service to the sick or the poor. They made the *votum monasticum,* or *propositum sanctitatis,* which implied asceticism, poverty, chastity, fasting, penance, obedience, and cultivation of all the virtues—an all-inclusive vow.

These early religious did not profess particular vows "out of fear of making what should be practiced freely and willingly out of devotion, a matter of obligation."[1] The monastic vow was the one vow, although it had many implications. It was the profession of a lifestyle which radicalized the common experience of all Christians. It was thus a truly explicit and public vow.

That action then, as now, denoted consecration. The religious is, in St. Augustine's phrase, "the person consecrated in the name of God and dedicated to him" (*homo Dei nomine consecratus et Deo votus*).[2] Being a total consecration, the action implied renunciation of the world, which was the proper meaning of the term *apotaxia* used by the cenobites of Egypt to denote this aspect of community. The religious was set aside for God.

But this renunciation and reservation were not the same as a flight from the world. This would be a false interpretation of the life of the first anchorites and cenobites as a flight from, or despising of, earthly realities. Every Christian loved creation because it was seen as the work of God. Religious were, and are, no exception. But the realism of religious cut deeper, aware that the real state of creation was marked by sin. Thus their relationship to the world was always a dialectical one, one of both yes and no. There was always a place for asceticism, renunciation of the world. The Pauline command would always be valid: "Do not conform yourselves to the present age" (Rm. 12:12). Only thus could creation recapture, through human beings, its authentic nature: its essential and radical dependence on God. From the moment disobedience took place as an attempt to emancipate humanity and creation from God, renunciation of the world, as total consecration to God, became necessary.

What, then, does renunciation mean? There is no doubt that the first anchorites claimed to interpret it most authentically. St. Anthony, the first Christian religious, abandoned everything and distributed his wealth to the poor. But he did not abandon labor, because to labor is to be positively related to the world. He made baskets and sold them to pilgrims who came into the desert. His work became so productive that once a year he sailed down the lower Nile to sell his baskets and then distributed the proceeds to the poor.

> If you do not want to teach what is superficial or false, take care not to describe the monks as always on their knees in their cells with their arms extended to form a cross and with their eyes closed, pretending to be, as they certainly were, contemplatives. We should rather present them as seated in their cells next to a mound of palms and rushes, weaving crude strands which they would later weave into baskets and mats.[3]

. . . *And Its Deeper Significance*

Certainly consecration implies the idea of total reservation to God, but what does this mean? God, being infinite and self-sufficient, needs nothing and no one. If someone is then set aside by a consecration to God it is to be sent back into the world in God's name. It is not God, but the world, which needs salvation and people to bring that salvation and make it real and visible. Consecration (reservation) means mission to the world in the name of God. Religious are taken from the world but only in order to be sent back to it in a deeper way and with a specific mission: that of announcing and creating a world reconciled, freed from all alienation, rebellion, and sin.

This is the reason why, even historically, religious were people of deep commitment and instruments of reform and renewal in the world. Permeated with the awareness that they were sent by God, they tried to make the world more human and more open to God.

Total consecration to God implies, then, a totally new attitude toward all the dimensions of the world, which is now contemplated from the perspective of that consecration. Thus consecration does not separate religious from the world. It is impossible to leave the world or flee from it because we are always within it. What religious consecration does is forge new relationships with things, people, society, and God. This is the core of what real religious, whether or not they constructed a spirituality, lived radically. Without proposing explicitly to fulfill certain vows, they lived their entire lives as a consecration to God.

Not so much to the extent that they follow their founder or foundress but to the extent that they reproduce or relive the experience of that founder, religious are discovering their own pathway within that basic charism. Rules and constitutions have to be catalysts for religious experience, not substitutes for it.

The task of forming religious in the charism of the founder or foundress does not consist primarily in transmitting to them the customs and traditions proper to the order or congregation. It consists rather in creating a climate in which each one can have (in accordance with what was said in the previous chapter) an authentic religious experience, which is now to be translated into a total gift of oneself to God. Self-giving, because it is total, embraces everything that belongs to God: people, things, all the vastness of reality—in short, the world-of-God.

Thus religious life is based on a single, all-inclusive vow: total consecration to God.

The Three Vows Detail and Concretize the Vow of Consecration

We must now ask how religious life came to be organized around three vows.

Let us begin by taking a look at history again. The three vows (poverty, chastity, and obedience) are the fruit of reflections made from the ninth through the thirteenth centuries in polemical and homiletic tracts on the rules of the early founders, such as Pachomius, Basil, Benedict, and Augustine.[4] Delving into these rules, as well as into the lives of the great religious of the past, we see that three basic dimensions stood out clearly among the welter of spiritualities and observances: poverty, chastity, and obedience. This intellectual reductionism aimed at orienting the interior dispositions of religious.

Moreover, in the eleventh and twelfth centuries new religous movements arose, springing up spontaneously among the laity or encouraged and led by especially charismatic individuals, almost always from among the laity themselves. The problem of the religious state became acute. Were the participants in such movements religious or not? What does the monastic vow imply? It was in the twelfth century when the Augustinians, in their commentaries and discussions on the Rule of St. Augustine, began elaborating the monastic vow into the three vows of poverty, chastity, and obedience. Later, in 1202, Pope Innocent III, in a letter to a monk of Subiaco, mentioned the three vows, the first time they appear in an official document.[5]

Initially there was no intention of reducing the one vow of consecration to these three concrete manifestations. Consecration continued to be treated as a totality which extended to all life and included all virtues. It still demanded a life of prayer and meditation, fraternal charity, and daily asceticism in order to curb all desire for power and all covetousness, until one was completely identified with Christ naked and abandoned on the Cross.

Taking this twelfth-century elaboration or concretization, the structure of the three vows was established canonically, particularly in the mendicant orders of St. Dominic and St. Francis, and endures through our own day.

We must ask if this historical answer is sufficient. Is being content with historical data not the same as remaining on the level of externals when we really want to discover the hidden logic of the vows? History consists not only of brute facts (which really do not exist) but above all in the deeper meaning implicit or revealed in the facts. It is this meaning that gives events their true historical character and a meaning for human life.

The vows of poverty, chastity, and obedience detail the total self-giving of the person to God and translate into human terms the totality and the radical nature of that gift. Let us try to clarify this.

The Threefold Structure of the Human Person

Human life incarnates itself in the context of an extremely complex web of relationships. Our destiny and the achievement of our identity are contingent on these many relationships: we attain our identity by being open to, and encountering, that which is different from ourselves. Insofar as we can assimilate and accept what is different, both inside and outside ourselves, we can succeed in establishing true communion with everything and in creating a community along with other people and things.

To live humanly is always to live-together-with. Within our web of relationships we discover our self-identity, our being-in-itself and our being-with-ourselves. The human self exists and acts in relationship with the non-self of the other thing, and the "thou" of the other person. Human life, even for religious, is realized in this context of openness and "pan-relationality."

In one dimension, we stand in relationship to the world of things as their master, taking from them our material and spiritual nourishment. Between us and our world a deep, mutual interaction takes place, since by virtue of our bodiliness, and yet without being an object, we ourselves are part of the world. Things allow us, moreover, to exercise our freedom and creativity. Yet at the same time things have an identity and an effect; they can seduce and even enslave us. By possessing them we become their master, and yet, by the very act of our possessing them, we can become the slave of the very things over which we are master. Rather than possessing them, we become possessed by them.

In a second dimension, we are situated within the sphere of distinctions between masculine and feminine. The masculine emerges in relation to the feminine and vice versa. This is a basic component of the human person that allows us to share profoundly with another; in dialogue and mutual sharing of our own richness the growth of the human personality occurs. It is important to observe that, from here on, masculine is not merely a synonym for male and feminine for female. Masculinity and femininity are basic dimensions of each individual's being and are not totally objectifiable. The male has a feminine dimension (without being a woman) and the female a masculine dimension (without being a man). A woman more profoundly incarnates the feminine dimension, and a man the masculine.

Masculinity is characterized by objectivity, clarity, mastery, and order, which manifest themselves in the human life of both men and women. Femininity is characterized by mysteriousness, depth, obscurity, intuition, and creativity, which are likewise found in every person. Integrating these two facets of our personality more and more harmoniously is the task of all personal growth. To the extent each of us knows, within himself or herself, how to accept and integrate these differences, he or she is enriched, even without being challenged by the masculine and feminine incarnations we each encounter in one another. This is the deepest meaning of sexuality as a structural-ontological category. While we will return to this in greater detail, let us say for the moment that the manifestation of sexuality as genitality is no more than one concrete way, given its specifically reproductive function, of becoming a person. Sexuality is not necessarily genitality. To integrate genitality into the wider context of the masculine-feminine reciprocity is the deeper and more human meaning of chastity, for married people as well as for single people and celibates.

In a third dimension, we find ourselves moving in a communitarian dimension of the "us" which is the basis for the family and the community, no matter what that community may be. This is not merely a group of people, but personal intercommunion, since the human person is by nature relational or communitarian and open to intercommunion. Community is thus the existence of identity-indistinction. Living-together-with, that is, living in community, each person open to the others, is the way we fulfill ourselves and others. Each of us is the way to humanization for the other. Community is the bearer of tradition, culture, and values. Through it and in it we achieve a collective consciousness of "us" as a common destiny, as solidarity in relation to the past, present, and future. Thus, to become part of the community means to accept and share in the appropriate social roles, and so to discharge the debt of coresponsibility to the community.

The Vows as Particularizing This Human Structure

Careful reflection shows that the three vows correspond to these three structural dimensions of the human person. Basically they particularize the consecration to God and give a new coloring to all effective human relationships. They form the basis for a total conversion, which springs from the relational roots of the person in his or her contact with things and with others, totally referred and oriented toward God.

The vow of poverty corresponds to our relationship with material goods, or, if you prefer, the world of things; the vow of chastity with the dimension of the masculine-feminine reciprocity; the vow of obedience with the person-community relationship. Each one, and all three together, detail and make explicit the one vow of consecration.

Thus the vows have not been invented by human beings, but spring out of our own life when we try to live it in all its radical meaning. Thus true religious have no problem with the vows; they simply live their consecrated life. Logically, this consecration, lived fully, tends to reflect, and will reflect, its religious character in those three relational dimensions of the human personality. Then a new mode of living or of existential relationship arises, translating itself effectively into characteristics of poverty, chastity, and obedience.

The Essential Content of the Vows: The Divine Sovereignty

People who consecrate themselves to God have the intention and the basic commitment to make God the point of reference in every dimension of their lives. Thus the core of the vows, not their historical concretization (which varies according to the age and the institute), will be invariable in religious life. The purpose and the dynamism of the vows aim at restoring the full sovereignty of God over everything, opening pathways for the realization of that lordship of love according to the demands of his original act of grace.

Although we will discuss the vows at greater length, let us now briefly explain their deeper significance in the human perspective we are moving in now.

To Be Poor Is to Experience Everything as Gift

Poverty does not consist in seeking misery or in despising material goods. Poverty must deal somewhat with material goods, but it cannot be defined solely in terms of these goods.

The concept of poverty or wealth differs according to the age and is modified in accordance with economic systems, the motivation and function the person serves. A landlord, for example, is not considered poor because he wears sandals, nor a university professor rich because he has a good library which is indispensable for his work. In trying to catalogue the material goods that make us rich or poor, we get tangled up in endless casuistry, which is subject to endless correction to make it conform to the rapid increase of buying power in a particular region or country.

Thus the simple fact that a religious lacks material goods is not in itself an infallible guarantee that he or she is poor. One can be an ascetic and yet not poor because of one's secret ambition for power, one's covetousness, or even one's domineering attitude without judgment or discretion. These would be signs of a rich person. Originally poverty was not an acquired virtue or habit based on possessing nothing. It had a deeper root. From that root, both the rich and those lacking material goods could be poor.

Poverty is the proper ontological, creaturely condition of everyone. To be a creature means not to have. It is to receive unceasingly one's essence and existence from God. To be poor is to understand that everything that comes to us, everything we have, is given. Even the capacity to receive is a gift of God. To be poor is to experience concretely this umbilical dependence on God. Sin lies in wanting to possess what does not belong to us. It is to forget our creaturely condition, beginning to keep what is ours for ourselves, as if any of us could claim our own right or not be dependent on God.

Since we have received everything from God, and since everything is completely and radically the property and gift of God, everything becomes our gift to others. The poor person is not only one who asks, but also the one who gives and sets no limits to the giving. Poverty thus understood demands a permanent, basic attitude of radical availability in regard to all we are and all we have, of feeling that we are least of all and the brother or sister of all creatures, radically empty and dependent on God.

The better this essential truth is assimilated, becoming flesh of our flesh, so much better will it become incarnated correctly in each situation and deeply affect ourselves, our ideas, our possessing. The preaching or catechesis on poverty should not be primarily about having or not having, but about the need to live our creatureliness, seeing everything as grace, continually extirpating all desire for possessions or power. Only in this way does one come to be truly poor (and not merely an ascetic), one who has no right or power to control any goods and thus has little or nothing.

Religious who have consecrated themselves to God, making this consecration their basic life-project, are called to see everything from the divine perspective and from that original divine gratuitousness. Thus we can be related to the goods of this earth in a way that they become no less than a gift received, which must become a gift given to others. Religious strive not only not to possess. The decisive factor is how they behave toward things: refusing to possess things for themselves, giving up all ambition for power, and all attempts to be right all the time, as if they themselves were the only standard against which to evaluate things or people.

Poverty is such a difficult attitude to attain that, if a person says he or she has attained poverty, it is no longer true.

Chastity Is Not an Absence, but a Superabundance

The deepest meaning of poverty already implies chastity and obedience. Before everything else, celibacy or virginity means neither selfishness nor the despising of sexuality. It is not a vow not to love, but a vow to love radically. It springs internally from the very experience of human love, which in its depths is open to, and calling for, an absolute love. The beloved creature reveals and conceals absolute love and is the bridge to it, since only in absolute love does a restless heart find rest.

Religious do not renounce the masculine-feminine reciprocity; on the contrary, they try to transform it in such a way that they see the absolute love in people and live their interpersonal relationships out of that love. Religious try to live out of the radical love of God, incarnated in their own consecrated person. To live chastely or virginally is not simply to give up the expression of love proper to marriage, but to give up all drive to dominate and possess another, to give up the incarnations of absolute love we encounter in our lives, to seek endlessly for the immediacy of divine love, and to incarnate that surrender and searching in a concrete lifestyle.

Chastity thus is not born of absence or privation, but of the outpouring of a superabundance. The vow of chastity, as the concrete expression of a total consecration to God, does not separate man from woman or woman from man, but, overcoming all possible ambiguity, submits their mutual relationship to the imperatives or demands of the absolute Love, experienced as eternal life, already present and working in the world as an eschatological reality.

Chastity is not a depreciation of marriage, just as martyrdom is not a depreciation of life. Marriage is the way for those who give birth to new life, a way to the future, to the promises of a new humanity, to eschatological humanity. Chastity, on the other hand, is the experience of faith in eternal life already present in the world, definitively manifested in Christ and by him, bringing the future to reality and even now fulfilling the promises; it is, in short, the love of the sons and daughters of the resurrection even now being introduced into the world. Thus it is already the witness of Christian faith in its radicality and its ultimate projection in flesh and blood.

Obedience Is Authority over Oneself

Obedience is a way of living poverty in the interpersonal order and in the effective structure of a community. To adequately appreciate religious obedience we must understand the paradox—the dialectic of the Cross—evoked by St. Paul (1 Co. 9:1; Rm. 13:8): Christians are lords, thus free in relation to everything and under no one's control; but at the same time they are servants of all people and guardians of all things.

Christians are free beings; that is a fact. Such freedom is our birthright, received from God himself. No one can enslave another. The very love God solicits from us presupposes this freedom. Thus no one can be forced, since without freedom it is impossible to live obedience, daughter of the most authentic love and the most authentic freedom.

But the Christian is, at the same time, the server of things and the servant of others. Christians freely serve all. We can freely accept the will of another. That is what it means to obey. We thus obey not because the law commands it or the other demands it, but because we have chosen to obey (*quia elegi ea, observavi mandata tua*). Obedience has nothing to do with passivity and material conformity or blind identification with the wishes of another. It is, on the contrary, the dynamic of freedom in a decision to accept the will of the other person, not for reasons of convenience but because in this way we empty ourselves to accept freely the plan of another or of the community in order to achieve the common good.

The more deeply we live that dimension, the more moral authority we possess, since we are nourished, not by our own will and criteria, but by the mystery of God as it flows through others. We possess authority to the extent to which we know how to lead the other, rather than to submit to an external command, to listen (*obedientia,* from *ob-audire,* to listen) to the voice and the plan of God. To impose orders or strictures on others is to exercise power or some faculties, but not necessarily to help others to grow. Real authority (*auctoritas,* from *augere,* to grow) is that which makes the person over whom it is exercised grow. St. Francis of Assisi, during his lifetime, had no kind of power over the Church. Nevertheless he exercised an influence through an unsuspected authority, merited and won, not by the power he wielded, but by the experience of divine mystery that led him to consider himself less than everyone else and thus their servant. Only the person who has real authority can really obey, since he or she experiences this authority from a hierarchical perspective, already within the fraternal circle of coresponsibility.

The vow of obedience is not ordained to free us from all power and authority with their decision-making faculties. Through our consecration, we must open up a context and channel a dynamism through which we try to discover within these very structures and in the very exercise of authority the incarnation of the will of God. People and communities become the intermediaries through which the plan of God and human aspirations find their explication and their path.

The conclusion is clear. The vows contribute to the essence of religious life no new theological content. They serve only to show in detail the total consecration to God, through which we strive to make God, and not ourselves, the Lord and absolute God of our own lives in all their manifestations, especially in those areas related to the three axes around which human life revolves.

The public character of the vows does no more than give the religious a place within the Church, which knows very well, and thus accepts and defends, religious life as a precious gift of God to the whole community, "a divine gift which the Church received from her Lord" (*Lumen Gentium,* 43). Thus the juridical and canonical institutionalization of the vows, far from being an obstacle to new forms of religious life, better protects and defends it. What is most transcendent and important is not to profess various vows, but to live their full meaning and content as the concretization, on the level of daily life, of the one vow of radical self-giving and consecration to God.

Now we can proceed to analyze the vows themselves, knowing that they correspond on the one hand to our internal drives (as we have just seen) and, on the other hand, demand responses and concrete lifestyles, as we will see in following chapters.

4

Poverty: Commitment and Solidarity

The idea of poverty has become a fundamental issue in the entire Church in recent years, especially in Latin America and in religious life. We call ourselves a Church of the poor, by the poor, and for the poor. Religious life must reinterpret its vow of poverty, moving away from an interior, private, and ascetical meaning to one of public commitment to solidarity with the economically poor and socially downtrodden.

This need reveals the bad conscience with which the Church and religious life live. Are they really poor? Yes; they make a vow of poverty. Yet it is others who keep that vow, not themselves. The simple fact that poverty is a question perhaps demonstrates that we are not living poverty. The poor do not pose questions about poverty; they never think of achieving greater poverty. Their problem is how to escape poverty, how to regain their dignity which has been debased, and how to attain a better life that will allow them to live more humanly without a daily preoccupation with surviving. Only those who are not poor ask questions about poverty and wealth.

It is providential that the Church is now sincerely asking about the meaning of poverty, as well as questioning the forms of its Gospel witness to poverty.

First of all, let us clearly recognize that very confusing interpretations of poverty have been proliferating. The many varied aspects of the theme of poverty (spiritual, personal, corporate, socio-economic) often succeed in covering up the true significance of poverty found in the Gospels. The analysis that follows is an attempt to reflect on poverty in its most experiential dimension.

The real problem with poverty does not lie in ascertaining its precise Gospel meaning, but in really living poverty. Simple reflections achieve little or nothing. Poverty achieves significance only when it is practiced and lived. Many rich people offend the poor with lofty speculations about the riches of poverty and the poverty of riches.[1]

Poverty, an Offense against God and Humanity

From the outset it must be understood that poverty, in itself, is no virtue. Material poverty implies and causes hunger, need, illness, and a whole range of problems that can be eliminated only by eliminating poverty itself. There is no dearth of people who make reflections about poverty without ever knowing what they are really talking about. As Berdayev observed, the problem of our own poverty is presented as a material question, while that of others is presented as a spiritual one. In other words, when poverty besets us and we suffer its consequences, we lay great stress on the material, on the infrastructure of human life. On the other hand, when poverty affects other people, we tend to exalt their situation, going so far as to say, for example, "the *favelado,* or the worker without job security, is poor, indeed, but he is happy, and poverty with happiness is better than wealth with misery."

With such subjective and pseudomystical appraisals, the only result can be the anesthetizing of our consciences. Meanwhile, the table of the *favelado* or worker remains empty of the basic necessities of life, and his children remain undernourished and sickly. In the Bible the poor are the indigent, the humbled, the weak, the wretched, those condemned to misery. In the Bible all these things constitute an evil that debases humanity and offends God. We have been made masters of the earth, not its slaves. We are created in God's image and likeness; offending that image offends its creator, God. As José María González Ruíz says in his book, *Pobreza evangélica y promoción humana:*

> The poor and afflicted direct a bitter prayer to God, angry, and at times tinged with blasphemies. This implies, naturally, that material poverty produces a religious vacuum in the human heart.[2]

Ecclesiastes observes very accurately:

> Do not turn your eyes away from the beggar, nor give anyone the occasion to curse you. For if he curses you in the bitterness of his soul, its Maker will hear his curse (Qo 4:5–6).

Exodus says touchingly:

> You shall not wrong a stranger or mistreat him, for you were strangers in the land of Egypt. You shall not mistreat any widow or orphan. If you abuse them and they cry out to me, I will surely hear their cry. . . . If you ever take your neighbor's garment in pledge, you shall restore it to him before sundown; it is the mantle for his body, in what else will he sleep? And if he cries to me, I will hear, for I am compassionate (Ex. 22:21–27).

Deuteronomy enjoins:

> For the poor will never vanish from the land; therefore I command you: You will open wide your hand to your brother, to the needy and to the poor, in the land (Dt. 15:11).

The curses and complaints of the poor in the Bible against God do not mean their rejection of God, but their unwillingness to accept dehumanizing poverty, because God himself does not want it to exist, since it contradicts his divine plan. God does not interpret their prayer as sin, but as grief-filled supplication.

The prophets oppose the poverty of the humble. Isaiah proclaims, as a basic thesis:

> Is not this the fast I choose, says the Lord: to undo the bonds of wickedness, to unfasten the thongs of the yoke, . . . to share your bread with the hungry, and bring the homeless poor into your house, to clothe the naked, and not to hide yourself from your own flesh (Is. 58:6–7)?

The Messiah will be the Liberator of the poor who cry out and of the wretched whom no one protects. The Kingdom implies freedom from poverty and its effects, since with its coming the lame walk, the blind see, lepers are cleansed, and the hungry are blessed because they will be filled (Lk. 4:2; 7:22). In Acts it is very positively observed that, in the primitive Church, "there was no poor among them" (Ac. 4:34).

Poverty is an evil. For the Bible it is a way death manifests itself in human life, since death must be understood not only as the final moment of biological life, but as everything that diminishes, limits, humbles, offends, and shortens human life. This poverty contradicts the historical plan of God. Thus it cannot be a human undertaking. If anyone is poor it must be for other reasons and must not be held up as human ideal. St. Thomas Aquinas correctly said, "Poverty is not good in itself."[3] In the Kingdom of God poverty will have no place; thus, it should be destroyed.

Wealth, an Evil That Dehumanizes the Person and Offends God

Depicting poverty as an evil does not mean that its correlative, wealth, is a good. It is interesting to see that both the Old and New Testaments condemn wealth as an evil which renders us unfit for God and his Kingdom. Amos, the shepherd-prophet, violently condemns the wealthy people of the Northern Kingdom:

> Woe to those who are at ease in Zion and those who feel secure on the mountains of Samaria, the first citizens of the first of nations, to whom the House of Israel comes! . . . Woe to those who lie on ivory beds, and stretch themselves out upon their couches, and eat lambs from the flock and calves from the midst of the stall . . . who drink wine in bowls, and anoint themselves with the finest oils, but are not grieved over the ruin of Joseph (Am. 6:1–6).

Habakkuk, another angry prophet, also curses wealth:

> Oh, certainly wealth is treacherous! Man is arrogant and greed is as wide as Sheol; like death he never has enough. He gathers all the na-

> tions for himself, and collects all peoples as his own. . . . Woe to him who amasses what is not his own . . . and loads himself with pledges (Hab. 2:5–6).

The New Testament is even more forceful in condemning riches: "Alas for you rich, you have your consolation now! Alas for you who are filled with bread, because you will go hungry" (Lk. 6:24–25). The rich man who says to himself, "My soul, you have goods stored up for many years, rest, eat, drink, feast," receives the following invective from Jesus:

> Fool! This very night your soul shall be demanded of you. The goods you have hoarded, where will they be? Thus it is for him who stores up riches for himself, and does not enrich himself with the things of God (Lk. 12:16–21). You cannot serve two masters. . . . You cannot serve God and riches (Lk. 16:13).

In Luke's Gospel, Jesus characterizes wealth, without qualification, as unjust and evil (Lk. 16:9). The Pharisees, who "loved money and scorned Jesus," heard, in a context critical of their wealth, this sentence: "What is exalted among human beings is an abomination in the sight of God" (Lk. 16:14–15).

It is said that the purpose of wealth is to give people security and make them free, but Jesus unmasks these pretensions in the parable of the Rich Fool (Lk. 12:16–21). At the beginning of the parable its moral is given, and the illustration follows: "Take heed and beware of all covetousness; for a person's life does not consist in the abundance of one's possessions" (Lk. 12:15). Right after the parable Jesus draws some beautiful lessons about human life and its true security resting in God alone: life is worth more than food, the body more than clothing, and people more than birds (Lk. 12:22–31). "Do not store up treasures on earth," Jesus tells us (Mt. 6:19; Lk. 12:33). The First Letter to Timothy, foreshadowing a radical condemnation of all plutocratic capitalism, says, "The root of all evil is the desire for money" (1 Tm. 6:10).

Justifying the Twofold Condemnation

This linked and equal condemnation of both poverty and wealth may seem surprising, yet there are profound reasons for it.

A Contrapositive Dialectic

Neither the Old Testament nor Jesus considers poverty or wealth in the abstract, as entities subsisting in themselves or as morally neutral situations. Neither poverty nor wealth is produced by spontaneous generation. In examining the Bible we see how infrequently poverty or wealth is used as an abstract noun. Yet we often find "the poor" or "the rich"—concrete nouns, historical realities.

Poverty and wealth arise from concrete, interpersonal relationships, mediated by material goods. Poverty and wealth appear in a dialectical relationship; one implies the other. Poverty is impoverishment; wealth is enrichment. There is a wealth that makes others poor, despoils them, grinds down their dignity, steals their goods, and thus deprives them of the material conditions necessary for a life worthy of human beings. This poverty is denounced as an injustice, just as dishonest riches are, since both poverty and wealth are the result of the boundless greed of the rich. This type of poverty is no good because it comes from evil.

That anyone in a situation of poverty can still preserve his or her human dignity, giving up all desire for revenge and all covetousness, is not the result of poverty but of the inexhaustible greatness of the human person, which is able to overcome and transcend any given situation. It is not by virtue of poverty, but despite it, that people preserve their dignity.

Thus we do not try to justify poverty theoretically, using human dignity which is experienced and preserved despite the evil poverty represents. Rather, because of the inviolable dignity of each person, we can combat every situation, not by holding up wealth as an ideal, but by seeking more just relationships among people, relationships that preclude the existence of rich and poor.

We want to recall the biblical texts, especially in the Prophets, where the dialectical relationship between poverty and wealth appears very clearly.

The prophet Isaiah proclaims:

> Woe to you who issue iniquitous decrees and their scribes who write oppression in order to keep the needy away from justice and to rob the

> poor among my people of their right, so that widows may be their spoil and orphans their prey (Is. 10:1–2).

Amos declares how poverty is engendered by injustice.

> Thus says the Lord: "For three transgressions of Israel, and for four, I will not revoke the punishment: because they sell the just for silver, and the needy for a pair of sandals—those who trample the head of the poor into the dust of the earth and turn aside the way of the afflicted" (Am. 2:6–7).

Job reveals the cause of poverty with prophetic indignation.

> Men remove landmarks; they seize flocks and pasture them. They drive away the beast of the fatherless; they take the widow's ox as a pledge. They push the poor off the road; the poor of the earth all hide themselves. Like wild asses in the desert they go off to toil, seeking prey in the wilderness as food for their children. . . . They walk around naked, having no clothes. . . . (Job 24:2–12).

Habakkuk points his finger at the usurers who amass what is not theirs and load themselves with pledges (Hab. 2:6–8).

All the prophetic literature abounds with condemnations of fraudulent business practices, exploitation, forcible land seizure, taxes and unjust burdens, and oppression by the ruling class.

The parable of the Rich Man and Lazarus clarifies the antithetical relationship between poverty and wealth beyond a doubt (Lk. 16:19–31). Zacchaeus is converted and redeemed, restoring the ill-gotten gains with which he has enriched himself.

The Letter of James points out that the rich oppress the poor and drag them into their courts, they do not pay the wages of the workers who have gathered in the harvest, they condemn and kill the just (Jas. 2:6; 5:4–6).

These texts are concerned neither with condemning worldly goods nor with praising poverty. Wealth is condemned as the cause of poverty, and poverty for being a social scandal and the indication and effect of an unjust situation. Material goods should humanize us and be equally shared by everyone. The condemnation of both poverty and wealth thus expresses the basic value of material goods; they are not distributed justly and equitably among people because of unjust human relationships. The biblical and human ideal is not the search for, or promotion of, a rich society, but the creation of a more just society. When justice is lacking, we end up lacking other goods and values: class distinctions come into being, hatred spreads, as do greed and idolatry. When justice has been established, there will no longer be rich and poor to be a scandal that humiliates people and offends God.

The Lukan Beatitudes (6:20–26) are clearly situated in the context of seeing wealth and poverty as equally to blame for the inequities they permit. By calling the hungry blessed because they will be filled and the persecuted blessed because they will have justice, Jesus clearly is rejecting hunger, persecution, and poverty. On the other hand, in the four Woes which Luke places immediately after the Beatitudes, Jesus just as clearly rejects wealth: woe to you rich, woe to you who are filled, woe to you who laugh now, woe to you people speak well of.

Life and happiness in the Kingdom and in human life do not reside in either wealth or poverty. They are found in a life of justice toward God and other people. Wealth and poverty are both irreconcilable with God and his Kingdom; in the way these conditions exist in our society, they imply injustice and the willful violation of the fraternal relationships among human beings.

A Dialectic That Causes Alienation

There is a second reason for rejecting both wealth and poverty. Wealth, by virtue of the power it confers, tends to become an absolute value; money demands adoration. It tends to become life's major preoccupation, since one must always be concerned about retaining it and increasing it; thus Jesus observes that one cannot serve two masters (or, in modern terms, one cannot have two absolutes in life): God and money (Lk. 16:13; Mt. 6:24). Wealth offers a false security which Christ himself warns us against (Lk. 12:15). The author of the First Letter to Timothy urges us not to set our hearts on uncertain riches, but on God (1 Tm. 6:17). Wealth dehumanizes. Material goods make the spirit materialistic and cause the destruction of our capacity for openness and communion.

Poverty generally causes all kinds of misery: illness, hunger, psychological disturbances, destruction of the individual and the family, hatred, theft and other crimes, blasphemy against God, despair. Since poverty is the result of sin, it inclines and impels one to sin. The unjustly rich are those responsible for the evil and violence perpetrated by the poor and humbled.

In conclusion we can affirm that for the Prophets, Jesus, and ourselves the poor constitute the starting point for evaluating and judging society and its wealth and comforts. In the poor we see the inhumanity and injustice of poverty and the evil and indignity of wealth. Let us realize that one causes the other. The cause of poverty is not lack of opportunity, laziness, nor lack of motivation to work, but lies in unjust relationships, in unbounded acquisitiveness, in despoiling and robbing, in fraud, in extortion, and in the exploitation of one person by another. This is the spirit that gives rise to rich and poor.

Society will not become more human, just, or fraternal without a deep conversion, renouncing the spirit of acquisitiveness. Only in a society where relationships among people are completely loving and just will wealth be a good thing, not because of the power and status it confers, but for the relief and the true freedom it provides. It will free us from the necessity of having to live preoccupied with survival. It will open new possibilities for us. It will guarantee health, adequate education, better communication, and fuller communion among individuals, nations, and continents.

The ideal Christianity proposes is not a society that exalts either poverty or wealth, but one that creates justice and fraternal love. It is the Lukan ideal of Acts 4, found in the sharing of goods by the early Christians in such a way that there were no poor people among them (Ac. 4:34). This Lukan ideal is not detachment and collective poverty, but fraternal love. Such an ideal, as Jacques Dupont affirms, "translates itself not into love of poverty, but into love of the poor, and does not aim at making everyone poor, but in seeing no one suffers need."[4]

"Blessed Are the Poor"

Before we discuss the new spirit of justice and fraternal love, which is needed in order to overcome both poverty and wealth, it is necessary to consider a question that has been the source of great misunderstanding and has been used theoretically to justify, and even idealize, poverty. The question concerns what Jesus means when he says, in Luke's Gospel, "Blessed are the poor, for theirs is the Kingdom of God" (Lk. 6:20).

Who Are the Poor?

The first question raised is: Who are the poor? Are they perhaps the materially poor in relation to whom our duty to give alms is defined and because of whom Jesus says to the rich man, "Sell what you have and give it to the poor"? (Mk. 10:21; Lk. 18:22 and par.; Mt. 26:9–11; Mk. 12:42, 14:5–7; Lk. 16:20–22; Jn. 12:5–6, 8; 13:29).

The noted exegete Gelin asks:

> Can we believe Jesus exalted a social class? Does the Gospel ever appear to be a social manifesto? No social condition has been canonized by it, or, insofar as social structure is concerned, directly related to the Kingdom. Only a spiritual situation can be related to a spiritual gift. Only confident faith opens people to the grace of God. And this openness is called the openness of spiritual poverty.[5]

According to Gelin, Christ directed himself to all social classes, not only to the poor. The real poor, to whom Jesus proclaimed the Gospel, are those who are dispossessed and open-hearted, without being tied necessarily to an underprivileged economic class. The poor, according to this interpretation, are the poor in spirit.

This interpretation seems false, moralistic, and spiritualistic, not situated in the concrete ambit of the Beatitudes. The Beatitudes do not speak only of the poor. They also speak of the hungry, the sorrowful, the persecuted, and the slandered or proscribed (Lk. 6:22). In other passages there are references to the blind, the lame, lepers, the oppressed (Lk. 4:18–19; 7:22; Mt. 11:4–5). Christ's mission is to the humiliated and outraged. He comes to free them. Salvation is prefigured by liberation from such situations, those of hardship, not those that spiritualize human life.

Thus the poor are those who are economically poor, and those marginated because of illness or social and religious prejudice. Joachim Jeremias, a specialist in the social and economic problems of Jesus' time, wrote:

> For Jesus, the poor, most certainly, are the oppressed in the broadest meaning of that term: those who, having been humiliated, cannot defend themselves, the despairing who have no salvation. . . . For Jesus, "poor" has the meaning, already used by the Prophets, of the disgraced or outcast person, including the humiliated and poor who know they must rely entirely on divine help. All who suffer need—the hungry and thirsty, the naked, strangers, the sick and imprisoned—are among the "least ones" and are his brothers (Mt. 25:31–46).[6]

The Beatitudes affirm that the Kingdom of Heaven belongs to these concrete poor. This is the key to understanding how the poor are privileged. It is essential not to lose sight of the image the expression "Kingdom of God" conjured up in the Jewish people who heard it from Jesus' lips. For the entire ancient Near East, as well as for Israel, the basic function of the king was to secure justice for those subdued, oppressed, and exploited by the rich and powerful. According to the Psalms and the Prophets, especially Isaiah (61:1–2) and Micah (4:6–7), the longed-for Messiah will be a Messiah of the poor.

> He secures justice for the humiliated of the people and will save the children of the poor and crush the oppressor (Ps. 72:2–4). He will free the poor who cry out and whom no one protects (Ps. 72:12–14, Is. 9:4–5).

Thus the Messiah will be

> anointed by the Spirit of Yahweh to bring Good News to the poor, to mend broken hearts, to proclaim liberty to captives and freedom to those imprisoned, . . . to console those who weep, to give them a garland instead of ashes, the oil of gladness instead of mourning, songs of joy instead of a downcast spirit (Is. 61:1–3; 11:1ff.).

The messianic king will secure justice for the poor in the face of their oppressor. The magnanimity of the king extends to all. This Good News is for all the poor: the day of justice has come. The injustice of wealth and oppression will be revealed; this will in turn reveal the injustice of poverty. The Messiah upholds the right of the weak against the strong and the oppressor. "Theirs is the Kingdom of Heaven" means that the poor will be the principal beneficiaries of the inbreaking of God's Kingdom, which is a new order of justice and equality and the overcoming of the distinction between rich and poor.

Their Blessedness

J. Dupont writes:

> The reason for their privilege should not be sought in their spiritual attitudes, but in the way God exercises his kingship. The poor are blessed, not because they are better than others or are better prepared to receive the Kingdom, but because he wants to make his Kingdom a dazzling manifestation of his justice and love for the poor, for those who suffer any kind of affliction. The privilege of the poor has its theological basis in God. It is an error to place it in the moral attitudes of the poor, which makes us spiritualize their poverty. The poverty of those to whom Jesus announced the Good News is centered in a wretched human condition, which makes the poor victims of hunger and oppression. Poverty is an evil; and, precisely for this reason, the sufferings and privations of the poor appear as a challenge to the royal justice of God. Thus God has decided to put an end to it all.[7]

Poor, then, has a concrete, historical meaning: that of a situation caused by injustice, which offends God and debases the image of God that is the human person.

Preaching the Good News to the poor, Jesus guarantees them that they will be liberated from their humbled condition. To be poor, for St. Luke, is not an ideal; it is something to be overcome, just as injustice and sin are.

What then does the Matthean version of the Beatitude mean: "Blessed are the poor in spirit, for theirs is the Kingdom of Heaven" (Mt. 5:3)? Before we give an answer, we must emphasize that, of the 24 times the word *poor* appears in the New Testament, 21 times it means lacking material goods, worthy of help. In the First Letter of John this meaning also appears: "If anyone who possesses the goods of the earth sees one's brother or sister in need and closes one's heart to him or to her, how can the love of God remain in that person?" (1 Jn. 3:17). This is one meaning of *poor*.

In St. Matthew we find another meaning of *poor* as a positive, spiritual mode of being. To be poor is to be humble, meek, to be a beggar before God, to the extent that one can receive everything from the Most High. Such a meaning is already present in the Old Testament tradition, where the word *anaw* (poor) is used to describe this spiritual disposition. This new meaning taken up by Matthew is found in all the Beatitudes. Just as they speak of the poor in spirit, they speak of those who thirst for justice, and those who are persecuted for the sake of righteousness (Mt. 5:10–11). Thus we encounter, on another level, a condition not dependent on having or not having.

Why does Luke adopt one meaning and Matthew another, since undoubtedly both meanings are correct? Exegesis confirms that Luke's formulation refers strictly to the poor; this is the older meaning and comes from Jesus. This formulation, which does not add "in spirit," was also known to Matthew, as we can see in the passage in which John the Baptist sends people to Jesus to ask if he is the one to come, and Jesus gives them the answer, "The blind see, the lame walk, . . . and the poor have the Gospel preached to them" (Mt. 11:5). The addition of "in spirit" is proper to Matthew, and very probably did not originate with the historical Jesus. However, it does conform to Jesus' thought, since Jesus sought to give a new spirit that made wealth and poverty impossible as two sides of a dialectic. Such a spirit is clearly defined and explicated in Matthew's version of the Beatitudes. Moreover, both meanings of poverty are deeply rooted in the theological tradition of Judaism: poverty as oppression and poverty as humility.

Concrete circumstances may have moved Luke to adopt one meaning (oppression) and Matthew to adopt the other (the spirit of humility). In Matthew's community, where there were many Jews and Judaizers, there was the danger of falling into the trap of phariseeism, linked to seeking one's own justification, to pride and self-sufficiency before God. Thus Matthew emphasized poverty as humility of spirit, as hunger and thirst for justice, to combat the tendency toward pride. In the Lukan community, on the other hand, there were sharp class distinctions between rich and poor, and real oppression existed. Thus Luke strongly emphasized poverty as injustice and the need to bring about the Kingdom of God, which is one of justice, love, and peace, and which manifests the power of God who repairs and transforms unjust relationships, freeing the poor from oppression.[8]

Both these meanings of poverty, although different, are essential and imply each other, as we will see below. On the one hand, a commitment to eliminate poverty (oppression) without an attitude of poverty (humility) would not be true justice and liberation for the poor. On the other hand, poverty (humility) without a commitment to eliminate poverty (oppression) would be no more than a mysticization of the Gospel meaning of poverty, and a refined way of carrying on the beautiful discourses of the rich about poverty.

A Poverty That Is Treasure Desired by God and That Ennobles Humanity

The preceding reflections show that the kind of poverty that pleases God and ennobles the person is certainly not material poverty in itself, given the unjust conditions it implies and the dehumanization it causes. The poverty that ennobles is in the Matthean concept of poverty as humility of spirit, which the Latin-American theologian Gustavo Gutiérrez calls "spiritual childlikeness." The expression "spiritual childlikeness" is perhaps better than "poverty of spirit" since it cannot be misunderstood and is not open to theological mysticization, which seeks to justify both poverty and material wealth.

Poverty as an Attitude of Humility

Poverty means the capacity to welcome God, recognizing the creature's radical nothingness, the human emptiness before the riches of divine love. Poverty in this sense is synonymous with humility, generosity, spiritual emptiness, renunciation of all self-sufficiency. The opposite of this type of poverty is not wealth, but pride, self-sufficiency, self-affirmation, a being closed to God and to other people. Evidently one can be materially poor and lack this other type of poverty, since a poor person can be proud, conceited, and egotistical. On the other hand, we can be rich materially and be poor in spirit insofar as we are open to God and to others, living in solidarity with those who lack material goods, and using our wealth for social betterment. This type of poverty is held up as an ideal by the Bible and the masters of spirituality. The Prophet Zephaniah warns the people: "Seek God, all of you, the poor of the earth who fulfill his commands, seek righteousness, seek poverty" (Zp. 2:3).

Poverty as humility, in contrast to pride, is clearly attested to by Zephaniah.

> On that day you will not be put to shame, Daughter of Zion, because of the deeds by which you have rebelled against me, for then I will remove your proudly exultant ones from your midst, and you shall no longer be haughty on my holy mountain. For I will leave in your midst a humble and lowly people who trust in the name of Yahweh (Zp. 3:11–12).

In texts like these the opposition between the proud and arrogant, who trust in their own power, and the humble and lowly, who trust in the power of God, is abundantly clear. The latter, not the former, is the poor person.

We emphasize that this meaning is not an idealizing of material poverty. This kind of poverty embodies a new relationship with things, considering them as coming from God. It is an ontological attitude, not merely a psychological one, which allows us to remain in union with, and open to, God no matter what our social condition is. Evidently the materially poor find themselves in a situation that favors openness to, and trust in, God. Having nothing, they are more disposed to put all their hope in God who provides. Those who are materially rich encounter greater difficulty in doing this. They have goods that satisfy them, preoccupy them, and keep them busy. They do not need God in order to survive economically. Thus Jesus says, "Woe to you who are happy now. . . . It is easier for a camel to pass through the eye of a needle than for the rich to enter the Kingdom of God" (Lk. 6:24; 18:25).

Material poverty continues to be an evil. But, despite this, it can be the source of unexpected spiritual riches, since it gives people the chance to give themselves over confidently to God who secures justice for them.

The Psalms elaborate the meaning of the poor as the humble still further. In Ps. 34 the poor are "those who take refuge in God" (v. 8), "those who seek him" (v. 10). In Ps. 37, the poor are "those who wait for the Lord" (v. 9), the "just" (v. 17), the "blameless" (v. 18), the "faithful" (v. 28), the "blameless and upright" (v. 37). Included in this psalm is the assurance that "the poor will inherit the land and defend themselves in abundant prosperity" (v. 11). In Psalm 34, it is said that "when the poor man cried out to the Lord, he heard him and saved him from all his troubles" (v. 6). González Ruíz observes:

> There is no room for doubt: the God of the *anawim* (the poor) does not want, as a starting-point, the social condition of poverty, and so its conquest is identified with the saving action of God himself.[9]

Material Poverty: The Ascetical Path to Spiritual Childlikeness

Humility of spirit is not a matter of mere desire or will. One must be realistic, without forgetting the historical meaning of poverty. Thus it is necessary to provide material conditions that make the experience of humility possible. This is where asceticism comes in. This does not imply a despising of material goods, which would be bad, but a sparing and moderate use of them, freeing ourselves from all wretchedness and all acquisitiveness, which always enslaves.

The warnings of Jesus about the amassing of riches must be understood in this context. Desire for riches becomes an excessive preoccupation, encourages neglect of God, and makes it easy to succumb to the temptation of idolatry (Lk. 12:15, 22; 18:25). The degree of asceticism in regard to material goods cannot be determined a priori. It depends on the economic system of the area, the times, and of the people involved.

In every case the degree of asceticism must be such as to allow us constantly to remember and to live for God as the only Absolute and Necessary, and for the other, the neighbor, as the presence of the Absolute in our lives. Only with an ascetical attitude can one live this poverty of spirit. Such asceticism can be practiced even by one who has great wealth, being freed from attachment to the wealth, having the possibility of using it for social betterment and for greater communion with the rest of humanity.

Poverty as a Commitment to Oppose Poverty

Poverty as total emptiness and complete availability before God cannot, in its own turn, be mysticized or idealized in order to preserve a de facto situation of a few rich people and many poor. People who are really open to God feel impelled to commit themselves to establish justice in the world. The encounter with God spurs one on to encounter the many in whom God is offended by misery, hunger, and the violence of which they are the victims. The encounter with the poor provides the occasion for the encounter with what God demands of us. The poverty-which-is-sin demands from the poverty-which-is-humility a commitment and an effort to overcome that sinful condition. The fight for justice in relationships among people, and a more equitable distribution of earthly goods are, or should be, two concrete expressions of poverty-as-humility.

We have already seen that, in the New Testament, the poor are the privileged people in the Kingdom of God because the real meaning of the Kingdom is manifested and realized through them. God comes to establish justice and restore their dignity which has been stolen. We must not think of this as being accomplished through divine intervention in the sense of miracles to be experienced day by day. Rather, this comes about through the historical process; God intervenes sacramentally, i.e., through human commitment. Believers have the greatest right to be these sacramental instruments through which poverty is overcome. In the people who make this commitment, and in the work they do, God's action is concealed. In the history of liberation we find the concrete history of the Kingdom.

The commitment to overcome poverty-as-sin is fulfilled on two distinct levels, both of which are based in Scripture.

The first level is almsgiving. Scripture abounds with invitations to give alms to show solidarity with the poor: "Give your possessions as alms and everything will be clean for you" (Lk. 11:41). Jesus advises us to give to those who ask and not hope for return (Lk. 6:30–38). Yet almsgiving has a limited effect; it does not eliminate the division between rich and poor. It gives the rich a generous spirit, but they remain rich and in the same social class.

The commitment to eliminate poverty tries to go further than almsgiving. Those who commit themselves to eliminate poverty take up the burden of the poverty they are committed to eliminate. They do so not because poverty is good in itself and thus a good they should strive for, but under the impulse of grace to show commitment to the poor, which causes them to unite themselves with the poor in their struggle to change the dehumanizing effects of poverty. Poverty is wiped out by poverty. Since sinful poverty is engendered by the lack of love and solidarity, only committed love and solidarity can bring about effective liberation. Gustavo Gutiérrez writes:

> There is no attempt to idealize poverty, but, on the contrary, to see it as it really is—an evil—in order to protest against it and strive to wipe it out. As Paul Ricoeur said, it is not a matter of remaining with the poor but of fighting against poverty. Thanks to this solidarity—the necessary actions, the lifestyle, the break with one's inherited social class—one should make the poor and the despoiled aware of their exploitation and foster their desire for freeing themselves from it. Christian poverty, the expression of love, is solidarity *with the poor* and a protest *against poverty.*[10]

The total detachment Jesus demands must be understood within the dynamic of total commitment to the poor of the Kingdom. This commitment, in Latin America today, is demanded of us as the contemporary incarnation of the

Church's mission and the legitimation of the vow of poverty in religious life.

Jesus, the Rich Man Who Became Poor

The three positive meanings of poverty—humility, asceticism, commitment—were lived radically by Jesus of Nazareth. His family was poor and he lived in a way that resulted in his having nowhere to lay his head. He lived off alms and the fish his disciples caught. He went around preaching and doing good to such an extent that he had no leisure even to eat (Mk. 6:31). He was even poor in regard to his time, since he never failed to receive and welcome anyone who sought him out: "If anyone comes to me, I will not cast that person out" (Jn. 6:37).

Nevertheless, the lack of goods was not, for Jesus, a value in itself. As we have already seen he exalts the poor, not because they have nothing, but because they can receive everything from God and long for justice. Because he is free, he accepts dinner invitations from rich friends to such an extent that people become suspicious of him (Mt. 11:19). In accepting these invitations he incarnates the love of God for all people, which does not exclude even rich sinners.

The Son of God humbled himself by taking on the condition of a mere mortal (Ph. 2:6–7). He lived in the closest intimacy with God the Father, from whom he received everything—his mission, his disciples, his Kingdom, his glory: "I have nothing of myself" (Jn. 5:19, 30; 8:29). All his life he realized poverty-humility in its radical meaning and not just in a moral one. He lived with such dependence on God that he felt himself God's Son. Conscious of having received everything from the Father, he likewise gives everything to others. He gives his life and his death. He conquers people, not with an arrogant power that subjugates, but with a generous service that attracts and captivates everyone.

He committed himself to the poor of his times and always came to their defense, avoiding no arguments or conflicts, defending the man born blind, the lepers, the prostitutes, the woman who perfumed his feet, the sick, and all those considered public sinners by the accepted standards of his times.

St. Paul reminds us of "the generosity of our Lord Jesus Christ who, being rich, became poor *for our sake,* so that by his poverty we might become rich" (2 Co. 8:9). The majority of the conflicts that brought about Jesus' death were caused by the liberties he took in favor of the marginated. His death was a worthy one because he died for all those for whom no one would die. He did it through solidarity—for our sake—as St. Paul emphasizes.

To follow Jesus is to pursue his life and his cause; it is to have the same feelings he had (Ph. 2:5), which led him to take on the condition of the other (Ph. 2:6), that is, of the sinner. He assumed it, not to idealize it, but to overcome it from the inside, in order to infuse a new mentality that would make the existence of rich and poor, oppressor and oppressed, impossible.

Poverty-as-commitment is the highest form of love, since it encounters the other as the other and not as some kind of extension of ourselves. To be poor, for the Church and Christians of today, on the personal level, is to commit oneself to justice for the vast numbers of the economically impoverished whose dignity as human beings and as brothers and sisters has been outraged; to place one's consciousness, words, social influence, goods, and historical presence in Latin-American society at the service of these people who constitute the masses—everyone—for whom Christ also lived and died. For the Church this means an unavoidable call to conscience, which serves as a criterion to judge the evangelical and liberating character of its action in the world.

For religious life a reflection on poverty in the light of the demands of so many people who live in a state of underdevelopment—of inhuman conditions—necessitates a rethinking of the character of the vow of poverty. This is needed both on the personal level of not-having and the demand for asceticism, and on the community level of having-in-common and in a sense of sharing. It also must have a spiritual dimension of availability and openness, in the sense of spiritual childlikeness, as well as a sociopolitical dimension of not-having-for-oneself in order to enter into solidarity with the poor, journeying with them toward a more just and fraternal society.

To take the vow of poverty implies a commitment to justice in human relations, a commitment so urgent today on all levels. Religious life must open itself to new forms of presence in the world, which grow out of the determination of new demands. The poverty of the majority demands a missionary self-understanding on the part of religious. In the coherent understanding of the vow of poverty in a new way is most likely the way a new shape of religious life will arise in the near future.

5

Chastity: The Integration of the Masculine and Feminine

The vow of chastity has many facets, analyzed by theology and spirituality, religious psychology, and other sciences. Within that diversity, in our analysis we attempt to highlight a very valuable and important aspect, studied with particular interest by modern anthropology: chastity as the integrating of the masculine and feminine elements present in each person. There will also be a very brief outline of the ontology of the structure implied in the vow of chastity.

This analysis we believe will shed new light, making us able to understand the full scope of this vow. We will not form any specific conclusions for religious life. But personal and community reflection will discern in this analysis fruitful avenues toward both a personal and a community experience of consecrated chastity, which, when vowed, provides a special approach to the task of integration, bringing about, and witnessing to, the achievement of full personhood by the content and spiritual values within the vow.

The Endeavor of Ontological Reasoning

In this era of "planetization" and scientific endeavor, the attempt to make an ontological reflection obliges one to begin by explaining what this means and to justify its validity for understanding the problem at hand.

The sciences—differential psychology, biological sciences, cultural and social anthropology—provide us with an abundance of data about man and woman. These data are of great importance, since they depict man and woman in concrete historical and cultural milieu, that is, in the arena where they actually exist and discover who they are. Such knowledge, critically systematized, makes up the universe of the human sciences.

Ontological reflection must begin with the question of how we are to understand the scientific knowledge about man and woman. At first the data would seem to express that man and woman are two different modes of human existence. But what is the human? This question transcends the data of science, since the human as such is not the object of scientific research. Scientific investigation does not reveal what a human being is, but what concrete men and women are. The human is not an existential reality, as concrete men and women are. Yet it is correct to say that male and female are two different modes of being and of realizing the human. The human does exist and is incarnated as male and as female.

One cannot answer the question about the nature of the human merely with scientific data, no matter how detailed. The data are always about concrete men and women in their concrete historical situation and in their process of humanization. Undoubtedly these data reveal much, but much remains obscure. The scientific method, which discovers many important dimensions or perspectives, is powerless to express or reveal other, more essential ones. Thus no science can claim to have exhaustively investigated, or to have given the definitive word on, man and woman. On the contrary, it is by virtue of these scientific data that we realize that the realm of our ignorance is much larger than the realm of our knowledge. Moreover, as our knowledge increases, our ignorance increases along with it—an apparent paradox. *The Mystery of*

Man is the title of a book by Alexis Carrel. Despite sounding a bit like a movie title, this title precisely expresses our situation in regard to ourselves.[1]

This ignorance is not surprising, since we observe in the depths of our humanity a mystery that is inexhaustible.[2] Yet what we think we know about the human, and its incarnation as male and female, which always exceeds our knowledge, continually challenges us to know more, to research further, and thus provide more and more data. It is an illusion to think that one day science will come to know all the secrets of man and woman.

After what we have said, it seems the only answer we can give to the question about the nature of the human is that we do not know. However, we do know that the human is a permanent openness to new possibilities, which causes the human reality to transcend its present incarnation. Man and woman are not exhausted by our knowledge of them, but are an ongoing mystery that demands our rethinking. Thus they reveal an unsuspected, living transcendence of whatever we can discover or posit about them. They are fundamentally mysteries, always eluding human knowledge, a darkness which nurtures science and yet which science is powerless to illuminate. The human as such is always referred to, and projected toward, a beyond, toward the mystery which is both revealed and hidden in man and woman. The human is more than one or the other taken separately. It is thus an identity being realized in distinction.

An ontological reflection must surely begin with scientific data, since, without that data, metaphysical knowledge is impossible. At the same time such an analysis obliges us to transcend the data, reminding the researcher not to become locked into his or her findings about man and woman, since their most valuable and essential part cannot be observed by science. Ontological analysis is not so much concerned with man and woman as with the mystery distinctly incarnated by each, a mystery that transcends the domain of science and is thus unknowable by anthropology. It is the mystery of the human, which our logic wants to grasp. Thus ontology comes into play as an analysis of the radically human.

Sexuality as an Ontological Structure of the Human Person

In the light of ontological analysis, sexuality is not an isolated characteristic of the person: his or her genitality. Thus it is not merely a biological dimension. It permeates every aspect of a human being. All the human person is and does is marked by sexuality, since we are always sexual beings. Sex is not something a person has, but something a person is; he or she is a sexual being. In other words, a human being is male or female. Male and female constitute two different modes of being and of situating oneself in the world. In whatever he thinks, feels, expresses, undertakes, or plans, the man manifests his being-a-man, his masculinity; likewise a woman manifests her being-a-woman, her femininity. The two can do the same mechanical, artistic, or scientific things, they can coordinate the same impulses and movements, but they do these things in different ways because of the differences between them. Although they are different, they nevertheless experience a deep complementarity in their beings: man is for woman, and woman for man.

This was already intuited in the Old Testament by the Yahwist's theology: "It is not good for man (*ish*) to be alone. Let us make him a companion who will be female (*ishah*), in all ways similar to him," that is, his reciprocal being, entirely complementary (Gn. 2:18). Only in being man or woman does the human appear as the image and likeness of God in biblical anthropology: "male and female he created them" (Gn. 1:27). The human exists only as being one or the other.

Let us inquire into the meaning of this. This may mean that each one, taken in isolation, is incomplete and that, in order to be perfect, one needs to be completed by the other, like two incomplete things that mutually complete each other. Current discourse on man and woman seems to suggest this. But can the human mode of being be compared to a thing's mode of being? As spirit, even though incarnate, man and woman possess a unique mode of being, which is not comparable to the mode of being of the purely material.

Ontological analysis focuses on the nature of the male-female complementarity and on what makes their mode of being different from that of inanimate objects. In this way all inadequate or false depictions of that relationship are avoided, depictions that result only in misrepresenting the male-female reciprocity. Is this reciprocity merely a superficial, biological one? Is it one that brings about the completion of each one's incompleteness? Is it one of two distinct and separate entities who are radically open to one another? Or is it a complementarity based on the fact of each being immanent in the other, in a real but mysterious sense, and each self-transcendent, such that the male carries the female within it, and the female the male?

These questions are not as theoretical as they appear. One notices, for example, that they have an immediate bearing on whether chastity is lived in an internal or an external dimension. Given the mysterious immanence of the male in the female and the female in the male, the relationship between the two is not established from the outside inward, but from the inside outward. The man enages in dialogue with, accepts, and is related to the female within himself, and from this point relates to the concrete individual woman he encounters. The same can be said of the woman.

One might conclude from such an analysis that each person is male and female at the same time—a concrete and universal hermaphroditism. This is not the case, since neither is both masculine and feminine in the same way at the same time. Masculinity, although it contains feminine elements, assures that the person is a man, not a woman, and vice versa. What this means is that male and female are not totally objectifiable realities, nor can they be circumscribed by physiological and psychological data. Maleness does not exhaust the subjective incarnation of masculinity; thus it may also be found in the woman, and vice versa. The human person is male or female according to whether masculinity or femininity predominates.

Thus instead of saying that man and woman are mutually incomplete, it is better to say that they are relatively incomplete. Each one possesses the characteristics of the other, but they do not possess them in the same proportion or in the same way. Thus individuals are not self-sufficient, nor can they be confined to their own person and personality. Since they are relatively incomplete, they are ordered to, and open to, interrelationship, reciprocity, and complementarity with each other.

What does being a man or a woman imply? Perhaps if we introduce a new category (already hinted at above) we can better understand the problem of masculinity-femininity. Masculine is not exactly or absolutely synonymous with male, since it is also found outside the man, in the woman. The same can be said about the feminine. This is an important observation, since it has serious consequences for relationships between men and women. The identification of masculine with male and feminine with female gives rise to numerous discriminations and to a notion of complementarity between men and women that is too external, objective, and material.

To clarify what being male or female implies we must first inquire into what masculinity and femininity are. However, since these are not entities in themselves, but dimensions of being human, let us first consider the basic structure of the human personality.

The Basic Structure of the Human Personality

What constitutes the human is always defined and revealed through a dialectic between the data of the social sciences concerning what the human is and people's latent possibilities, which always go beyond scientific descriptions. The human is always both what it is and what it can become; it is both the charted and the unexplored, both described and indescribable or mysterious. It is light and, at the same time, the darkness from which the light springs. It is the word and the silence that gives birth to the word. It is order and systematization, but also the chaos out of which order arises. In short, the human personality is a mystery, which can always be explored further without thereby losing its mysterious character. This dialectical and seemingly paradoxical, though real, unity of all these dimensions constitutes the subjective nature of the human, which is incarnated as male and as female.

The human is an identity being realized through diversity. It is essentially unified and multiple. It is itself and its psychological, sociological, historical, religious, cultural, internal, and external circumstances. The experience of the human on any level is the experience of a plurality sustained by a fundamental identity. The human person can be incarnated, and effectively is incarnated, in a variety of circumstances without its human identity's becoming lost in them. Despite the circumstances, the human personality can still realize its potentialities.

All this is to say that what is human in oneself is never encountered as a perfect identity, but always in a difference. We can only encounter the image or idea a person has of himself or herself or the work or task a person performs. The identity always appears hidden, and yet is revealed in what issues forth from it. From this point of view, we can truthfully say that the human person lives with its circumstances, thinks with its representations or ideas, works with its works. The person lives in perpetual communion: the communion of identity with diversity and diversity with identity.

In its primary sense, that communion is not something that is established, but that is discovered. The communion can be constructed or facilitated at a later time, that is, when one accepts the identity, lives with the differences, and does not attempt to suppress them. The human, then, presents itself as essential communion: a conjoining of identity and difference. To the extent that one can accept and live with what is different in oneself and in others, so much is one communitarian or involved.

The basic structure of the human person consists in the "and." It consists in being itself and also being different from itself by entering into communion: male and female, the person and the world, the "I" and the "not-I" within me, I and thou, the individual and society.

In dialogue with all these differences the person constructs himself or herself and grows. The ability to accept, share and communicate with what is different constitutes the strength of the human personality or one's personal identity. The task of personal growth obliges us to be constantly open to what is different and what is new, to be mobile and willing to take risks. This dialectic is the basic structure of the human personality. It is full of creative tension, yet constantly threatened by the danger of becoming locked into its own little world and rejecting what is different. Its synthesis is never perfect and complete. To be a person is to be a world that is constantly coming into being, since no matter how much we know or do, we never come to exhaust the mysterious depths of ourselves, precisely because these depths are inexhaustible.

Masculine and Feminine as Different Dimensions of the Human

In light of these somewhat detailed reflections, we can try to understand better what the masculine and feminine are in the human person. It would be good to repeat here that we consider both these aspects as dimensions realized in each man and each woman. The feminine expresses the side of the human person which is obscurity and darkness, mystery and depth, death, interiority, earth, emotion, receptivity, generative power, human vitality. The masculine is the other side of the person: light, time, impulse, sustaining power, order, exteriority, objectivity, and reason. Repose, permanence, obscurity which defies curiosity and investigation, immanence, longing for the past belong to the feminine character. To the masculine character belong transforming dynamism, aggressiveness, transcendence, precision which distinguishes and separates, the capacity to impose order, projection toward the future.

The feminine constitutes the original source of life; the masculine is life coming into being and evolving. In the feminine resides the power of life-giving fullness; in the masculine the power to organize and dominate. In the feminine, repose and preservation; in the masculine, conquest and acquisition. In the feminine, defensive struggle; in the masculine, offensive combat.

Notice once again that man is not defined only by the masculine and woman only by the feminine. Such identification of man with masculine and woman with feminine, although done in literature, psychology, and the social sciences, has actually prevented the possibility of giving a clear theoretical formulation to the problem and has had grave social consequences. We can say that the usurping of the masculine by men made them come to consider themselves the only ones who possessed reason, command, and active presence in society, and to relegate the woman to the home and to tasks of dependence, men often considering her to be no more than an appendage, an object of adornment and pleasure. This cultural obstacle has been sustained even in theology, as can be seen in the Church's discussions about the ministry of women. Overcoming that obstacle is the first condition for a more human and more equal relationship between men and women.

It is the task of each person, in the context of his or her own personality and gender, to integrate masculinity and femininity in his or her own concrete way. The process of individualization or, better, personalization, is carried on in dialogue between the nebulous and obscure, the emotional, the profound and mysterious, and the rational, objective, and ordered, that is, with the principle of order, in human life. Each person is that totality which forms the world, the drama, of human spirituality. Each person is called to realize his or her masculinity and femininity in the best possible way.

Cultural Manifestations of the Masculine and the Feminine

Human groups historify or embody the masculine and feminine aspects of their humanity in many varied forms. In Western society the masculine predominates to such a degree that "man" is a synonym for human being. The masculine is so dominant that it has created a truly patriarchal culture of logic, reason, power, and domination. The feminine is present, but repressed. The values of all Western social organizations, including Christianity, are marked by the predominance of the masculine.

There was a time in human history when the feminine had greater cultural expression. This was seen in the matriarchies, which found in the woman their modes of expression. Historically, although not ontologically, woman continued to be a synonym for the feminine.

The identification of masculine with man and feminine with woman is a cultural phenomenon. Ontology does not authorize that total identification. In actuality, both aspects are conjoined in the human personality, to such an extent that the masculine can be manifested and predominate in a woman, and the feminine can be manifested and predominate in a man.

The studies conducted by Margaret Mead have demonstrated to perfection that masculine and feminine are combined in different ways in men and women, for example, in three primitive tribes of New Guinea that are geographically contiguous. She cites real case histories that show how, independently of biological sexuality, the masculine and the feminine are historified now in the man and now in the woman. In our culture femininity is systematically expressed in the woman. Through relationships with women, men enter into a mysterious world they find fascinating and disturbing. Using the categories of Western mythology, we can say "the brightness of the masculine, solar sphere does not succeed in grasping the mystery of the feminine, lunar realm," and vice versa.

In reality the woman in Western culture explicates and exteriorizes in the world what is implicit and interiorized in the man. By encountering this in the woman, the man encounters his own depths. The woman finds realized and externalized in the man the masculine segment of her own personality. Carl Jung affirmed, with deep insight, that each man possesses within himself his *anima,* and each woman her *animus.* In the woman the man experiences his own feminine unconscious. In the man the woman experiences her own masculine unconscious. The integration of the two in the human psyche, in tandem with the cultural incarnations of the person as man and woman, forms the challenge of the call to human fulfillment.

Studies based on depth psychology, especially those of Erich Neumann, have demonstrated through detailed analysis of the great myths the ambivalent nature of the masculine-feminine dimension. The feminine incarnated in the woman can be, for the man, mother and lover, sister and daughter, queen and slave, saint and she-devil, angel and witch, maiden and prophetess, friend and enemy, day symbol and night symbol, reality and dream, heaven and earth. Simone de Beauvoir accurately observed: "Man sees Woman as Nature with its procreative forces and its dark, destructive elements."[3] In short, the feminine can provide, for the man, an influx of positive, beneficent forces that open a path for him toward undreamed-of horizons, or an influx of negative, sinister forces that can enslave him.

Mythologies, with their wise interpretations of the deepest realities of human nature, always show the constitutive duality, now for the man, now for the woman. The positive aspect of the Great Mother is depicted by Isis, Demeter, and Mary. The negative aspect is represented by the Gorgon, Hecate, and Kali. The feminine gives life and growth, elevates, and transforms; it leads to the vision of the undreamed-of and initiates into the mystery; it is depicted by Venus, Urania, Sophia, and Mary. The feminine that seduces and enslaves, that blinds and maddens, is embodied in Venus, Circe, Astarte, and Lilith.

The growing consciousness of women, during the last decades, of their dependent status in a predominantly patriarchal culture, as well as the social transformations of relationships between the sexes, allow us to see the dawning of a great revolution in the cultural focus of humanity. The schema is delineated for a new manifestation of the masculine and the feminine, in which men and women appear, and are understood, in the context of a deep, personal equality of origin and destiny, of searching for and committing themselves to building a more fraternal society, less dominating and more democratic, one that draws fewer distinctions.

Myth as Expressing the Masculine and the Feminine

It may seem strange that when we come to sketching the masculine and feminine in their concrete reality we abandon abstract language and ontology and have recourse to myth. Yet, in the preceding reflections we have sketched a concept of masculine-feminine that goes beyond the dictates of biology, one which only the figurative and symbolic language of myth can translate adequately. Paul Ricoeur noted:

> Sexuality basically remains impenetrable by human thought and indomitable by human mastery; possibly it is a reflection . . . of that which cannot be captured in either an ethics or a science, but only depicted symbolically by virtue of the mythic which perdures in us.[4]

The mythic within us is not a vestige of the past, but a factor in our present consciousness. The primitive patriarchal and matriarchal elements of our humanity are not relics of a bygone age, but treasures uncovered by spiritual archaeology that still live and motivate us today, according to the findings of psychoanalysis. Personal growth and sanity largely depend on how one relates to these primitive realities, as well as to the unconscious motivations they give rise to, and on whether or not one accepts them and integrates them.

The realm of the masculine-feminine, rooted in the depths of the human personality, is not accessible to the simplifying schematizations of discursive reasoning, but only to incisive exegesis of the ancient myths. The myths expressed, in symbolic and imaginative language, the richness of the mystery incarnate in man and woman better than conceptual, analytical discourse—which always proceeds by definitions, explanations, and epistemological divisions of reality.

The unity of the masculine and feminine in each man and woman is depicted in almost all ancient mythologies and religious cosmogonies. Chinese thought pictured the masculine and feminine as a circle composed of two equal parts of light and darkness (Yin-Yang). Babylonian and Egyptian culture expressed the unity by elaborating the hermaphroditic nature of all reality as born from a principle simultaneously masculine and feminine (Ishtar). Chaos, earth, and night are grounded in the feminine principle; order, day, and air in the masculine principle. In the *Symposium,* Plato presents the myth of the origin of man and woman: in the beginning Zeus created androgynous human beings with two faces, four ears, four hands, two sexes. They sought to rival the gods and Zeus split them in two "as a piece of fruit or an egg is divided with a horsehair." Separated male and female endlessly seek to recover their original unity through Eros and thus complete themselves. There is a Hebrew midrash that says that man and woman originally had one body with two faces. God separated them, giving each one a back, but they instinctively seek to be one body again. Genesis (1:27) presents humanity as a symbiotic unity manifested as male and female. The unity-in-diversity of each human being as masculine and feminine is as old as humanity itself. The psychological study of complexes by the Jungian school confirms the basic truth of the ancient myths.

The truth depicted symbolically in the myths conforms to the truth discovered by ontology: the person is always masculine and feminine. We are not simple beings as the gods are. We are a pluralistic, complex unity that constantly realizes itself in difference, engaged in an unending process of moving from identity to difference to identity. The masculine-feminine in each man and woman manifests the dialectical unity of the human person.

The data of human biology confirm the intuition of the myths, verifying the findings of ontology at the same time. In the first stages of life immediately following conception, the zygote has no sexual determination expressed as male or female. According to biology, chromosomes contain the genes, which transmit hereditary traits. The minute difference in one chromosome determines the sexual structure of male or female, along with the distinctive anatomy, physiological processes, and biochemical composition.

What is the ultimate source of masculine and feminine? We do not know. It is a challenging mystery. We only know how masculine and feminine are culturally incarnated in the historical process of humanization and how they survive in the vast storehouse of human experience, assimilated well or ill—that is to say, as they survive in the individual and collective unconscious—and how, even today, these unconscious elements remain relevant to our social life. Existing forms do not exhaust, in our opinion, the possibilities and potentialities of the masculine and the feminine. History, of itself, is neither repetitive nor routine. It tends to be creative and to bring to realization what has not yet been experienced. The masculine and feminine are thus open to the unknown dimension of the future, whose incarnations will still be seen even if we cannot plan for them or bring them about today. Yet we must prepare for their arrival, which is a way of anticipating them and going forth to meet them.

The Ontological Vision of the Masculine and Feminine and the Future of Relationships Between Men and Women

Despite the mechanisms of repression and tradition, one notices today in society a qualitative and quantitative advance of women. Slowly but surely women are achieving greater decision-making power and corporate responsibility. Positions once held only by men are, more and more, coming to be held by women. This is a sign of a cultural change of direction, in which new relationships between men and women are occurring, based on freedom, on personal worth, respect, and acceptance of their basic equality.

In this way the range of possibilities for self-realization, self-esteem, and mutual respect is being widened. The slow transformation of a system in which men dominate women increases each person's responsibility for a real and personalizing sharing of gifts through the free discovery that one is enriched as one accepts the other's differences and becomes richer as one gives of oneself.

Research carried on by depth psychology and other social sciences on the affective life of the person has revolutionized the concept we have had of ourselves, making us aware of aspects of our being that previous cultures had not revealed to us. Thus we have come to understand that sex is not explicable solely in terms of a genitality exaggerated by its exploitation in a consumer society. Rather, men and women are only such by realizing in themselves, through mutual and complementary relationships, basic ways of being which come to be expressed as masculinity and femininity. They must mutually free themselves from models that keep them in a dominant-submissive type of relationship.

Women can achieve their true identity and freedom only when men come to see their own cultural deformity, that is, when men rediscover their true relationship with the feminine in themselves and with the women who embody that femininity in the world. But woman also must engage in overcoming her archaic concepts of what she is that were inculcated in an age of patriarchal domination and that keep her in an accepted, and consented-to, spiritual dependence. In equality with men, women must assume a cultural role of equal importance in the new society that is coming into existence.

Ontological reflection on the masculine and feminine thus does not lack value or interest. On the contrary, it is more necessary and urgent today than ever before.

Theological Implications of the Masculine and Feminine

According to the Bible, the human person is the image and likeness of God, historified as man and woman. If we come to know God only in and through human mediation, then we can well affirm that human beings can come to know him only through the masculine-feminine structure that defines the human person. From this double aspect values are expressed and horizons opened that cannot be discovered in any other way.

God is certainly outside all human categories, including that of masculine and feminine, which are human, not divine, modes of being. Nevertheless, God reveals himself using masculine and feminine metaphors. God calls himself husband (Is. 54:5) and can speak with infinite tenderness to his people, Israel, depicted as his wife: "I have loved you with an everlasting love and I have kept my affection for you" (Jr. 31:3). However, in the feminine Wisdom imagery, God and his Word are personified (Pr. 8:22–26; Si. 24:9; 1 Co. 24:30). God reveals himself as a mother who consoles and is incapable of forgetting the child of her womb (Is. 49:15; 66:13; Si. 25:6). With a mother's love God wants Jesus to reunite the children of Jerusalem. In an action characteristic of the Great Mother, God will be the one who wipes away every tear from our eyes when he appears at the fullness of time (Rv. 21:4).

In the New Testament, the theme of Christ the husband appears: he saves and sanctifies his bride, the Church (Ep. 5:23–27). The Church is no longer the slave wife, but the freeborn one, the Jerusalem on high (Ga. 4:22–27; Rv. 21:2–9), celebrating her eternal marriage to her husband (Rv. 19:7; 22:17). The theological meaning of these images parallels that of the masculine and feminine: only through the different modes of human existence is the full revelation of God's plan actually communicated to the world. Thus, the woman is for the man, as he for her, the sacrament which reveals aspects of God that can be known and lived only because of the differences in human beings.

The masculine-feminine unity and reciprocity calls to mind that no one is self-sufficient; one does not live only for oneself. The man is open to a transcendence that allows a personalizing encounter with the woman; the woman is likewise open to a transcendence that allows a personalizing encounter with the man. Together they form a two-sided unity, which oneself can never fully incarnate. Pleasure, eros, encounter, love, and joining are also symbolic and figurative; they deal with incarnation, yet also with an aspiration to share in a fullness which both long for and yet which is never fully realized in this world. Man and woman only become fully personalized by together immersing themselves in a transcendent mystery which is greater than their mutual love. They thus open themselves to the Absolute, to God, having had the courage to accept the absolute which they experience in their own lives.

The male-female sexual reciprocity demands consideration of sexuality from an ontological point of view and acceptance of sexuality as a constitutive structure of the human person. We have already observed that sexuality is not mere genitality; thus it can be reconciled with virginity and celibacy. Indeed one of the concrete ways of living one's sexuality is as a virgin or celibate. Religious take a vow of chastity for the sake of the Kingdom of Heaven. This certainly implies a renunciation of the genital expression of love that characterizes marriage, but does not imply a renunciation of love. The vow of chastity is not a vow of "un-love" of "non-reciprocity."[5] Rather it is a vow of more radical love and reciprocity. It is not a vow born of absence, but of superabundance, which permits the exclusion of no one from the sphere of the religious' love, and of radicalness, which transcends flesh and blood without denying them.

Thus the vow of chastity is not a vow against ontological sexuality or despite it. Rather it is a vow that consecrates interpersonal relationships, that places oneself at the service of others in a dynamism of universal love which is sacrificial and personalizing, a love defined by *agape* rather than *eros*.[6]

Virginity or celibacy in the sense just defined, and as a means of being faithful to a commitment, becomes a sacrament of what life will be like when the Kingdom comes to fulfillment, when God is all in all (1 Co. 15:28). Then the masculine-feminine complementarity will find its source and its definitive meaning, becoming transcendent and, in a certain way, transcended.

6

Obedience: A Way to Personal Fulfillment

Personal Fulfillment and Its Depictions

Among the themes usually treated in every discussion of religious life, one is sure to find that of personal fulfillment. All religious, especially younger ones, are more or less explicitly aware of this conviction: I must be fulfilled completely and in keeping with my personality. Religious life, like any other vocation, should offer everyone the possibility of the greatest personal fulfillment. Otherwise why would anyone choose religious life? As the very term "religious life" suggests, it must nourish life. This is especially important since, over the past few years, religious life has been criticized as dehumanizing, encouraging infantilism and naivete, a life that enslaves and reveals the bankruptcy of the religious dimension. The entry of religious into the modern world of work, study, and secular pursuits has awakened a strong consciousness of, and desire for, greater personal fulfillment.

We must start by asking what personal fulfillment is. To ask the question is to form some idea of what fulfillment is. To varying degrees, everyone projects an ideal and establishes goals and objectives in accord with that ideal, as well as determining the behavior patterns necessary for realizing it. In setting up an ideal, one also establishes a system of values in accord with the ideal and values opposed to the ideal.

We must now ask how personal fulfillment is usually depicted. In asking this question and critiquing the answer, we are not trying to destroy any ideal or any noble aspiration. We simply want to refine our ideals, to reveal their most valuable parts, to probe deeply into the quest for personal identity. Furthermore, criticism has the function of discovering where the real values lie, in preserving and fostering them, and of discovering debilitating elements so that these may be overcome.

In its most commonly accepted sense, personal fulfillment is the realization of latent possibilities in our personality. The human person is a unique being who lives a multidimensional existence: intellectual, emotional, moral, professional, artistic, recreational, religious. What we might call the task of human life is the development of everything God has graced each of us with. The Parable of the Talents, in which the master entrusts his servants with money in accordance with their ability (Mt. 25:14–30), coincides with this observation. On his return the master receives double what he has loaned each one. Thus we must develop and increase our talents, making them productive. In other words, we must actualize the potentialities locked up in the mystery of human existence. This is what the process of personalizing humanization involves. The person is never finished being born, but is always in the process of coming to birth. We each strive to achieve, in accordance with the talents we have received from God, our full human potential. Entitatively and dynamically we are God's image and likeness to the extent that we fulfill our own personality during our lifetime.

The model used for this depiction is that of efficiency-output. It is a typically modern model. Sciences, converted into technologies, attempt to obtain the maximum output from materials: more than thirty products can be obtained from soybeans, more than a hundred from petroleum. Such products represent the multiple possibilities latent in those materials. It might be said the materials achieve fulfillment by becoming their products. Now certainly people are not comparable to soybeans or petroleum. The human is a person, not a thing. What, then, is specifically human or personal about us that makes us infinitely different from petroleum or soybeans?

Questions Based on the Evidence

We have begun asking questions, and we will keep on formulating them. These questions will basically confound us, since what at first seemed familiar and quite evident ends up being obscure and imprecise. What does it really mean to radically actualize human potentialities? What potential does the person have? The Western tradition, from Aristotle to St. Thomas to St. Bonaventure to Teilhard de Chardin, affirms that a human being is "*quodammodo omnia*"[1]: the person, in some sense, is everything. Can a human personality realize everything latent in it?

We are going to be realistic and concrete, since each person lives in an existential and historical situation. I live in mine, you live in yours. My situation is created by choices and decisions I have not made and that antedate my existence. I find myself in a situation I have not chosen: my family, my body, my intellect, my education, my friends and neighbors—all that I inherit and all that befalls me. I must determine myself in that situation: this is how my personal fulfillment comes about. The situation limits me since every concrete situation is limited. How, then, can I realize my limitless potential within those limitations?

We go on asking questions. When can I say that I am, and feel myself, fully realized? When are my aspirations satisfied? Who or what can limit them? To be satisfied with realized desires or plans is the same as becoming stagnated and, in a certain way, means the death of the spirit. Have we not said that the person, in some sense, is everything? Human feelings seem embroiled in contradictions: we experience desires of the flesh and of the spirit, desires for death and for self-realization, altruistic urgings and selfish urgings. What must I foster and what must I not? Is there a hierarchy among these desires and urgings?

Now think about people who live in the same situation (members of the same order, community or house). If the situation is always limited, how can propitious conditions come about so that each member can fully realize himself or herself? How do we proceed when something becomes an obstacle? How much does what becomes an obstacle depend on each person's reaction to the situation? For one person, living with a particular confrere is an obstacle to his or her development, while for another person, living with that same confrere is an opportunity for discovering new dimensions and for acquiring new attitudes that would never have been discovered or acquired in any other way. What, then, is a favorable or unfavorable climate for full personal development? Is it not true that, in regard to human fulfillment, each person has a particular path, rhythm, temptations, and opportunities and, in the final analysis, a personal pace? Thus, what does it mean to say that the congregation, the diocese, the community should provide each member with conditions favorable to the attainment of personal fulfillment? It is generally understood to mean that the group must give everyone the opportunity to study, specialize, and become professional. What is modern is characterized by specialization, increasingly more necessary and urgent, given the explosion of knowledge and the demand for more and more specific kinds of activity.

Does personal fulfillment necessarily demand specialized study and professionalization? Does what position I have and what I do determine my identity? Or is it rather the way I am what I am, and the way I do what I do? Evidently one could use specialized knowledge and a profession for self-advancement, self-enrichment, and self-affirmation at the expense of others—in other words, for professional pride. How does all this enter into the task of becoming a person? Does all this not rather imply a denial of personal fulfillment?

The really important and critical factor, therefore, is not the study or the profession, but the spirit with which one undertakes study or the motivations one has for becoming a professional. What is that spirit? One could say that the studies and professionalization mean a greater service to others. Indeed, but how do I concretely realize such service? Do I help others as a social worker, doctor, lawyer, or artist can? Or do I do it in my concrete situation as a religious? Or is it necessary that my character as a religious not appear? In that case, why have I become a religious and why do I remain one? Is it necessary to be a religious to help others? Could I not simply be a doctor, lawyer, social worker?

Well now, if my religious identity must be apparent, it means that professionalization and study must be undertaken with a religious spirit. Only this gives a different modality and a special coloring to my study, my work, or my possible profession. The problem then is not with study or profession, but with creating and promoting this being religious in such a way that the religious aspect is clear. How can this spirit be created? Can it be created merely by studying and undertaking a profession, or is it rather by looking beyond everything for the deeper meaning of my life, promoting this meaning tirelessly, making it the point of reference for all my other personal realizations? It is in the latter way, because human fulfillment is real and gives my life meaning only when everything I undertake is done with, or permeated by, the religious spirit.

The Negative Aspects of Fulfillment: Obedience

In the model of human fulfillment that we are studying, the guiding factor is the efficiency and output of the person. The person has become a kind of knowledge machine or a robot used for mechanical activities. In order to more fully create the *homo productor,* the most refined methods of human relations and group dynamics (especially of communal creativity) have been created. The person possesses fourteen systems and must use them all. Only then can the person be considered fulfilled.

We must then ask in what system the spirit and religion belong. The answer would be that they have no system because they enter into all systems and are not limited to a single aspect. The spirit has a place in all the systems—domestic, relational, emotional, recreational. Indeed, what would the concept of the human person be that left out what is most particular and most typical of the human being?

There is still more. What happens, for example, in the efficiency-output model, when people break down, get sick or old, and cannot continue to adapt to the situation? Do they no longer have to fulfill themselves? Should they be separated from the group? What bearing do the negative aspects of life have on the process of self-realization? How do we evaluate the cross, sacrifice, humility, patience, awareness of sin, pardon, the burdens of inevitable imperfections and of irreformable situations? Are they obstacles to the development of human potentialities? Should they be repressed when they cannot be removed or overcome?

All these questions only make another question apparent: is it not only in the face of these negativities that the inadequacy of our depictions of human fulfillment merely as the total development of our latent abilities is revealed? Such depictions seem to neglect (and it is always a serious neglect) the truth that freedom and the spirit can also transform the negativities encountered along the road to fulfillment and to more authentic humanness. This was the path of Christ, and almost all the great saints who came after him. The person is not like a plant. When a plant is diseased and does not produce flowers or fruit, but uselessly wastes sap, we cut it down, following Christ's advice in the Parable of the Barren Fig Tree (Lk. 13:6–9), and throw it into the fire.

It is evident that the image of a tree's output cannot be applied to a human being too directly. The tree that does not produce fruit loses the meaning of its existence. People give meaning to their lives not only through productivity—unless of course we understand them, and they understand themselves, only in terms of the model of fulfillment we have called into question. Negativities can represent a fertile peat that makes humanity improve and makes the life-giving sap flow. Freedom can transform them, like the best of the alchemists; the spirit can restore life to them. The evil person or the sinner is for the good person and the saint a great occasion for accepting someone who is different from themselves, and for converting that other person into a neighbor, for pardoning that person and loving him or her. The rock in the roadway can be an obstacle, but it can also help me build my house.

We can go on to ask concretely: what meaning does obedience have in the model that interprets fulfillment as actualizing all my potentialities? Is it the subject who must obey the superior, or is the superior the one who must pay attention to the qualities of the subject and give the subject the chance to use and fulfill these qualities? How can a superior make everyone happy and reconcile individual differences when the superior's own possibilities are also limited? One cannot suppose that he or she will be able to send everyone to the better universities and to create all the material conditions in which everyone can realize what is most to each one's liking in every aspect of each individual's personality.

Such questions may seem ridiculous. But there is no doubt that they serve to pose the basic question clearly: do we know what we are looking for when we talk about fulfilling ourselves completely in every dimension? We honestly and truly do not know. Clearly it is not a matter of an ignorance that brings about skepticism and inaction. It is rather an ignorance that opens us to the calling and creating of our own life with every imaginable richness, in what pertains both to its concrete aspects and to its meaning. It is sufficient for us to take up the task without forcing life to conform to fixed schemas. Life for us is what we live. The road to personal fulfillment is the road we are walking on now and the life we are living on our daily journey.

Thus it is on this road of mine, of yours, of ours as religious that we become aware of, and open to, our surroundings and to the multidimensional context of our fulfillment. The road goes through fields, over rocks, and across rivers. It passes through cities, schools, churches, factories, and hospitals, and through cemeteries. In other words, everything is along our road and we must confront everything: life and death, health and disease, work and prayer. We do not need to leave our chosen road, nor should we leave it. Indeed, if we no longer travel along, we no longer go anywhere. Only by traveling along our road can we enrich ourselves with the many riches the countryside offers.

What is the significance of the road? What are we looking for when we look for fulfillment?

Situational Living: The Way to Fulfillment

Personal Fulfillment and Radical Meaning

The road to fulfillment is one's own life in the concrete situation in which we happen to be. The road is not something that joins two points at a distance from one another, but it is traveling at one's own pace. Life itself is a journey; life is incarnated in concrete individuals. The journey is made by living. "One travels without travelling; the journey is made by living," as the poet Machado said, very practically and very metaphysically. Life is lived, but it is lived in a concrete situation and amid circumstances, that is, amid everything it carries with it from the road already traveled by others, and from a situation which predates me and in which I find myself. We always find ourselves traveling some road; we do not build the road and we are not the first to journey down it. We have been born with a direction already determined. There is no contradiction between the fact that each life is unique and the fact that it is largely predetermined.

In our concrete instance, we find ourselves as religious. Thus we are already within a determined context and traveling in a certain direction. Even when we ask the most concrete questions about our personal fulfillment as religious, we are asking about the radical meaning of our life: what fulfills what we do; what illuminates our past, present, and future; what gives us the strength to suffer the vicissitudes and conflicts of life; what makes us grow in every experience we have and every experience that happens to us; what gives an existential unity to our whole life?

As religious, what is the absolute in our life? Let us be candid with ourselves once again. The vast majority of the crises in religious life do not arise because its structures are out of touch with real life, or from lack of dialogue in community, psychological problems, lack of involvement in the world. The crises come from lack of an absolute that is capable of giving unity to all our actions and all the concrete situations inherent in human and religious life.

Naturally God must be our absolute as religious. Yet this cannot be like a catechism answer one has had to memorize.

To say that God is the Absolute and Radical Meaning of our life is only possible if one has had an experience, the experience we have spoken of before: of all life's being open to something beyond ourselves and to a deeper meaning which sustains life; this experience is the experience of what we call God.

Religious are people who make the experience of God manifesting himself in the world the point of reference for their whole lives. To say God exists is not the same as saying a tree exists. Saying a tree exists and knowing it exists do not commit me to it, since my life is not changed because of it. But to say and know God exists means that an ultimate meaning exists, which snares me because it means rest from my endless search; it knows the tentativeness of my endeavors; it contains no ambiguity of good and evil or meaning and absurdity because it is beyond all that. This faith and conviction deeply change my life, and the way I view and interpret the world. To live from this perspective is to live religiously: to see and live all life as permeated by the presence of God.

The Dialectic of Fulfillment

Since God reveals himself in our concrete experiences, it is logical that he always reveals himself in a concrete way. We have already said that God is not the image we have of him, and yet we need images to be able to approach his Mystery. Images allow us to talk to him, pray, petition, establish a relationship, and find the strength we need for daily life. Most likely at the beginning of our Christian initiation, God was presented to us as a generous Father, who creates us, sustains us, and cares for us at every moment. This image gave meaning to what was happening in our lives as children. Later in our life, when faced with sorrow, absurdity, and sin, we may have asked how God could be a loving Father and still allow such things. We mentioned this in Chapter 2. Let us say here that even religious life could not avoid this problem. Rather it was in religious life that the problem arose most acutely.

We pray and meditate, and still God does not speak. We feel our lives are going nowhere even when we participate in and receive the sacraments. We are mired in certain faults and imperfections that seem insuperable. This is the primary frustration in religious life, which perhaps already seems so very little religious. The rocks have appeared in the road, the obstacles we ourselves have created by our lack of self-denial and openness, by our lack of understanding in regard to other people.

When we valiantly take up the burden of life, a light may begin to shine, giving us hope, a light in our dark, pathless wilderness: we discern Christ as God incarnate and suffering. We come to discover the God of the New Testament. He is no longer the God the Psalmist prayed to, recognizing only his grandeur: "Great is the Lord, wonderful beyond measure." He is the God of whom St. Bernard said, "Humble is the Lord, lovable beyond measure." God does not simply tell us why sorrow exists, he becomes the Man of Sorrows (Is. 53:5). He does not tell us why people are humiliated; he humbles himself. He does not provide information about our insignificance and weakness; he becomes insignificant and weak. Here the intellectual inquiry, which always wants to know why and which invents a theodicy to exempt God from the world's problems, ends.

The intellect is silenced. The history of the coming of gentleness began when God identified himself with our misery and our sinful flesh. Thus God's love for humanity was revealed to us: he loves enemies and sinners (Mt. 5:45); he loved us even when we were his enemies (Rm. 5:6–10); far from being vengeful, he bears with us with infinite patience. He is willing to forgive and accepts all the evil directed at him without taking revenge. Christ incarnated the love of our God. In short, we know how Christ wanted to show God's love for us and in what ways he did it. Thus he could ask us to imitate our heavenly Father whose love is so strong that he can give himself and, we can even say, live with all the negativities of life (Mt. 5:48).

If we come to understand all this, perhaps it will reveal to us what God as Father and Love means for us in the human drama incarnate in the experience of our own weakness. In refining our image of God and by imitating Christ, we will come to discover a new aspect of him. This discovery makes us strong and helps us see the riches in the negativities, which teach us to be humble, to tear up the scripts we have written for our lives, to experience death every day so that we can experience the resurrection of life every day.

For Dietrich Bonhoeffer, a theologian who experienced life's absurdity perhaps better than anyone, the essence of the Christian is to be able to live with the suffering of God in this world. God did not call us to a new religion, nor did Christ call us to observe a more holy Law or a more rigorous discipline. Rather he calls us to share in the death of God in the world, in suffering, in accepting enemies and sinners as he always does.

That experience of God enables us to live the actual ups and downs of our lives. That is the way to our self-realization, the wisdom to accept the challenges life keeps on presenting to us. This is the dialectic of the Cross and Easter: one must die in order to live. Every situation is good, every time and place favorable, every circumstance suited to encountering the self within me and God within myself "higher than my heights and deeper than my depths" in order to encounter, in short, my salvation or even my damnation. No one can take another's place in this regard, no one can act for another. Each individual is the only one who exists. Everything depends on me. That is the task of my life. Yet, if I am faithful to my own path, I can find that I am in the company of others making the journey, and I can join myself to them in that center where all are met and become one. The geography of the spiritual differs from that of the physical world. In the physical world countries touch at their boundaries; in the spiritual world they touch at their centers.

It is indifference, mediocrity, and the absence of ideals that alienate us from ourselves and from that center which joins us all together. These things isolate us from others, even though we are standing next to them or among them or giving ourselves to serving them. The best service I can give people is to be radically what I should be and what they expect me to be: a person of God, for God and with God, a person who sees in everything, even the most absurd, the presence of God. People do not long for material bread so much as they long for that essential bread, which satisfies the deeper hunger and brings salvation. In doing this the religious plays his or her trump card, which assures personal fulfillment.

Personal Fulfillment and Taking Up the Cross

From what has been said, it is clear that personal fulfillment does not lie in the number of potentialities realized, but in the quality of one's interaction with life and what life in our concrete situation presents to us. The acquisition of more degrees and vague planning for the future—adding up numbers—can mean (and does mean for many religious) that one is trying to avoid the encounter with one's basic task in life: to confront oneself, to interact with and evaluate oneself with all one's aspirations, problems, limitations, assets and debits, always keeping in mind one's ideal as a religious. Many times this avoidance is taking refuge in a heap of useless knowledge which only succeeds in increasing one's pride and which makes one more distant from other people rather than helping one to understand others better. It can become a matter of knowing myself, creating myself, advancing myself—others are no longer my primary motivation. What counts is only myself, my personal fulfillment, a real, but hypocritical, individualism.

Personal fulfillment is not primarily a work of discursive reason that moves from one thing to another, but of the recollected spirit that knows how to profit from the riches hidden in each situation. The spirit is not something alongside the body, nor is it a higher form of reason. Spirit is the human mode of being, which knows how to discover everything's meaning. The wisdom of life, the experience of the mystery of God, which illumines every situation, belongs to the spirit. In it resides one's ability to become fully whatever one becomes. Spirituality is the power to live for God in everything. Spirituality is not a science or a technology, but the way one lives out of the spirit.

The Job of Self-Fulfillment

The first task in self-fulfillment is therefore to accept the limitations of one's own existential situation, knowing that within those limits one encounters everything, not as quantitatively distributed, but as collected in single concentration. To encounter that center within ourselves is to encounter everyone and everything. The ancient wisdom of India said, "If a person thinks correctly, recollected in his cell, his thoughts are heard a thousand miles away." If you want to change others, begin by changing yourself.

A second, and no less indispensable, task is to know how to live with death. People who see the meaning in death live their lives with true meaning; those who do not see the meaning of death cannot give life its true meaning. Death is not the final moment of life, because life itself is dying. We are dying slowly, bit by bit, even from birth beginning to wear away and to take leave of life. We begin by leaving our mother's breast, dying to it. We go on taking leave of infancy, childhood, adolescence, school, youth, home, adulthood, jobs, and each passing moment, finally taking leave of our own life. Such leave-taking is not only leaving behind things and situations, but also leaving behind a little bit of ourselves. We see we must despoil ourselves, impoverish ourselves, empty ourselves. This process helps us see everything's meaning. But is that meaning simply that dying cannot be stopped? No, the meaning is mysterious, but it is real and positive. We surrender everything, even ourselves, in the last moment of life—in death—because we have not been created for things (not even for ourselves), but for the Great Other who should fill our lives. During our lifetime he goes around taking everything from us and taking us more completely for himself, taking away even the security or conviction of our goodness and virtues.

Some of us are called to imitate Christ even to the point of giving up the certainty that our trust in God is stronger than the power of pain, like Jesus on the cross crying out, "My God, my God, why have you abandoned me?" (Mt. 15:34). Christ on the cross is totally stripped interiorly and exteriorly. But accepting such an extreme situation is the way perfect life and resurrection (total communion with God) come to be realized. We are not saying that this sets up the conditions for total communion with God, but that total communion with God occurs in this situation. The *Little Flowers* of St. Francis on perfect joy illustrates this: in being sent forth to be punished, in being expelled by God, perfect joy and life fulfilled in God are achieved. In that complete emptiness the person no longer even has his or her own self to lean on, but must lean completely and only on God.

Thus, life is dying; but in that daily dying another, more authentic, immortal life comes to be seen. The negativities and crises we pass through teach us the lesson of self-denial and prepare us for total and complete living with God. We ultimately find ourselves consumed in him. Perhaps an old parable can illustrate what we are saying.

The Lesson of the Man of Salt

Once upon a time there was a beach. A man made out of salt had been wandering through the desert and suddenly came upon the sea. He had never seen it and could not understand what it was. "Who are you?" the man asked. "I am the sea," it replied. "But what is the sea?" the man demanded. "I am," the sea answered. "I don't understand," the man sighed sadly. "How can I understand you, because it would make me so happy?" "Touch me," the sea told him. The man of salt timidly touched the sea with the tips of his toes. He was starting to understand the mystery of the sea! But he quickly noticed the tips of his toes had disappeared. "What did you do, Sea?" "You have done something to be able to understand me," the sea answered. And the man of salt began to slide slowly and gently into the sea, as one does when performing the most important action on one's pilgrimage of life. To the extent he enters the water he is going to be dissolved little by little. But to the same extent he has the impression of knowing more and better what the sea is. The man continued to dissolve, all the while asking himself what the sea was, until a wave completely washed him away. But in that final moment he could make the sea's answer his own, "It is I."

The man of salt began to understand the sea by giving something of himself, by giving up himself. Thus also the person, to the extent the person gives himself or herself up, becomes identified with God. In this total self-denial is identification with (not the identity of) God given. God is all in all (1 Co. 15:28). Death is that crowning and definitive moment.

The crises of life prepare us for death. Crisis originally meant purification (the Sanskrit *kir, kri,* means precisely to purify or cleanse). The crises of life can be occasions for the purification of our innermost being, which is very often shrouded in a mantle of earthly attachments and created interests. We must give up superficial and transitory things, putting our efforts into an increasingly deeper and more authentic fulfillment—just like the man of salt who became identified with the other, the sea, to the extent that he gave up himself.

Life undoubtedly will present us with difficulties, situations of external and internal crisis, always giving us the chance for further growth. Knowing how to avail ourselves (which is in our power) of the riches of all those moments in order to grow in our identity, in our capacity to accept and take on what is different from ourselves (the sea), this is where our personal fulfillment lies.

To run away, to blame the past, to place the responsibility on structures for always being ineffective, to criticize others, is basically no more than an infantile device instilled in us. It shows we have not yet become open to the search for true personal fulfillment, because we have not yet been able to discover the riches of real life, which, although beset with many stones and potholes and twistings, is always a road toward light and truth.

Knowledge acts as a springboard projecting us toward deeper and more authentic fulfillment, which is the basic task of our life. Only the valiant and the venturesome find success at that task. Only those who, like the man of salt, accept death, self-destruction, succeed in understanding it. The Lord put it this way:

> One who does not renounce oneself, take up one's cross, and follow me will not enter the Kingdom of Heaven (Lk. 9:23). If the grain of wheat does not die, it does not bear fruit; but if it dies, it bears much fruit (Jn. 12:24–26). If anyone wants to save his life, he will lose it; but one who loses his life for my sake will save it (Lk. 9:24).

Religious Obedience as the Way to Hear God

One who has decided to face whatever life offers, both external events and internal happenings, who confronts life as the way to self-fulfillment, as the way God manifests himself as always beckoning, calling us to new and self-transcending decisions, this person understands what religious obedience means.[2]

Religious obedience is more than obeying a superior, observing rules or constitutions, or doing what a particular situation demands of us. The word *obedience* comes from the Latin *ob-audire* and means listening to the voice of God who calls us forth, allowing ourselves to hear his voice in our situation. St. Francis strove to be the obedient servant of every creature. By saying this he showed how he saw God in every creature: animals, people, and even the bad superior who served that God. Such an ability demands radical self-denial and a great concentration on the One who is present in all things. Obedience, then, does not refer only to subjects, but also and especially to superiors who as such are the ones most obliged to obedience, to listen (*ob-audire*) to God who can also manifest himself in the life, desires, aspirations, and talents of the subjects.

To understand this obedience better we must not forget that it is the greatest expression of freedom, and not a limitation on freedom. If it sets limits to freedom, they are only the lowest limits. At its upper limit freedom is perpetually open to the infinite. By nature and grace, the person is a sovereign master, subject to no one (1 Co. 9:1). Thus no one must enslave another. Without freedom there is neither obedience nor love. Obedience is servitude only to those who do not understand the spontaneity and freedom of love. One can, however, freely become the servant of everyone out of love. With sovereign freedom, one person can accept the will of another. I do not obey merely because the law commands or because you want me to obey, but because I myself have chosen to obey: "Because I have chosen to, I obey your commands." I have decided to do this because I have understood that nothing can keep me from God who is manifested in everything.

The problem of obedience lies in the freedom that disposes me to do another's will. The motivation for this is not the will of the other, which gives rise to a kind of legalism. It is the free "I" who determines this myself for the sake of God, and not solely or simply for the sake of the superior. Obedience is thus synonymous with pure freedom understood as full control over oneself. Only those who know how to give orders to themselves are capable of obedience. Those who can do this possess authority; they grow and help others to grow.

Obedience, then, has nothing to do with the selfishness and passivity of people who submit to everyone in order to avoid having to think or make decisions of their own. Obedience is the greatest free decision one makes for God. Seen in this way, obedience is a way of permanently searching, of listening to God in the communitarian obligations of my life. But to progress along this path toward God requires a healthy idealism, that idealism that made the great prophets of religious life progress by following this path.

The Religious, True to Oneself

We have seen how the identity of religious does not lie in the many things they do or should do, but in the way they do these things. That way is the one their experience of God dictates, sought and loved amid the tasks they are confronted with in daily life. Everything, positive or negative, is seen as an invitation to grow for God.

It is in this school that God educates us and purifies us every day, thus preparing us for the definitive encounter with him in death. Death will be the moment of supremely personalizing and fulfilling encounter, in which, without losing our identity, we will identify ourselves with the immensity of the divine sea. No, we will not embrace God with our own experience, but, as tiny as the man of salt, we will enter into the infinite being of God, and we will be able to exclaim at last, "It is I," drowning ourselves in the greatest self-fulfillment possible in the unfathomable mystery of God.

This experience is what defines our life and gives harmony to our work. What we do within a religious context will be, or can be, more or less relevant, but it is not decisive. The problem will always be how we do it and what motivates our work. Professionalization is, in itself, indifferent. It can be, and perhaps should be, the way we take our place in the modern world. Yet we still experience the urgent questions: How do we professionalize ourselves? How do we exercise our profession? Is it to evade our true religious identity? Have we taken it on in order to hide our fear of asking ourselves about the radical meaning of our lives, about what is most specific in it, and about what must fill our days, even the darkest and grayest, until the moment of complete and definitive giving of ourselves to the Mystery of God?

Thus there is an enormous difference between a professional religious (social worker, engineer) and a religious professional who works as a social worker or engineer. It is not merely a matter of semantics. The motivation is completely different. From one's religious experience one should do something or be something, but this means that one should do and be everything from one's religious experience. Externally a religious will do the same things the others do, but a religious will be different because the motivation and the way will also be different. A profession presupposes an immediate, earthly goal; religious life responds to the radical and ultimate meaning of life as such.

Often the crisis in our activities and our feeling of being socially useless gives the opportunity for the question to arise concerning the meaning of religious life outside or beyond other ecclesial or social goals. We are not going to repeat what has already been said elsewhere. It is enough to recall that it undoubtedly has a meaning in itself as the search for the Absolute in life, for God who transcends all practical goals, all social and economic meanings, and who is purely and simply the supreme meaning of everything there is in regard to what is most human and personalizing (such as love, friendship, encounter)—an encounter with the infinite and absolute Thou.

To a disciple who complained the road was long, rough and difficult, the Buddha answered:

> Friend, the road is long and difficult because you are trying to reach the end ahead of time. The true purpose of the road is not to reach the end, but to make the journey.

3

The Existential Situation

In the preceding section we dealt with general expressions of the fundamental reality we had considered in the first part of this book. We must now consider these general expressions in the concrete situation we find in the modern world. We must consider the framework in which our religious life must be lived and incarnated.

In terms of structure, our age defines itself as non-religious, as an historical epoch governed by secularity. The *saeculum* (world), with the process of secularization that goes along with it, is the guideline for interpreting our experiences, as well as for determining which of our schematizations of reality are valid.

This provides a challenge to religious life. Religious life need not fear this challenge, nor collapse in the face of it, for the challenge provides religious life with a great opportunity to reveal its deeper riches and meaning which are valid in every period of history. This revelation will in turn become a challenge to the world, or, if you prefer, a response the world needs even to its most cherished premises.

How then do we live our religious life-project in an historical context defined by secularity? Does religious life continue to have meaning and purpose today? What risks do we confront and what concrete challenges do we face? What is our message to today's world? Does prayer still have a meaning, and how do we pray in a secularized milieu? This series of questions demands a swift and positive answer today. The following two chapters seek to orient our response.

7

Religious Life and Secularity

The lack of harmony—and of a synthesis—between religious experience and its forms of expression on the one hand, and the experience of the world with its manifestations in human life on the other, is a major factor in the crisis religious life is experiencing. We could also add that it is a major factor in the crisis the world is experiencing.

If we consider religious life concretely we see that our practices and structures are largely inherited from a past, rural world which had a sacral view of reality. The world which was brought into being by the Industrial Revolution is technological and urban. Its attitudes are completely different from those of the former world, no longer considering reality from a religious perspective but from a viewpoint called secular.

In order to understand the present crisis, let us first consider the model religious life uses, or presupposes, for understanding the world, as well as the model proposed by secularization. We will then examine the differences between the models and see that these differences are only analytical, differences in emphasis, and basically complementary.

We will next proceed to consider the major ramification of the secularization process for religious life, the challenge hurled at it by the process. Secularization thus invites religious life to a basic reform, especially in regard to its forms of self-expression and presence in today's world, which is understood and defined secularly.[1]

Finally, we will highlight the contribution religious life can and must make to the secularization process so that the process can remain truly one of secularization and not degenerate into secularism.

We accept as given that religious life is possible and legitimate in the secular world. Religious life is not, and must not be, an anachronistic remnant of the past. It is the institutionalized experience or the incarnation of the Christian religious experience in a unique way. As we have said earlier, religious life, prescinding from its cultural and historical forms, has a theological and anthropological significance that is paralleled in all cultures past and present. Within Christianity, religious life emerges as a concrete, charismatic response to the Gospel message.

When we use the word *world* we mean the unified totality of the experiences we have of people and earthly realities. The world is "the concrete unity within which people of our culture today think and organize their lives."[2] Sometimes we will use the word in the sense of all creation: the universe, the human person, history. *World* thus has an eminently positive meaning here.

The Relationship Between Religious Life and Secularization

Between these two models (religious life and secularization) of representing and interpreting the world, there are many tensions and even contrary positions. These problems should not be treated as if they do not exist.

Religious Life's Understanding of the World

Consecration as Mission

Religious life has been, and continues to be, understood as a total consecration of the person to God, thus implying a renunciation of the world. The consecrated person is set aside for God and for the fostering of religious values. Nevertheless, according to the Christian understanding, this reservation does not intend to separate the religious from the world, but rather to send the religious back into the world.

Consecration and its attendant reservation does not mean God needs people for himself. What God needs are signs of his presence in the world, signs that make the promises of his Kingdom visible among human beings. Thus consecration fundamentally implies mission. Renunciation of the world is not isolation from the world which makes one unavailable as a sacrament of God, that is, a sign and instrument of his action in the world. The religious is taken from the world in order to be given back to it again.[3]

The Vows as a Basis for a New Relationship with the World

This consecration, which involves renunciation and mission, is expressed through the vows of poverty, chastity, and obedience. We have already seen that the vows do not end religious' relationship with the world, but give that relationship certain special characteristics. The vows make the person available, placing him or her in the service of God's cause in the world.

> Service or worship is not offering God things he must have to satisfy his needs; God needs nothing. Service is being an instrument of God to save people. The needy party is the world to which God comes through human agents.[4]

In the preceding part of this book we have seen how the vows correspond to dimensions of the human personality and transfigure these dimensions.

The Sacramental Function of Religious

Living a life transfigured by the vows, the religious assumes a sacramental function. Religious are signs to the world of the eschatological realities proclaimed and promised in Christianity, realities whose fulfillment comes only in heaven but which begin to be realized here in universal love, deep fraternity, profound freedom, and the overcoming of all the alienating elements in human life.

Be that as it may, we must note how, historically, by emphasizing its consecrated nature, and forgetting its missionary and sacramental character, religious life has been upheld as a value in itself, apart from its relationship to the world.

Religious life is not so much something that exists for itself, but a way of being-for-others. It cannot deny the world. On the contrary, it must be related to the world, although in such a way that it demands that the world transcend itself and keep the absolute future promised it by God constantly in mind.

A Primarily Sacral View of the World

Defending religious life as a world within the world kept religious communities closed in on themselves or open only to other religious. They carried out works (apostolates) chiefly of a religious or ecclesiastical nature, usually within institutions or organizations maintained by their own religious. Consider the following aspects:

1. The world, for communities of religious, was most often seen in reference to God and not in its own autonomy or secularity. One approaches the world through God. The world is the great sacrament that reflects the goodness, beauty, and wisdom of the Creator.
2. Religious operated in the sacred, cultic sphere of liturgy, sacraments, and community prayer. They thus developed a spirituality of representation: religious represented the Church and all humanity in their duty to praise God.
3. The virtues most called for in religious life were imitation of the poor, humble Christ, meditation on his *kenosis* on the cross, which is a scandal to the world (1 Co. 1:23), renunciation, and disinterested love, as well as the other virtues that went along with, or were a consequence of, observing the evangelical counsels.

If we define the person biblically as one situated between God and the world, then religious take the God to whom they have been consecrated as the starting-point and from it derive their self-understanding and their involvement in the world. The values of religious stress relationships with God and neighbor rather than relationships with the world and earthly affairs.

How Secularization Understands the World

From the very start let us make clear that secularization does not mean atheism, indifferentism, or loss of religious sensibility or faith.[5] Nor does it imply hostility toward moral values and the message of Jesus; that is secularism, not secularization. By secularization we mean the worldwide historical process by which human beings, *in their relationships with the world,* free themselves from mythic, metaphysical, and religious interpretations.

Secularization means rationalization or the rational explanation of phenomena of the world, using principles drawn only from the world and from data controlled by scientific methods. We need not resort to myth, religion, or metaphysics to interpret the world around us scientifically. Secularization demonstrates that we are not slaves to the laws and secret forces of the universe, but masters who have been charged with dominating and subduing the world, placing it in service to our needs. This domination is achieved through exercise of our reason and other human faculties.

In this sense secularization is no more than a consequence of the biblical command to subdue the earth (Gn. 1:28). The world is profane, not divine. It is a created thing given to us so we can exercise our freedom and creativity. The concept of the human person as the image and likeness of God (Gn. 1:26) is basically secular, since the expression, in its biblical sense, means that the person is a representative or lieutenant of God in the world.[6] Just as God created the world and gave it order, so must we, through our work and our creativity, impose on it a human order, grounded in rationality, and one for which we are immediately responsible.

It will truly be necessary to Christianize the world (to use a classic phrase), understanding this to mean that we must see to it that the world continues being what it is according to God's plan, namely, territory entrusted to the care of reason and human endeavor. The modern secular world is not the decaying remnant of the *corpus christianum,* as has sometimes been thought. Rather it manifests a biblical perspective in regard to worldly realities in the vast panorama of culture and history.[7]

Moreover, secularization is one of the shapes faith can have in the world. Faith can and should be lived in the sacral world of rituals, worship, and prayer leading to communion with God. But this faith can be lived outside the sacral realm in the midst of the secular world in labor, society, economics, or politics. The signs that express it are certainly different from those of the sacral: fostering the world's natural goodness (which God also wants), honesty in one's profession, respect for human dignity, courage to accept the world as relative and not absolute, and the strength not to absolutize the goods of this world with ideological statements.

God communicates himself both in the divine and in the secular. Both domains are under his providential care, and both are different forms of his self-communications—forms not antagonistic, but complementary. We can touch God in both realms. We can thus see that secularization is not opposed to religion or faith; it is rather a different way of living out faith and our relationship to God.

In the secular world, the only sacred creative power that exists is the human person—in the final analysis, the image of God—which must always be revered and respected, treated always as a person and never as an object to be manipulated. Our sacredness comes from our being the image of God, which results in our ability to enter into a relationship with the Only Sacred and Holy (*Tu Solus Sanctus*), God.

The sacral person expresses faith through actions, objects, and people, thus giving these things—in themselves profane or secular—a sacral character. Thus sacralization arises as a countermovement to profanization or secularization.

Up to now religion has been expressed in sacred signs. Today it feels called upon to express itself in secular ones. This is also true of religious life, which is challenged today to re-express the service of God and of people in secular terms. Later we will see how this is done.

The following are the most outstanding features of secularization:

1. The world has a value in itself which has been conferred on it by God, since the very act of creation confers on an object its own truth, goodness, identity, laws, and order.[8] Vatican II emphasizes this more explicitly:

> All which makes up the temporal order: knowledge, the good things of life and prosperity of the family, culture, economics, the arts and professions, political institutions, international relations and similar things, as well as their evolution and progress, are not only aids towards humanity's ultimate goal, but have a God-given value in themselves, whether considered alone or as part of the whole temporal order.[9]

2. The individual, in relation to the world, is in the same position Adam was. The person gives everything a name and thus controls it. For the secular and autonomous individual the world is not a predetermined, preordained cosmos in which everything already has its fixed and immutable position in an order established from all eternity, which must simply be accepted and allows no room for creativity. Rather the world is entrusted to human beings who, in God's name and in his place, must establish an order in conformity with humanity's historical task and responsibility. The order people give to the material world is always an historical order in a constant process of evolution; it must continually be adapted and gradually invent new forms. Today's demands are not those of yesterday, nor are those of tomorrow necessarily those of today.

God is not immediately apparent in the secular world. Indeed the secularized world says more about humanity than it does about God. Certainly we are working for God, but we are also working for humanity. Wherever we look we see the imprint of human hands.

3. One gains access to the world not through God but through reason and experimental science, by scientific analysis and verification. Here rationality and objectivity rule and dictate the critical attitudes and conduct of modern men and women toward things.

4. The modern secular world is a complex of interrelated functions that are carried on in a context of organizations, social structures, centers of production, and large masses of

consumers. Everything must be functional and fit harmoniously into the total complex or system. A characteristic of this functional world is that, in order to be maintained, there must be continual renovation and constant progress, as we have already suggested.

5. In the secular world efficiency is one of the basic criteria. The determining factor is not knowing what things are, but what purpose they serve; not what their meaning is, but how they function in life.

6. In the secular world of work, as well as in social relationships, neither honorific titles nor the idea of established authority are worth anything. The only thing that matters is professional, technical, and scientific competence.

The Relationship Between the Two Models

While the relationship between the sacral and secular models has already been made clear, or will be made clear in what follows, it is not superfluous to state that relationship explicitly here. Secularization refers to humanity in its relationship to the *saeculum* (the world), which has already been demythologized and desacralized by critical reason. Just as religious life is defined principally by starting with our relationship with God and other people, so secularization is understood by starting with the openness and relationship of people with the world. Religious life and secularization are situated on different levels.

There are tensions always possible between them, but these are not, of themselves, denials or oppositions, but merely different points of view and different ways of situating oneself within the same total reality. Both models are completely valid and legitimate. The tensions alluded to come about only because the concrete individual can simultaneously be both religious and secular. It is evident that both models, taken either separately or in relation to a totality, present pitfalls that can denigrate each other as well as enhance each other because of their mutual complementarity. As we will see, it is a question of how secularization impinges on religious life and vice versa.

We will briefly consider the pitfalls that are characteristic of religious life and of secularization. To fall into these traps is to destroy the totality, which never can or should be split apart.

The Pitfalls Inherent in Religious Life and in Secularization

While entirely valid and legitimate in themselves, both models can lead to a debilitating polarization. These pitfalls are on the one hand escapism, and on the other secularism.

The Pitfall of Escapism

Religious life can fall into this trap by emphasizing its consecration to God as a renunciation of the world rather than as a mission. This emphasis leads to a downplaying or denial of the value of the inevitable relationship between ourselves and the world. The world, its realities and occupations, are tolerated but not loved. This represents an escapist attitude, and even an affront to the plan of the Creator, who wants us to be his agents or lieutenants in the world in order to carry on his creative and transforming activity. Vatican II, always careful and sparing of condemnation, says very sternly:

> They are mistaken who, since they know they have no lasting city here but look for one which is to come, think they can shirk their earthly responsibilities. They forget their own faith demands they fulfill these demands more perfectly, according to the task to which each person has been called.[10]

By becoming escapist, religious life becomes alienating, and places religious in opposition to the times and to history, and even to the very meaning of their faith. This meaning points to, and concerns itself with, freeing people from all slavery in its mission and task of overcoming and transforming the world. As we have pointed out above, the human person, in the biblical view, is a being who lives between God and the world. Thus we should live this dialectical tension, which may be difficult. We must not lose ourselves in the world so much that we forget about God, but we must not dedicate ourselves so exclusively to God that we forget our obligations toward the world of work, progress, and human development.

In relation to God, we must conduct ourselves as sons and daughters, living out our filial obligations of love, obedience, trust, and dedication. In relation to the world, we should be masters, and not become slaves either to work or to any other elements that are hostile or alienating to the human person, such as sickness, underdevelopment, and poverty. We should master these alienating elements and thus bring about a more human and more fraternal order which benefits everyone. In relation to other people, we must behave neither as master nor as child, but as brother or sister, rendering mutual assistance as friends. Every person, and even more every religious, must live this mysterious and sublime dialectic of being son (daughter)-brother (sister)-master.

The Pitfall of Secularism

Secularization can fall into the opposite trap. It can succumb to the pitfall of seeing only the relations between the person and the world, considering as unreal and empty any relations between the person and other people, or between the person and the Great Other, God.

Be that as it may, we must emphasize that it does not mean in itself a denial of God or the supernatural if one makes no explicit reference to God when one examines the person in relation to the world, or if one restricts religion to the human arena without appealing to the supernatural in wordly pursuits. This merely indicates that God, the supernatural, grace, salvation, are not quantifiable phenomena and cannot be verified scientifically. These are realities situated in another dimension, different from those of the person and the world.

Silence about God can sometimes be an indication of deep religiousness, as well as of the validity of secularization. Simone Weil observed, "to know if someone is really religious it is not necessary to observe how they address God but how they address the world." But if the secular world becomes one-dimensional or is rooted only in a relationship with things and ignores other dimensions of the person, it becomes ideological totalitarianism, although it is actually splitting up the totality of life. This is then secularism, not secularization. It is true atheism rather than religious silence about God.

Furthermore, secularization as desacralization or demythologization of the world runs the risk of creating (as it has done or is doing today) a new myth and new divinization: the myth and divinization of power. If such power were restricted merely to a mastery of nature, it would not be so reprehensible. But it has been extended to all relationships, even those among people and nations. Everything proceeds by legal, bureaucratic, and institutional channels, ignoring the fact that love and the appreciation of each person's unique character belong to no bureaucratic or political domain, to no facet of production or consumption.

What then are the limits of secularization? Here is where the concerns of religious life and secularization intersect in the area of common demands and mutual implications.

The Interrelatedness of Religious Life and Secularization

Legitimate secularization, the autonomy of the individual in relation to the canons of religion and metaphysical interpretations of the world, along with the proper respect for earthly values, can only take place correctly and be correctly lived out when the individual remains master, brother (sister), and son (daughter). We remain masters of the world as long as we are not dominated by our structures, by the allure of science or technology, by legalism and established systems of domination, by myths created by big business, politics, and the entertainment world. But this mastery is attained only by people who succeed in understanding themselves also in relation to other people and to God. Only the person who is also religious can be truly secular, because only that person, through faith, has achieved true freedom.[11] We will now consider the nature of that freedom.

Freedom from and Freedom for

Human beings are essentially and naturally free; we have been born to be free. We have been called to fulfill ourselves freely. Freedom, viewed this way, is the midwife of our personal history. But freedom must begin for us as liberation that frees us from all slavery, internal and external, so that we can effectively be what we should be by nature and should be in relation to things, to other people, and to God.

Freedom from the World

This title might also be expressed as freedom from the world while within the world, or freedom in the world. Faith demands that we not consider the world as an end in itself, or as a human paradise, but as our territory. We must subdue it and rule over it by our work, our science, our technology. Thus we must not become trapped or enslaved by the world, nor by the entire complex of means we use to dominate the world and transform it. We cannot be free for the world unless we have first been freed from the world. Without being freed from the world, we would not be free in ourselves.

Freedom for Other People and for God

Only by being free or freed from the world can we be free for other people and for God; for the former in a spirit of fellowship, for the latter in a spirit of sonship. It is only by being free for the other and for God that we can be worthy of salvation and of the fulfillment of the promise of a perfect and happy future. In this dimension we discover, and truly encounter, ourselves, since only there can we realize, on the one hand, love, friendship, fraternity, and encounter and, on the other hand, the goodness of God and others, grace, and salvation.

Freedom for the World

By virtue of the salvation that comes from our relationship to God and our brothers and sisters, we experience ourselves as free for the world. Now we can work and exercise our creative responsibility as a duty carried out to further the humanization of life. Within that existential framework "all is permitted" (1 Co. 8:1–23, 10:14–33; Ga. 4:1–7). The objects and laws of nature are at our disposal so that we can enhance our mastery, fellowship, and sonship without any limitations other than those imposed by good sense, right thinking, and charity (1 Co. 8:1–13, 10:14–33).

Thus we can organize our world. But we must do it rationally and responsibly, not at the expense of others, but respecting the dignity of our brother or sister, the son or daughter of God, and in creating greater and greater opportunities for the humanization of life and the real liberation of each and every member of the human family.

Only in faith can we live these three freedoms. Only in faith can we live secularized without falling into secularism and losing ourselves in the world of things. Thus we can see that secularization not only does not exclude faith and religious life, but rather demands them in order to maintain itself as secularization.

The Mutual Openness Between Secularization and Religious Life

That religious life implies in itself no depreciation of secularization is, in the first place, demonstrated by the principle—and even the fact—that the religious is the person who can live secularization in a preeminent way. By the vow of poverty lived in its full authenticity, we can demonstrate human mastery over things, using them without losing our hearts to them and without building walls between us and our brothers and sisters. Through the vow of chastity we propose to love everyone without distinction, respecting and honoring the one sacred thing in the world—the human person, who is the image and likeness of God. Through the vow of obedience we dispose ourselves to serve God and other people better. In short, religious give priority in their lives to relationships between people and between people and God.

In a similar way, that the secular world is not insensitive to spiritual values is demonstrated by the fact that the more the process of secularization advances the more the sanctity of the person is advanced. Today one is very aware that the person is not a thing to be used or manipulated, but a being worthy of all respect. That the secular world is sensitive and open to the religious dimension of life is shown more concretely by such phenomena as the new mysticism and the new religious experience arising among the young and the Hippies. Despite their imperfections and even aberrations, these movements are a basically sincere and passionate search for the transcendent, the religious, for the person of Christ, which influences vast segments of the population who are more or less ignorant of mainline Christianity.

These groups, furthermore, manage to restrain the world of business and consumerism by creating a new symbol system that sees the human in terms of love, fraternity, universal reconciliation, solidarity—all of which are genuine Gospel values. Feast days and rituals, formerly set aside by the theoretical, rational, and objective world of technology, are again finding a place.[12] It is especially in feast days and rituals that we discover and reveal our peculiarly human character and thus give meaning to our lives, which are so often torn apart by excessive pragmatism and apodictical science.

In regard to this human aspect, it is particularly significant that in many places houses of prayer and recollection have been established. Secular people continue to be people of eternity who seek silence and prayer to find themselves and the indescribable, absolute Mystery which we who believe call God and Jesus Christ. The contemplative life, far from perishing at the coming of the secular world, is rediscovering its meaning, value, and function by facing a new future, which holds new opportunities.

One can readily understand that secularization and religious life, situated as they are on different levels, in themselves only try to accentuate different perspectives: the former, the perspective of the person-world relationship; the latter, the perspective of the person-person and person-God relationships. Any opposition or tension between the two models can only arise in superficial areas. When we reflect on them and on our actual experience deeply, we see that each demands the other. Secularization needs the religious dimension in order not to become corrupted and degenerate into secularism, which forgets about God or transcendent values. Here religious life plays a decisive role. Religious life, if it does not want to escape into an idealistic supernaturalism and commit sins of omission against the world, must open itself to the secular dimension of autonomy, rationality, and the critical spirit that defines the world of today. It places great emphasis on the incarnation and development of the person-world relationship as a way of being human, or better, as a way of fulfilling human life through mastery of the world.

Ramifications of Secularization for Religious Life

Let us begin by recognizing that secularization, in the sense in which we are using the term, is an irreversible conquest of the world. The characteristics of secularization are already elements of our culture and form a vast sociocultural framework in which we are situated and in which the religious is called upon to bear witness to the vertical dimension of the human person and to the coming of the Kingdom of God, which is not a world opposed to the present one, but a world that is even now coming to birth within the present world.

In this context it would seem to be romantic nostalgia to long for the sacral world of the past (and it is definitely past). Faith should embody the phenomenon of secularization as a new chance to manifest its interior riches (riches so vast they can never be exhausted by a single historical expression) just as it could and did in the sacral world of the past. The God who is manifested in contemporary history wants to be recognized and accepted in the context of secularization. It is proper to faith to accept this challenge and discover a new opportunity for it to be creative, for it to reveal God in the world and in the human secular phenomenon.

More specifically it is incumbent on religious life to take up the enormous task of becoming present in the secular world "so that the value of life consecrated by the profession of the counsels and its essential function in the real world redound to the greater good of the Church,"[13] and even to the greater good of the world itself. This is even more urgent since we know that religious life somewhat instinctively has tended to confuse the historical forms of living out its consecration with the consecration itself. This imposes on us a rethinking and a deeper understanding of some of the essential elements of religious life so that it can better respond to the demands of secularization. We will now list specific elements.

Consecration

Rather than placing the emphasis on the person consecrated and set aside for God, we must emphasize the sense of mission that the religious, precisely because of his or her consecration, must carry out in God's name. Certainly the mission of today's religious is not to compete with those who control the world through science and technology. It is rather to live humanly in the secular world with all that implies: a conscious, explicit reference to God and to Christ, as well as a radical orientation toward other people shown in the way we use earthly goods, considering them, and using them, as instruments to serve humanity.

The concrete form of consecration today is definitely not flight from the world, but participation in it through jobs carried out within secular structures. Apostolates carried on within the religious' own institutions seem to be irreversibly disappearing as ways of organizing secular society. In reality society itself is assuming the task of education and welfare, as well as other roles. We religious must prepare ourselves to work, without privileges and as equals with the rest, in public and private pursuits. Within these secular structures we can and must bear witness (this is our calling) to God and his grace in Jesus Christ, recalling to everyone the existence of other, transcendent realities that are not extraneous to our human vocation and that must not be forgotten in our earthly lives.

Yesterday's religious were undoubtedly teachers and saints of the flight from the world, and in their way and according to the signs of the times, they also transformed their world. The religious and saints of today must teach participation in a common situation that is gradually becoming everyone's world. By working in the secular world we will have an effect on the spirit of the modern age. Religious will experience at close range both the needs and limitations of the secular world and their own, more positive values. In this way we can create, out of our own lived experience, new forms of religious life demanded today, or we can discover the walls that separate us from other people.

Where life is lived authentically, structures of religious life that better answer the spiritual needs of secular society will be authentically and spontaneously created. What these new forms should be cannot be determined a priori. They will flow out of the life that inspires them.

The Secular Aspect of the Vows

The vows up to now have been interpreted almost exclusively in terms of the sacral world. We sometimes forget that, if the vows make a person sacred, it is only to free him or her for a more extensive and more intense service to others. Secularization of the vows, then, must be integrated into the perspective that sees consecration as mission to the world.

The secularization of chastity demands that chastity be lived not only as a value for the individual. It is certainly that, but it also has an essentially ecclesial and human purpose. Chastity is the preeminent form which love for others can assume, characterized by disinteredness, universality, availability, and renunciation of all personal considerations in favor of the testimony we intend to give through our vocation. The life of virginity or celibacy does not limit or do away with the psychological, emotional, and social dimension of the person. The practice and experience of chastity will undoubtedly impose sacrifices, but it should not become neurotic by being overprotected. The safeguards that were so earnestly taught and recommended, especially to religious women, must be adapted to keep pace with their evolving social position, their maturity, and their liberation. It would certainly be ridiculous, for example, that a religious woman could not frequent a place that a good Christian laywoman could frequent without danger.[14]

The secularization of poverty consists not so much in having less as in a commitment to solidarity with those who suffer from poverty, so that one can be able to battle against it. The poor of today are the oppressed and marginated of society, workers expected to live on a pittance of a salary. To be one with them is to practice vowed poverty today. This demands a deep social awareness that may involve personal and communal risks but that must be assumed with boldness and serenity. Even so, the most concrete form of poverty in the secular world is undoubtedly the work by which religious, taking their place in the world, earn sustenance for themselves and their religious family.

The secularization of obedience presents more acute problems, since this was the area most influenced by sacralization, the will of the superior too facilely identified with the will of God. Religious obedience in the secular world must be oriented toward imitating Jesus, who was obedient even unto death on the cross. Jesus never let his mission of redemption be determined by the world around him or by the religious and social traditions of his people; rather he looked at the signs of the times and current events in which he read the salvific will of the Father with whom he identified himself.

Religious obedience should respect the values inherent in temporal realities. It must be more rational in relation to the project and mission of religious and to the way these can be carried out within secular structures. In the vow of obedience, besides supernatural criteria, there can be internal demands imposed on the religious by the earthly realities the religious is committed to, realities from which he or she cannot separate himself or herself in the name of a poorly-understood supernaturalism. In relation to such demands and realities, both subject and superior must be obedient. To the superior falls the task of unifying and leading the community for the benefit of the common mission. Subjects must cooperate actively and responsibly in that task of unifying and fulfilling the common mission. Obedience seen in this way is concerned with, and presupposes, dialogue among members and the maturity of each one to sacrifice personal convenience for the sake of the common apostolate or works taken on and supported by the community.

Being the Sign of God amidst the Profane

Religious, by their function in the world, their language and lifestyle, are among the signs of the sacred. The secular world considers the presence of such signs as an abuse of sacral power when they are not necessary for human and religious activities. In the sacral world the traditional signs were perfectly understandable, since they appeared in a sacral context. The context of these signs in the secular world is different; only secular signs can speak to today's secular world.

To be a prophetic, eschatological sign today means that religious must live in secular society with the joy and the abandonment of those who know this world will be transfigured by God into a new world, and that everything here thus has only a relative value and meaning.

Religious can become signs of the eschatological situation of themselves and their world in a secular way, which is fully in keeping with their consecration. They do this not so much by flight from, or renunciation of, the world as by the correct use of things, carrying out their mission without losing themselves in the world or becoming enslaved to its goods.

On the concrete level, every community or institute must reflect on its use of a habit, and see to what extent the habit continues to be a sign that a group of people or an area understands and accepts, or whether the habit has become a countersign. Such reexamination is also necessary in relation to other aspects and practices of the community. Still, the community must avoid complete radicalism. The important thing is that the sign, be it sacred or profane, speaks of the transcendent realities promised us by God.

Concentration on What Is Essential

Perhaps we have become occasionally lost in too many accidental things. The secular world obliges us to center ourselves on what is essential, constantly transcending forms and structures which were valid in the past but are not today. What is essential in religious life, as we have said before, is the lived experience, the fostering and the deepening of the religious dimension as the basic life-project of religious.

Our principal task is to live our being-religious, and then to embody it and give witness to it in a particular pursuit. The forms of expression of Christian and religious experience can and must change to conform to the times. But we must not forget that a renewal that concerns itself only with historical forms and does not consider the experience of God and the communicating of Christ to other people, to the Church and to the world, remains empty. It is incapable of, and perhaps even detrimental to, on the one hand, satisfying the aspirations of religious themselves and, on the other hand, withstanding major crises.

In short, religious life only becomes a sign for today's world by critically accepting the new sociocultural context, attentively reading the signs of the times but intepreting them in the light of the Gospel, and taking its place in urban society—compartmentalized, pragmatic, dynamic, and self-creating—aware that it is part of that society in the same way that it is aware of its religious nature.

Ramifications of Religious Life for Secularization

We have already alluded to the demand for the secular to be inserted into the religious and for the religious to be inserted into the secular. We have insisted on an interpenetration of religious life and secularization so that each may clarify for the other what it is and what it is called to be, so that secularization does not fall into secularism and religious life into flight or isolation from the world.

Religious life, giving up its ghetto mentality, should make its apostolic and evangelizing efforts a corrective to the excesses that can, and actually do, take place in the secular world. What influence then does religious life have on secularization or how does it impinge upon it?

Elevating Humanity: Subjectivity and Personalism

The secularized world tends instinctively to overemphasize the value of the individual in terms of the individual's specialization or ability to produce more and thus to gain competence. The human person today is defined exclusively in terms of one's relation to the world: the economic individual, the political individual, the progressive individual, the genital individual. There is a great proclivity toward the quantitative without great concern for the choice and selection of more basic human values.

The basic aspiration of society lies entirely with increasing the GNP and the per capita income based on the model of American consumer society. Every occupation tends to be integrated into the collective enterprise of producing and consuming. The culture born of this society is poor in typically human values such as love, fraternity, hope, the understanding of the individual in terms of social relationships, the fostering of subjectivity, and personalism understood as the capacity for self-giving without consideration of productivity or wealth.

There is a vast, overriding task for religious who have been integrated into secular society. By their fundamental option for others and God, as well as by their lifestyle which flows from that option, they can and should testify to the value of love, tenderness, and hope. They can thus overcome, help to overcome, or at the very least criticize, "the competitive isolation of today."[15] Religious, like all Christians, are called to proclaim that all productivity and progress should lead to a deeper fraternal communion of all people and a qualitative increase in humanization.

Exercising a Prophetic and Critical Function

By their integration into, and work in, the secular world, religious can be aware that, in a certain way, they are also actively participating in the evil and social injustices of today—structural injustice which cannot be corrected merely by individual effort. But this must not be a reason for shying away from the task of correction, nor a reason for creating a closed world within the world. Their taking their place in the world demands from religious a critical attitude and a denunciation, often very strong, of the real structural injustice that occurs in the world.

Carrying the cross of Christ today means needing to live in an unjust and discriminatory social situation, aware both of its injustices and of the short-range impossibility of overcoming them. It is a question of living with an awareness of paradox, challenging and criticizing the situation from within, while at the same time trying to make it better or to renew it. This is the task to be undertaken by religious integrated into secular structures.

Giving Witness to the Meaning of God and Jesus Christ

The secular world is essentially a world compartmentalized and functional, one that lacks a deeper sense of things other than the sense things have in their respective systems. The meaning of the totality of the world and of the person has largely been lost.

In what direction are psychosocial evolution and technical and scientific progress headed? What are we trying for with such great activity and productivity? Why should we work so hard and buy so much? To raise these or similar questions—which will often be disconcerting because they do not fit into the economic system, the political system, or the system of interpersonal relationships—is to place being human in relation to our absolute future.

God, the absolute future of humanity and of history, must be present in the world through religious, not through frequent mention of the holy name or the placing of crucifixes in public places (which seems implausible), but through living out what that name signifies for us in its radical and absolute meaning, without which everything would be absurd.

This radical meaning is not something abstract or totally other-worldly, but has been incarnated and made a living and intimate reality in Jesus Christ—God-with-us—who came to the world with a message of renewal and complete liberation, called the Kingdom of God and given reality in Jesus' life, words, works, and, definitively, in his Resurrection, which gave a new meaning and a sure hope to the world. The world will not be destroyed but will take its place in the Kingdom of God when it has been definitively freed from vanity and bondage to corruption in order to share in the glorious freedom of the sons and daughters of God (Rm. 8:19–22). The Kingdom is already mysteriously, but really, present here on earth and will reach fulfillment with the coming of the Lord.[16] Religious are called in a special way to bear witness to that fact and to make it visible.

Attesting to the Joy of Life

Consumer society celebrates to the full the triumph and the prosperity of the individual. Yet it has hardly any room for accepting and appreciating the brokenness, disillusionment, and suffering that are also part of life. The host of diversions that try to handle these realities is nothing more than an illusion of happiness. These diversions cannot understand or touch the deepest part of people who feel themselves victims of brokenness and suffering.

In light of all this, religious must be prophets of the joy of life, of hope, of the natural goodness of things, by the way they act in the face of sorrow and the brokenness of life. Religious must truly struggle for the development of each and every person. But it must above all be their special task to proclaim the riches of God that infinitely transcend our poor wealth: the riches of living as those who share in God and his goodness, open to the joyous future built on fraternity that God has promised to everyone.[17]

Even brokenness and disillusionment can be a way of becoming a person and growing spiritually,[18] and the chance to leave a superficial and narrow context and to enter a more personal and fuller one, which transcends the considerations that animate the neurotic activity of the world.

Testifying to the Value of Prayer

The secular world easily comes to lose its sense of transcendence and thus its sense of value and the meaning of value. Religious, as signs of transcendence in the world, must be people of prayer and meditation who devote a large amount of time to these activities. Prayer represents the interior aspect of human life. In prayer we find ourselves and God, and can then unite our interior world of silence and listening with the exterior world of activity and work.

It is significant, as we have suggested elsewhere, that the compartmentalized and fragmented world of today, eager to reconstruct its spiritual life, seeks to do so through systems of meditation, yoga, Eastern mysticism, and even drugs. Religious, with their special lifestyle, can help point out a better and surer road to satisfying longings like these, at the same time showing that such an adventure brings with it hidden joys that can fill the heart with undreamed-of fullness. It can do this because it brings the fullness of encounter with God, brought about not by artificial techniques but by an ascetical spirituality that is deeper and makes a person gradually more open to the mystery of God discovered in oneself, in others, and in all things.

If in the past there was an immense contribution by religious to culture and humanism, there is no less demand and need for this today. It is a task not to create and promote consumer society, but to humanize, spiritualize, and give a transcendent context to structures that threaten to dominate the very people who created them by secularizing those people and turning them into objects.

Likewise, within the secular city, religious must announce and proclaim the heavenly city "which has indestructible foundations and whose designer and builder is God" (Hb. 11:10). This is a way of spiritual, but effective, cooperation "because the building of that earthly city is always founded on God and directed toward him, so that those who build it may not labor in vain."[19]

8

Prayer in the Midst of the Secular World: Challenges and Risks

It is undeniable that prayer life today is undergoing a crisis. Yet this is no more than the symptom of a deeper crisis affecting the very roots of our faith and the principles that orient our Christian life. Attempts to resolve the crisis have been made with varying success:

The archaizing solution: This solution tries to reform existing models through a strict return to primitive forms. It is a flight into the past.

The futuristic solution: This is a reaction to the existing situation of searching for a new order in a future whose outlines can be discerned. It is a flight into the future.

The escapist solution: This solution is an attempt to resolve the crisis by taking refuge in a private spirituality. Small, closed groups are created, isolated communities are formed, giving rise to something like an underground church.

The solution of challenge: In this solution we begin by accepting the crisis just as it is, analyzing the factors in it so we can arrive at an adequate solution. Every crisis is a process of purification, examination, and decision, according to the original meaning of the Sanskrit root *kir, kri,* and the Greek *krisis*. Through the crisis, prayer forms are examined, purified, and reconstructed. Nothing accidental or merely decorative can stand up to the test; only what is substantial, appropriate, and valuable remains. Thus every crisis has a tragic aspect. It is really a break. The old is in ruins and the new is being born.

Every crisis has forces in it that can lead to reform, revolution, or a process of transformation.

Reform is no more than reaffirming the existing situation and trying to improve it. This succeeds only in prolonging the crisis, since it does not get to its roots. For example, the Divine Office is reformed: it is said in the vernacular, the hours and the psalms are shortened, the rubrics simplified, and substitutions allowed. The result is that a new crisis arises as soon as the reform has been instituted. Why? Because structure as such is not the real problem.

Revolution tries to eliminate the existing structure by creating something entirely new. Revolution generally rails against all tradition, and thus does not make use of past experiences, which, despite having been fossilized, always have, as experience, many useful values.

The process of transformation, also called ongoing revolution, seeks to improve the situation as it exists, but at the same time to create something new—not only a particular goal, but a continuous process of renewal of the system and its actual structures. Such a process of transformation seems to us to be the most promising, since it makes use of all viable elements but gives them a different interpretation. As a permanent process, it never stops at a particular goal already achieved, but maintains an openness to all new things that are valuable and viable.

In the prayer life crisis, all these approaches have been used: archaizing, futuristic, escapist, reformist, revolutionary, and challenge. We would like to reflect on the last one, taking our theme from Karl Rahner: "Since we must not fail to pray, we must not stop talking about prayer, good or bad, in the way it is given to each of us to."[1]

The Origin of the Prayer Crisis of Today: Positive Aspects

The Passion for Authenticity

Our age has, more than any other, experienced mendacity and hypocrisy, from manipulations by dictatorial regimes to commercial propaganda. People today are skeptical about any kind of truth, and yet they feel a passion for sincerity and authenticity. One can be mistaken, but one must be authentic even in error. The search for authenticity reveals itself in architecture, painting, and the other plastic arts, and in sociology and psychology. Iron should be iron. Wood should not look like marble. Myths, dreams, and people should be recognized as myths, dreams, and people. We find an analogous search for veracity in religion itself.[2]

Until recently we said that Catholics possess the truth without being true, while Protestants are true without the truth. Today we are aware that one cannot live apart from the other. In the council hall, one bishop passed a note to another with this message: "The synod does not make mistakes. If it does make mistakes, they are not corrected because they do not appear to have been made."[3] This statement has no validity for today's Church. We have learned to be authentic, to recognize our failures and our errors not only in relation to the Church but also in regard to prayer life.

Our liturgical prayers are too archaic, Roman, and Byzantine. The Breviary is largely a hodgepodge of pre-Christian Semitic piety and expressions taken from the court of the Roman or Byzantine emperor. There is little reflection of New Testament piety.

Likewise it is easy to see that a rigid concept of the Word of God is outdated. The Mass comes from a rural world, a juridical one with pagan terminology. The formulas are too objective and seem to come out of a Roman mind-set where piety and its expression were the province of jurists. The majority of the official prayers do not express our communitarian experience of God, but the experience of those of the remote past which is no longer ours. The verbosity of the liturgy is not compatible with our religious experience, which seeks fewer words and greater simplicity.

Today we experience the silence of God in a vivid way: God the Father allows so much death, allows two out of every three people to go hungry, permits 20% of the world's people to eat 80% of the world's food. The liturgy presents a God who talks about himself too much and reveals too much. We need and want more silence and meditation. We cannot talk a lot about the problem of the absence and silence of God, but we can pray in silence and with acceptance like Jesus himself who, when confronted by evil, did not teach us to interpret it, but to fight it and to accept it with peacefulness and patience.

Thus it is our passion for sincerity that has revealed the crisis that already existed in our prayer life. Many people do not pray because many prayers do not express their deepest concerns. We are on our way to becoming new Jobs or new Psalmists who pray to God with sincerity, even to the point of rudeness, even daring to question him, but always with hearts full of enthusiasm, gratitude, and sincere love. Many have abandoned the old formulas without substituting new ones. A recent survey that points this out was taken of Italian ex-priests. It shows that their leaving the priesthood was primarily the result of a twofold spiritual deficiency: abandonment of prayer (90 out of 100) and the lack of inner peace caused by the spiritual and moral ambiguity in which the priest lived (83 out of 100).[4]

The Experience of the Death of God

The theology of the death of God has become a fad and, on the level of theological reflection, already passé.[5] The experience of the death of God is, nonetheless, a common one for religious and other people concerned with deeply living their faith. In speaking this way we do not want to say God has died, since a God who ends by dying never was God to begin with. With this Hegelian expression we mean the silence, the hidden and enigmatic face of God. Religious, for example, profess a greater communion with God. But this God is, most of the time, a hidden God. He does not speak; he does not intervene. There are times when he does not even give an inner security that the pain of having renounced everything we have renounced for the sake of his love is worth it.

In the secularized world the silence of God is even more startling. The texts of our prayers and our hymns find no verification in our experience. They facilely proclaim God is Father, Love, Lord of life and history. Yet how little we experience this in our own lives and in the events we witness through the mass media. That God is Father and that all he created is good is not a human experience but an act of faith.

How then do we pray when God himself and the meaning of things come to us enveloped in contingency? Faith needs to be recaptured as a vital dimension of our experience of the world. God himself must be a unique and irreducible experience in human life. If he is not, then neither a deeply Christian life nor religious life can exist, since these are no more than making explicit the experience of God and of Christ. Faith is a becoming aware of the meaning we find in life, explicitly proclaiming the natural goodness of things, accepting that the meaning of life is not an abstract idea but a person very close to us, God-with-us called Jesus Christ; the meaning became flesh and blood and lived among us (Jn. 1:14). Christian faith, then, does not claim to add something new to the reality we experience. It only tries to make explicit what is already hidden and implicit in all human experience.

Prayer is always an expression of the whole person before God. Can we say that our prayers express our experience of God both in his presence and in his absence or silence?

The Inevitable Fragmentation of Life

In a world that is growing smaller, where, for example, 700,000,000 can observe the same soccer game at one time, there is also an opposite phenomenon of a fragmentation of life. Modern life is based on specialized segments. Approximately 20,000 professional occupations exist. Each person plays various roles: one is a sister or a priest, one prays, one administers the sacraments, one is a teacher, a worker, a chauffeur, a student; one is part of an anonymous crowd when one takes the bus, a fan when one goes to a football game, a customer when one goes shopping. All the roles one plays have neither a unique starting point nor a unique, separate goal. They lack a frame of reference that coordinates them. Our life is pluralistic. Each role has its own logic.

Until not long ago a framework existed that unified them all, the *corpus christianum*. Christianity was a common environment: in the church one prayed, outside one made ejaculations, in the workplace one lived one's right intentions, in schools the crucifix was prominent, at crossroads chapels were built. In short, everyone had a common Christian faith. Today all this is dissolving.[6] The factory, the family, the person are no longer blessed, nor must they be blessed. Secularity possesses its own teleology and its own holiness, which should not be "profaned" by the sacredness of the sacred.

What all this means concretely for prayer life is that what we would call praying is a period in life and not all of life. When we fly, work, travel, or teach, we live as if God did not exist (*etsi Deus non daretur*). The many roles we play have their particular and legitimate autonomy, as Vatican II recognized and demonstrated.[7] We do not need praying to be good or pleasing to God. This fact obliges us to reflect on prayerfulness and devotional praying.

The Legitimate Secularization of the World

As we have already seen in the previous chapter, secularization is the term we use to express the legitimate autonomy of worldly values. It is not necessary to resort to religious principles to explain the phenomena or patterns of the life we live in relationship with the natural and increasingly humanized world. These have their own laws, as they also have, teleologically, their own innate goodness.[8] To live that goodness is already pleasing to God, who wants this to be.

Nevertheless, the realistic believer knows the basic ambiguity that pervades human reality. Secularization is good and desired by God. But we know that it can degenerate into secularism, which is no more than a way of proclaiming the relative values of the world to be absolute values. Christianity does not command us to choose heavenly values by depreciating earthly ones. It only demands that we distinguish between true and false goods, among both heavenly and earthly ones. The legitimate autonomy of earthly realities should not separate us from God, but should make us freer *for* him.

Thus a critical attitude in regard to secularization is always needed, since our heart has been created in such a way that when it loves it loves totally and undividedly. It can happen that the Christian, loving earthly things, ends up noticing that he or she loves only these things. God is no longer the center of one's fundamental life-project. He is merely the object of prayer forms and not the subject or end of one's aspirations.

It would seem then that only through prayer can we live secularly and not secularistically. Only our relationship with God allows the world to go on being a secular world without becoming a secularistic world.

The World of Noise: Images and Sounds

This is another characteristic of our times. Television, radio, and other communications media bombard our brains with pictures of the world, music of all nations, information of every kind. We are necessarily rapid thinkers. Our psychology and our mentality are dominated and besieged by the need to assimilate and digest the input from every medium. Fritz Leist has studied the way the invasion of archetypal images and motivations (conscious or unconscious) tends to dissolve our psyches.[9] All this has an effect on the person who wants to pray or concentrate on God, who has no image, no voice, no sound. How can one pray authentically and personally in this situation?

Modern Mobility: Speed and Acceleration

Harvey Cox, in *The Secular City*, emphasized mobility as one of the characteristics of modern life.[10] Everything moves rapidly, from our household appliances to our ways of thinking and acting. We live running from one occupation to another. This results in nervousness. Karen Horney finds in this a factor responsible for the neurotic character of our culture.[11] Such a condition seems to clash with prayer life, which demands an inner calm.

Thus it seems at times that the liturgy is synonymous with lethargy. The prayer crisis has come about from the simple fact of one's not being able to stay in one place for a long period of time. In religious men and women, the situation has been aggravated by their commitment to the general progress of the Church in the Third World and by their responsibility for so many tasks of human development.

The World of Occupied Leisure

Our civilization offers enough free time. But we have to have our free time occupied by the newspaper, radio, or TV, with this or that program, novel, or game. Often even the hospitality one should show to the stranger or one's brother or sister is sacrificed for these things. Family life has, in many places, been greatly damaged by television. Bernard Bro, the noted French spiritual writer, recently wrote: "When we think we are being generous, we have reached the point where we can always find in our availability an excuse to avoid prayer."[12]

In light of all this, how can we say that God is the most concrete being for the religious and the person of faith?

Conclusion

All these factors constitute a challenge to prayer life today. They do not keep us from praying, but challenge us to pray in a different way. The situation does not depend on us; we find ourselves immersed in it. We uselessly try to find out if it is good or bad, or what causes it. It forces us to take up the challenge, not to evade it or flee from it. It also demands that we develop the energies or powers hidden in the situation, turning it into a journey of the mind to God, just as St. Bonaventure did with the situation of his time. But how should we pray today?[13]

A look at Jesus' attitude of prayer will serve to clarify the reflections that follow.

The Prayer of Jesus: Sacred and Profane

The New Testament does not present Jesus as the person in history who prayed most outstandingly, as some have concluded,[14] nor even as one who prayed better than others did.

We know the origin and development of official and private prayer in post-exilic Judaism. The gospels never say Jesus went to the Temple to pray; Luke says only that Jesus, as was his custom, entered the synagogue on the Sabbath (4:16). The Synoptics record only two prayers of Jesus. One is the prayer of exultation (Mt. 11:25–27; Lk. 10:21) in which we find undeniable Johannine, sapiential, and apocalyptic elements. In connection with this prayer we see the theological work of the community, who placed the prayer on the lips of Jesus, possibly in the context of a missionary discourse.[15] The second prayer is the one in Gethsemane (Mk. 14:36 and par.). Here doubt arises as to whether Jesus used these kinds of formulas, since no one was at his side, the three disciples nearest him being asleep at that moment. This prayer seems to be a stylization by the early Church to express Jesus' very firm trust (cf. Hb. 5:6–7 and also 2:18). In addition, Luke (22:31–32) refers to Jesus' praying for Peter. There are also various other references to Jesus' praying in solitude (Mk. 1:35; 6:46 and par.; Mt. 14:23; Lk. 3:21; 5:16; 6:12; 9:18–28).

The Lord's prayer is a prayer typical of the historical Jesus. It is perhaps the most certain gospel text for knowing the message of Jesus of Nazareth. The frequent conversations of Jesus with the Father in St. John's Gospel, especially the high priestly prayer in chapter 17 (cf. also Jn. 11:14 and 12:27f.), are, as exegesis has recognized for some time, discourses of St. John about Jesus rather than discourses of Jesus himself.[16]

Among the evangelists, St. Luke is considered the evangelist of prayer.[17] Prayer is the customary attitude of Jesus and a characteristic element of Christianity. It is only Luke who, in order to demonstrate that one "should pray always and not get discouraged" (Lk. 18:1), refers to the parables of the importunate friend, the impious judge, the importunate widow who seeks justice, and the pharisee and the publican (Lk. 18:1–14). In these parables it is not the person, but God, who is the center. If the importuned friend and the godless judge grant what they are asked for, how much more will God grant what we ask him for.

Both Luke and Paul insist on prayer at all times (Lk. 2:37; 18:1–8; 21:36; 22:44; 24:53; Ac. 1:14; 2:42; 6:4; 10:2; 12:5; 26:7; Rm. 1:9–10; 12:12; 1 Co. 1:4; Ep. 1:16; 5:20; Ph. 1:3–4;

Col. 1:3–9; 4:2–12; 1 Th. 1:2–3; 2:13; 3:10–13; 2 Th. 1:3–11; 2:13) because both of them are preaching to Greeks and pagans who do not know a practice of prayer, as the Jews do. This explains their insistence.

Radbert Kerkhoff, in a classic study, has demonstrated that the expression "pray without ceasing" is not exhausted by praying at set hours according to the Old Testament tradition. On the contrary, and more importantly, it means the interior transformation of the person in a new attitude toward God and belief in the imminence of his saving intervention. This phrase inculcates an attitude of prayerfulness which extends to all of life, rather than a set of prayers to be recited at set times.[18]

We know that Jesus came from a pious family (Lk. 2; cf. 4:16). This means that Jesus, like all the Jews of his time, faithfully recited the Shema twice a day ("Hear, O Israel, the Lord is God, the Lord alone"—see Dt. 6:4–5), and that three times a day (morning, midday, and evening) he would say special prayers (cf. Dn. 6:11–14; Ac. 3:1; 10:3–30; Didache 8:3). Despite all this, the gospels show that Jesus was not satisfied with this tradition. Mark (1:35) says, "In the morning, when it was still very dark, he got up, left the house, and went to a deserted place where he prayed." Jesus stayed there so long that the apostles were looking for him. Mark (6:46) also says, "After dispersing (the crowd and the apostles), he went into the hills to pray." Jesus prayed for a long time and only returned from there at the fourth watch of the night, when the apostles met him again (Mk. 6:48). Luke says, "In those days he went into the hills to pray and spent the night in prayer to God."

These accounts testify to Jesus' custom of praying alone in the quiet of the night. This prayer is firmly within the tradition of his people, but it does not stay within the tradition. It goes beyond the tradition. We also know of Jesus' criticism of the Pharisees' ostentatious prayer, as well as of the Gentiles who used a wide array of devotional formulas (Mt. 6:5–8). Jesus himself taught us not to talk too much or with too much show, giving us the Our Father (Mt. 6:9–13; Lk. 11:2–4). In it there are no grand discourses nor an attempt to "wear God out," but a wondrous simplicity and naturalness. It calls on God with a profane expression, "Abba," the same expression children use when they call their father "Daddy."[19]

The Synoptics present Christ as preferring solitary prayer and constant prayer (not only at set times or three times a day) to temple and ritual prayer. He is indifferent to these kinds of prayer because the prayer of a child to his father in nothing like a cultic ritual. The results of prayer are not tied to set gestures, times, or places. The words of Jesus transmitted by Luke (18:1) say that what is necessary to "pray always and without losing heart," freeing prayer from a set time and place, placing the person constantly in the presence of God. John (4:21–24) recounts words of Jesus that need no explanation: "Woman, the time has come when no one will worship the Father either on this mountain or in Jerusalem. . . . True worshippers worship the Father in spirit and truth." Each person can be the temple of God (1 Co. 3:16; 6:19; Ep. 2:21).

Jesus thus freed prayer from devotional exercises, emphasizing the attitude of prayerfulness, the openness of the heart to God. From his time on the person could pray always and everywhere; the person is before God not only during certain actions. Christ thus made prayer profane, or rather, sacralized all human existence. Both in the sacred and the profane, the person is related to God and God to the person.

Two Solutions

Jesus' attitude can give direction to a style of prayer for today's situation. First, one needs to know what prayer claims to be. It is primarily a search for personal union with God. Prayer is only possible when one achieves an interior unity and a unity with the world. The person must be self-possessed. But one is often possessed by one's ideas, concerns, or interests. To pray is to open one's heart to God. Before we do this, we must possess our own heart so that we can succeed in opening it to God. Prayer is a dialogue with God. One must be in communion with God, one must assimilate God into one's own life, if one is to be able to converse with him anywhere and at any time. A prayer without conversation is impossible; it is not prayer. To pray is one of the ways to love, and to love is to seek union. When one person loves another, one thinks of that person continually; no matter where one is, no matter where one goes, no matter what one does, one's thoughts always return to the beloved and are united with the beloved. The same can be said regarding God. To pray is to "relax with God," as the ancients said, to reserve a time for God, to walk with him and feel oneself with him. The Fathers speak of *ruminatio:* to pray is to think about God in the way a child sucks on a lollipop.[20]

As one can readily see, prayer appears to be an attitude more than a devotional exercise. Now we must ask if it is possible to cultivate this prayerful attitude in the midst of our contemporary situation—secularization, the bustle of activity, the bombardment of sensory data—in the midst of a complex of factors that speak to us of the human person much more than of God.[21]

I do not believe any single model exists that will cure all our problems with prayer. I will thus confine myself here to presenting two models, which seem to correspond more or less with two types of people: the introvert or the person closely attuned to his or her inner self and its experiences, and the extrovert who is more attuned to the outer world and the experience of the objective world.

Prayer in a World Transparent to Christ and to God

For some people the attitude of prayerfulness is possible in today's compartmentalized and frenetic secular world through a profane, interior religious experience. There are people for whom God and Christ are concrete, lived experiences. This experience opens up for them a broad context in which to interpret life and in which to orient themselves. They see everything out of the center which unifies everything. The world, objects, events are seen and experienced as a manifestation of God, a theophany. Reality is transparent to Christ. Everything causes one to remember, or becomes a memorial, of Christ and his mystery, i.e., Christic transparency or diaphany. Some examples from the past and present will serve to illustrate this kind of religious experience.

St. Francis, the Newborn Man of Eden

Francis of Assisi, who went around with his friends spreading youthful enthusiasm and romanticism, fond of gaiety and parties, as were his friends, one day came to discover the religious dimension of his life. He thought he heard the imposing Christ of St. Damian speaking to him. On October 12, 1208 (or February 24, 1209), he attended Mass in the chapel of Portiuncula and listened to the Gospel of Matthew (10:5ff.). The message he heard translated itself into a rule and a lifestyle, because it awakened in him a deep religious experience. Throughout his life he experienced Christ in such a way that the universe became quickly transformed for him: sun, earth, water, death—everything was his brother or sister. Everything reminded him of the Father who was in heaven, who had a special love for all those who remembered Christ in a special way. Francis entered into cosmic communion with all nature. He appeared to return to the beginning, to the state of Adam in paradise, entirely at one with God, with other people, and with the world.

St. Bonaventure, in the *Legend of St. Francis,* commented: "By virtue of the familiar unity he entered into with all things, he seems to have once more achieved that primeval state of innocence."[22] St. Francis's *Song of Brother Sun* is not primarily a lyrical composition or a romantic flight of fancy, but a little theological work expressed in poetry. It sings of a point reached after a long and difficult process of overcoming the self through endless penance. Francis underwent a painful process of inner purification such that his eyes could come to see the cosmic presence of Christ and God at the center of each created thing.[23]

St. Bonaventure: The Journey of the Cosmos to the Omega Point

St. Bonaventure (1221–1274) had an experience similar to that of Francis, as we see from his work, *The Journey of the Mind to God,* a masterpiece of medieval Christian literature.[24] He had been general of the Franciscans for many years, had traveled all over Europe reforming the order, strengthening it in certain aspects by making them structured rather than simply charismatic. Weary from his travels, he searched for inner peace and serenity on Mt. Alvernia, where St. Francis had received the stigmata.

Meditating on how St. Francis had been given the stigmata by Christ in the form of a six-winged seraph, he discovered, using the analogy of the six wings, the six roads that lead to mystical union with God. He writes down his own experience as scholarly theology, yet the focus is still sharp and clear: everything is the reflection, the image and likeness of God. He examines the world around us, the world within us, and the world beyond us. God and Christ can be discovered in and through created things. The various classes of created things are like Jacob's ladder by means of which one ascends from the world to God and descends from God to the world.

Teilhard de Chardin: The Transparency of Matter to Christ

On September 19, 1919, while celebrating the Feast of the Stigmata of St. Francis, Teilhard de Chardin also had an experience of the cosmic Christ who transforms matter. He writes in one of his letters:

> Up to now this feast made little impression on me. This time, however, reading in the Breviary the account of St. Bonaventure's vision, I was struck by the symbol of the flaming, crucified spirit who appeared to St. Francis and filled him with a mysterious combination of pain and joy. I do not know whether this is the meaning of that marvel, but I have seen here one of the forms, and one of the most perfect and precise revelations such as the Church has never seen, of the cosmic, transforming Christ revealing himself as he did to St. Paul. Our generation needs this Christ very much. On this occasion I felt once more the desire to no longer live in any way except as a living force or a living idea. Such was the effect the One Necessary had on me, driving me to belong to him completely and annihilating me. What made me believe this desire is good is the conviction I live with that the call comes from on high and one cannot remain true to it except by the power of purity and humility.[25]

Until that point in his life, Teilhard had lived in a permanent conflict between his experience of the world and his experience of Christianity. Each of these wanted to win him over entirely. Christ in his cosmic dimension became the bond of union between his pagan self and his Christian self, in Teilhard's own expression. All his scientific acumen was used to discover the echoes of Christ in matter. Reality was not only a theophany, but also, and preeminently, a Christic transparency. The world, created in Christ, by Christ, and for Christ (Col. 1:16) is transparent to him.[26]

Prayer as the Cultivation of Inner Space

In these three examples, the world does not lose its worldliness or secularity. Christ, the Eucharist, and God pervade profane reality. For these men, and for those who have had similar experiences, the theology of the death of God or the experience of him is an absurdity that contradicts their own inner experience of him. One could say, with Carl Jung, "I do not believe in God. I know and experience him." It is a matter of existential evidence, not logical proofs.

It is clear that the world for these men is not less secular or less desacralized than for the rest of us. The sacred continues to be sacred, the profane to be profane. Thus the attitude of prayerfulness is actualized in both the sacred and the profane. God and Christ are seen in various ways in everything, in both the sacred and the profane. The bustle, the noise, the fragmentation of life, leisure filled with TV or radio, cannot destroy their interior unity. The unity is profound; the other things are superficial. Everything can be transfigured. The person has seized the inner dimension that allows him or her to discern the will of God and the signs of his presence in the signs of the times of his or her own life. Although still pilgrims, we feel ourselves as already in the Father's house, as already in the hands of God.

That people like this exist today is obvious. It is sufficient to recall the works of Michel Quoist, the published diaries of the great Christian philosopher Maurice Blondel, the prayers of Fr. Lebret, the spiritual diary of Dag Hammarskjöld, the famous prayers of Antoine de Saint-Exupêry in *La Citadelle*, and many others. The testimony of the majority of people who have made the Cursillo shows us that such experience is not the prerogative of the very few. For all these people the world becomes the great sacrament of God. St. Ignatius of Loyola understood this very well when he advised, "Look for God in everything." He went so far as to advise his students not to pray so much that it would become detrimental to their studies. His secretary wrote to the rector of the College of Coimbra, "Ignatius places greater value on the search for God in all things than in devoting so much time useful for this to prayer."[27] In another letter Ignatius wrote even more clearly:

> Study, when undertaken seriously, involves the entire person and one cannot devote oneself totally to it if one wants to dedicate too much time to prayer. Everyone should get used to seeing the presence of our Lord in everything, such as, for example, in dealings with other people, in walking or resting, in eating, in listening and thinking, in everything people do. This is because the majesty of God is in everything through his presence, his action and his essence. The way of meditating by looking for God in everything is easier than what we could attain by reflecting on abstract spiritual themes.[28]

Prayer appears here above all as cultivation of the inner religious space of the person. Formulas and rituals are undoubtedly important, but not unconditionally so. One has already achieved the important thing: seeing everything as transparent to God and to Christ.

Prayer in a World Where God Does Not Speak

There are other people, surely the vast majority of Christians, for whom the world is not transparent to God and Christ. The world is experienced more as the world and less as a sign and sacrament of God. One finds God not in an attitude of prayerfulness but in devotional practices and in a sacred place.

These people experience the reality of the world in its deepest worldliness where God really does not speak and is not easily seen. This world makes up the larger part of life. The hours of prayer and recollection are few in comparison to the other hours in which we live concerned and preoccupied with things.

What role does prayer play for these people? Can they also have a prayerful attitude in themselves?

Prayer as the Basic Life-Project

There is an attitude of prayerfulness that is achieved through the basic life-project of each individual.[29] Each person wants to be this or that in life. The believer will bring God into the life-project. Baptism and Confirmation already consecrate the life-project to God in some way. If one lives that consecration (which also implies a mission), it should make God present, although in a hidden way, in other things. This is what makes up the basic life-project in which God has a central place, and in turn constitutes the attitude of prayerfulness. Everything a person does in living out this life-project from day to day is being sanctified by the presence of God. Provided the life-project has not been corrupted in its essence, the life-project centered in God continues sanctifying and creating the attitude of prayerfulness as an attitude of openness to God.

These people, if they experience the God-given goodness and rightness of things and the goodness and rightness people attribute to God himself, are experiencing a sanctifying work. We do not need prayer to sanctify our daily work as if work had no religious value without prayer. Since it is naturally good, it is marked by divine grace. Doing this work is merit, prayer, and salvation.[30]

We do not want this point misunderstood to mean we are not praying. The secular world in the autonomy God wants it to have has its own sanctification. This is not a new idea. Sirach said of ordinary workers, "They give solidity to the created world and the object of their prayer is the tasks of their occupation" (Si. 38:34). Josiah receives the following praise from Jeremiah: "He defended the cause of the humble and the poor, and it was good. Is not this to know me? says the Lord" (Jr. 22:16). In the gospel of the anonymous Christians (Mt. 25:31–45), the eternal judge identifies himself with the humble: "I was hungry and you gave me to eat. . . . When you failed to do this to the least of my brothers, you failed to do it for me." This constitutes the task of people in the encounter with

God. To say "yes" to God I do not have to meet him face to face. It is enough to recognize him hidden in the sacrament of the neighbor. Thus the great Flemish mystic Ruysbroeck said, "If you are in ecstasy and your brother needs help, leave your ecstasy and go help your brother. The God you leave is less certain than the God you encounter."

In the Decree on the Apostolate of the Laity, Vatican II makes a very important statement about what we are affirming:

> Many elements make up the temporal order. . . . All of these not only aid the attainment of our ultimate goal, but also possess their own intrinsic value. This value has been implanted in them by God, whether they are considered in themselves or as parts of the whole temporal order. "God saw all that he had made, and it was very good" (Gn. 1:31). This natural goodness of theirs takes on a special dignity as a result of their relation to the human person, for whose service they were created. Last of all, it has pleased God to unite all things, both natural and supernatural, in Christ Jesus "that in all things he may have the first place" (Col. 1:18). This destination, however, does not deprive the temporal order of its independence, its proper goals, laws, resources, and significance for human welfare, but rather perfects the temporal order in its own intrinsic strength and excellence and raises it to the level of our total vocation on earth.[31]

In this passage it is said very clearly that to verify the autonomy of things is to realize something foreseen and desired by God himself. It is not by their explicit relationship to God that things acquire their natural goodness. They possess that goodness in themselves, in their autonomy before God, who originally wanted them to be so. The attitude of prayerfulness in the secular and autonomous world should be to do what must be done: to be honest, to be faithful, to be a partner, to be authentic, and to be open to all without discrimination. To be good is, in a secular way, to be Christian.

In this sense there are many great men and women of prayer in the world. Perhaps they are anonymous Christians, outside the sociological, or better, the theological, limits of the Church, but they live faithfully and according to their conscience and the natural goodness of things.

Be that as it may, we must once again recall that the secular world is ambiguous. It embraces the natural goodness of things and a legitimate autonomy, as well as institutionalized evil and secretiveness before God. In the latter case secularization becomes secularism. Autonomy degenerates into independence and neglect of God. In such a case the fundamental life-project that made God its center is destroyed. Humanism becomes merely humanitarianism.

The Need for Devotional Prayers

To avoid the degeneration of one's life-project, one should periodically undergo a renewal. Devotional prayer becomes an urgent need in this renewal.[32] Praying, meditation, an annual retreat and life review, and Sunday liturgy give us breathing room. These are the best times in daily life to accumulate the energy to be able to live the daily routine with meaning. Devotional prayer is like a holiday banquet: while no one can celebrate holidays or feasts endlessly, a holiday breaks up the routine and gives us the strength to live our other days with full meaning.

The attitude of prayerfulness is like a ship sailing the ocean. It starts to rust; barnacles accumulate on its hull. Reaching port, the sailors must paint and repair the hull, refurbishing it for a new voyage. This refurbishing is devotional prayer; it places us before God in an attitude of praise, petition, and thanksgiving, and renews our basic life-project, which is centered on God himself. If we omit this prayer, we quickly end by living in a kind of ambiguity, not knowing why we are doing what we are doing. Rivals come along and battle with God for his place in our lives.

Secular Religious Experience

In today's very secularized world, one notices a return to, and a sincere search for, the mystical dimension, religious and mysterious, which has been stifled and lost in the world of technology and in the activity of producing and consuming. The Hippies and the youth of other movements seek new symbols, new rituals, to express their religious experience, which is no longer lived in the sacral or cultic domain of the church or monastery, but in the heart of the secular city. For the majority of these people, Christ Jesus possesses a numinous, religious reality and exercises the fascination of a superstar. It is true that the search sometimes takes on orgiastic expressions in which the mystical experience is an illusory one provoked by drugs and other toxic substances.

Be that as it may, this phenomenon is still relevant. The secular world is not as secularistic as some would like to think, celebrating with too much abandon its conquests at the expense of religion. Prayer as openness to the transcendent, and ritual, symbol, and liturgy as expressions of human dreams, freedom, and the depths of the person, are rooted deeply in the core of our being. Thus they cannot easily be uprooted by the historical process of secularization. In reality they are gaining new strength today (thanks to a beneficent crisis) in new ways, greeted joyfully by certain proponents of the theology of secularization, such as Harvey Cox and Jurgen Moltmann.

Prayer and Prayer Forms: Their Unitive and Divisive Character

The preceding reflections we believe have made it clear that prayer is basically a way that people can be in themselves and exist in relation to God and the world. It is marked by an openness and an encounter with the mystery of God who is discovered in oneself, in the world of things, occupations, and people, and expressed by gestures, words, formulas, or silence.

Yet one must notice that the word is not primarily a means to communicate something to others. The word itself is communication; it already has an intrinsic value. Before it communicates this or that to another, it has established an interpersonal relationship, be it one of rejection, indifference, or openness. Thus the word is primarily the person himself or herself as communion and communication, as thought, reflection, and self-awareness.[33] From this perspective, one can say with complete justification that there is no thought without words. Not without reason did the Greek *Logos* mean both words and thought.

When we pray, we are being a word for God; that is, we are in a relationship of dialogue, openness, self-giving, and love. It makes little difference what one says to God—whether one's prayers are beautiful and rich in theological content, or merely repetitions of an ejaculation like "My Jesus, mercy." The dialogic relationship, the position one is situated in, already puts one in touch with God. From this perspective, one can see the inconsistency of many critics who oppose prayer forms. What is important is not the prayer but the praying. Praying can express an intimate relationship with God even in using impoverished verbal expressions or ones monotonously repeated.

In saying this we do not want to play down the criticisms mentioned at the beginning of this chapter. We simply want to delimit the problem properly. The word does not exclusively possess, as its primary or fundamental value, interpersonal communion. It is also a means for communicating and for understanding this or that thing. Thus it serves to unify norms, data, and people's interests, but not people themselves. Prayer forms arise within these limits, and are adequate or inadequate insofar as they adequately or inadequately express theological ideas and concepts of God, Jesus, the Church, grace, salvation, and communion with God. It may well happen that some formulas are objectively erroneous in what they say, and are not conducive to the search for God of one who prays. Other forms can objectify God in such a way that he becomes an idol, or depict him as if he were an object among other objects. God himself cannot be objectified; thus we cannot speak about God as if it were possible to stand above him and look down and describe him. We can speak only from, or starting with, God. If we do not remain in awe of his reality and, despite this, still dare to speak to him, we become atheists, even though we always have his name on our lips. But if we speak touched by him, then our word and language are the word and language of prayer, signifying and expressing a trusting self-giving, a humble search, an openness full of awe and sincerity at the same time.

A word spoken as a prayer can facilitate our communion with God, express it, or even bring it into being. Here we touch on a problem that is crucial to understanding prayer forms: every form has a basic, twofold aspect.

First, a prayer form can express objectively (and thus imperfectly) our inner religious experience and our living out of the divine reality, embodying it excellently. We know the classic prayers, deeply and essentially rooted in the awesome and numinous mystery of God, examples of which can be found in many prayerbooks already published. Such prayers transcend their age. They can be recited and meditated on endlessly. Their contact with the mystery makes them transparent; they communicate and create immediate communion. There are others, certainly the vast majority, in which one experiences the concerns and expressions of a particular historical period. They may beautifully express a generation, but they die with the generation that used them. Such prayers reveal their authors and say much more about them than about God.

Second, prayer forms have an evocative power. They do not reveal their author; thus they help raise to God the one who prays. Reciting the formula, grasping its content, the person is raised above the prayer's objective contents to the ineffable, the mystery of God which cannot be captured in any formula. The formula, then, makes us remember not the human author, but God himself. There can also be prayers that are so self-conscious that they cannot raise us to God.

We can thus say that all prayer forms have a symbolic (unitive) and a diabolic (divisive) character. The Greek *synballein* means to unify or to join together; thus a formula reveals a symbolic character when it helps the person to be raised to God, to be unified in the self, to make the self totally open to God as a son or daughter. The form reveals its diabolic character when it objectifies God or makes us think more about its human author and human things, dividing us and separating us from God. The Greek *diaballein* means to separate or divide.

The important thing is to try constantly to transcend the formulas in order to unite ourselves immediately and intimately with the divine. We may never be able to live without formulas, but we can never be satisfied with them. We will always be on a journey, involved in a process of expressing the inexpressible, of touching the inaccessible, of wanting to experience him who transcends all our feelings. This is our condition as pilgrims, who see God and definitive, divine realities as in a mirror and through signs (1 Co. 13:12). We cannot get out of that situation; we must accept it joyfully in all its limitations and in its symbolic and diabolic ambiguity.

Community: The Formula Creating the "We" of Faith

Word has two basic meanings: pure self-communication, and a way to communicate ideas and things to other people. This raises the problem of community and community prayer.

Every word presupposes, and creates, community. The universe of discourse embraces the world of people and things and forms a living linguistic community. The personality has a social structure because it is word and language. The human community is not merely the sum of the individuals. It is something richer, something rooted in the structure of the person, which is defined as being-for-others or being-with-others. Community exists or comes about only when we encounter people and not merely individuals.

Thus all personal prayer is already, in some way, community prayer. If it were not personal, it would not be communitarian. The structure of the human person that a priori provides the basis for community prayer is debated or denied by many people today. Be that as it may, the person is by nature a "being-with"; thus the person's prayer will take on the character of "prayer-with," community prayer, which is far more than the synchronization of individuals' prayers. Through that prayer we express our solidarity with God and our solidarity in the one faith. That prayer can also be the expression of our poverty or abundance, or of our seeking and our finding. Thus the Creed is one of the preeminent forms of community prayer. In it and through it we each proclaim aloud, for the benefit of each other and of all, the wonders God works for us and our response to his offer of salvation.

The real crisis in community prayer, especially liturgical prayer, is above all with the forms themselves, their rigidity, and their juridical character. Here we must be really courageous: the formula that can no longer express our "we" as believers, thus doing violence to the community, must be abandoned so that its diabolic character does not destroy its symbolic character, which creates community. This is the area that demands creativity. New forms should express the sensibilities of today's faith, concerns, and common beliefs. These forms should have an objective and flexible character so they can be recited by everyone without difficulty. Nothing is more unsuited to, and even destructive to, community prayer than the excessive subjectivism or conceit of the one who revises community prayers.

Within this context, let us make another observation. Perhaps today we should make a special effort to reevaluate individual and collective silence, which is punctuated by brief, incisive thoughts. This is needed because of the danger of the mechanization and objectification of formulas that can destroy prayer as a personal and collective encounter with God. Thus we should combine fixed prayers with periods of reflection and other activities that allow the words to be digested and understood in their effect on our daily lives. There are religious communities here and abroad where the recitation of the Divine Office is accompanied by meditative pauses.

Prayers should be short and simple, in the style of Jesus, without a pompousness that makes God laugh. In preference to many words (Mt. 6:7–8), God wants our humble hearts and the complete, unconditional surrender of ourselves. In general this cannot be adequately expressed in formulas without violating the intimacy of each person's mystery. This is where silence, out of which every creative word is born, shows itself to be a better form of communication and a better attitude of prayerfulness.

Celebrations and Prayer: The Nature of the Profane and Sacral Person

The preeminent form of community prayer is realized in the sacred, liturgical celebration. In this celebration the world of secularization is interwoven with the sacral world, the mythic in each of us with the secularized.[34] The celebration can be restricted to neither of these dimensions: each time the celebration takes place the person responds with a great "yes" to the whole of life and finds the opportunity to express it.

The celebration suspends the daily routine and clock time. It is a participation in eternity; thus, when we truly celebrate, we do not feel time passing. The celebration also has no goal or purpose. In it we do not come together in order to be taught by or to learn from others, but only to rejoice together, to be-with-one-another in harmony, friendship, and love. The celebration reconciles everything and for a short time creates a paradisiacal or eschatological world, a *mundus reconciliatus*. Plato phrased it that the gods made celebrations because "we need to breathe a little."[35] The Psalms affirm, "This is the day the Lord has made" (117:24).

The celebration is a human thing, but both its sacred and profane motivations seem to be a gift that no longer depends on us and cannot be manipulated. People can prepare themselves to celebrate, but the aura or spirit that pervades the celebration and enlivens it—its festivity — arises freely or gratuitously. No one can foresee it or produce it. We can only prepare ourselves interiorly and externally.

Among the exterior preparations are festal garb, music, and dance; among the interior, fasting, penance, and purification. Yet where does the joy or festivity come from? Nietzsche put it well: "In order for people to rejoice over something, they must say to everything, 'You are welcomed!' "[36] In other words, in order to rejoice, and thus to celebrate, we must be able to say "yes" to everything. "If we could say 'yes' to each moment, then we would be saying 'yes' not only to ourselves but to all of life."[37] This "yes" we say to life is already implicit through our daily work, our concern for our family and our community and for the common wellbeing of all.

The celebration is a privileged moment in which the hidden meaning of life springs forth incarnate and concrete. From the celebration we go forth better able to face the daily routine and other demands of living. We live in an environment inimical to faith, experiencing the challenges life presents to our religious convictions, hearing the endless debates about Christianity and its historical forms, and worried over the questioning in our own hearts. But on our feast days we celebrate the joy of our faith without doubts or questions, and we celebrate along with our brothers and sisters who profess the same creed, hear the same word, love the same Father, and feel at home in the same maternal womb of the Church.[38] The fixed formulas and the liturgical rituals free us from the need of having to express our personal faith in formulas acceptable and intelligible to others. In this way, free of worry, we can enjoy the happiness of our faith together with the whole community as we celebrate the feast.

In such celebrations we notice how the theology, which sensationalistically celebrates the death of God, is only the tragic symptom that society is saturated with material concerns and has already lost its ability to rejoice and delight in the goodness of life and of work, of the sun and the stars, of the oceans and the mountains, of the look of a child, of the caresses between lovers, of the joy of the celibate or virgin, and, finally, of the mystery (which is not a puzzle) whose presence in daily life the feast celebrates. Nietzsche well understood the essential truth of Christianity that is concealed in the many diabolic elements of our religious culture. He reflected on how the loss of joviality, that is, of divine grace (*jovial* is derived from Jupiter or Jove), is the basic consequence of the death of God.[39] By losing joviality, the vast majority of our culture has become incapable of celebrating. It certainly knows frivolity, gluttony, the popular feasts organized and directed by those who exploit consumers; but it has lost the joy or delight of the feast that makes us truly aware of the meaning of human life.[40]

The celebration, if it is to be experienced as something different from the ordinary or routine, must be properly prepared for both interiorly and exteriorly. We still have celebrations, and yet, because they are poorly or not at all prepared for, few people experience their festivity. These celebrations fail to be privileged moments or means to renew the rest of life.

Prayer and Ritual: A Forgotten Reality

Ritual is undoubtedly essential to a celebration. Celebration is not possible without it, because we always live in a symbolic world. Eating and drinking at a celebration are not intended to curb hunger or thirst—rather they are symbols of friendship and of delight at our being together. Singing is not an attempt at an artistic performance, but the expression of joy over our common friendship.

> "What is ritual?" the Little Prince asked the fox he had captured. "It is something much neglected," the fox answered. "It is what makes some days different from others, one hour different from all others. There is, for example, a ritual among the hunters. On Thursday they dance with the girls of the village. Thursday is a wonderful day! I go walking even as far as the vineyard. If the hunters danced on any day they chose, every day would be the same and I'd never get a vacation."[41]

Ritual, then, is what makes the feast day different from other days. But it only has expressive power when it translates or embodies the interior anticipation and preparation of the person. The fox, after the Little Prince captures him (the captor is always responsible for what he captures), advises:

> "You would do better to come always at the same time. If you come, for example, at four in the afternoon, I will start to feel happy at three. As the time passes I will feel happier and happier. By four I will already be jumpy and excited. Thus I will learn the value of happiness! But if you come at any time whatsoever, I will never know to prepare my heart. . . . Rituals are necessary."[42]

Only with preparation can there be a celebration, because then everything loses its natural qualities in order to take on symbolic and deeply human values. Things lose their purpose, become useless, in order to acquire their true meanings. The noise of footsteps (purpose) will not scare the fox, but will be like music, calling to mind that the Little Prince is coming (meaning). The wheat fields do not make the fox think of bread (purpose) but of the Little Prince's golden hair (meaning).[43]

Prayer, especially community prayer, should live joined with ritual, gesture, or symbol. These generally are more expressive and profound than words, which are the "source of misunderstandings" as the Little Prince tells the fox. The reason for this is that every symbol or ritual springs from the depths of the unconscious and translates it into a more suitable or more intimate form. Even the most secularized person is mythic, insofar as this word indicates the ritualistic and the symbolic: when we want to express who we really are or to express our love, friendship, joy, or sorrow, the mystery of our person, we do not use cold concepts, but images and metaphors. We recite histories and tell stories. Only these things communicate mystery without violating it. Something similar is involved in prayer and ritual.

Prayer, Play, and Humor: The Person as God's Plaything

In its symbolic and ritualistic aspects, prayer must contain a large element of play. Play has no practical goal, and yet has a profound meaning, as Romano Guardini[44] and, before him, the stern Thomas Aquinas,[45] saw very well. In the Greek and Latin Fathers, there is the theme of the *Deus ludens* (the God who plays), the *Ecclesia ludens, homo ludens,* and the cosmic dance.[46]

Some have seen creation as the work of God at play: God did not make the world because he needed it. It is a creation of his generosity flowing out of a loving fantasy. He made it to delight him, so that the world would be the *theatrum gloria Dei* (the playhouse of God's glory).[47] St. Gregory Nazianzus (died 390) wrote in one of his poems: "The sublime *Logos* plays. With vivid imagination he adorns and embellishes the entire cosmos in every way."[48]

Plato wrote, "The human being is the plaything of God. And this is the greatest praise that can be bestowed."[49] This is true because the plaything is the work of the creative imagination, of generosity, of a world free of pragmatic goals, free of profit motives, parochial interests, and special privileges. God has no practical goal; he is our absolute and eternal meaning. We have been invited to participate in God. "For God to be really at play, the person must be really at play," as Hugo Rahner, one of the finest theologians of our century, said.[50]

Such reflections attempt to show the serenity and joyfulness of the Christian concept of prayer. To pray is never to negotiate with God, since, before we ever ask him anything, he knows our needs. To pray is to open ourselves in praise, thanksgiving, and gratitude to God who created everything with such goodness and love. Christian prayer is thus always accompanied by a note of humor.[51] To have humor is to share in God's playing; it is to make life less dramatic, to be able to laugh at oneself even at the most serious moments. To pray with total seriousness is to know that everything besides God is relative—starting with our prayer forms—and that, even before we open ourselves to God, he has already come to us and directed our words.

A Christian philosopher wrote,

> As heretical as it may seem, the secret essence of humor lies in the power or capability of the religious attitude. Humor sees human and divine things in their insufficiency before God.[52]

The praying Christian is not anxious. He or she knows that the important thing is that we pray; what we pray is secondary. To this secondary level belongs our concern, at times neurotic, for the beauty and content of the formulas.

The Time and Place for Prayer in the Secular World

In the secular world where we spend most of our time, except for our sacred moments, devotional prayer is almost always carried out in the midst of the bustle of the world, for example, while traveling. Long hours of travel create an environment for most authentic prayer: there is silence, space, and calm. The long prayers of Antoine de Saint-Exupêry flying alone in his plane are well-known. I myself have a friend who read complicated exegetical works when he traveled by train or bus. Another used to read the Spanish mystics in the same circumstances. The speed characteristic of our times can bring concentration. The spiritual writer Jean Leclercq tells of a man who said he always used to sing "hymns and spiritual songs" while driving his car.[53] Do we not often sing hymns and psalms while we travel? And do they not ring out with a strange poignancy in a Datsun in the midst of the secular city? Traveling or walking alone often gives rise to free, spontaneous prayers and meditations on the mystery that is God and the human person.

For the person who maintains an attitude of prayerfulness, each moment can be transformed into an explicit prayer by anything whatever, as we can see in the young lay mystic Gabriela Bossis.[54] She traveled across countries and continents. She died in an accident as a young woman. Her spiritual diary is full of prayers written on boats, in train stations, in a cafeteria, in the foyer of a hotel restaurant, in a dentist's office, on the street, anywhere. We do not have to leave our world to meet God. It is sufficient to be quiet and try to recollect ourselves. God can, and will, surprise us with his coming. Moreover, we should not waste any opportunity, since God comes only once on each occasion.

Prayer is like love. It is an art. A person is always learning and never succeeds in learning enough, because prayer is looking for God, talking to him, being united with him. God is a mystery, not a puzzle, always capable of being known and loved more and more intensely and personally.

After all is said and done, perhaps each of us must experience what Dag Hammarskjöld, secretary general of the United Nations, wrote a month before his death in the Congo in 1961:

> Thou
> Whom I do not know
> But Whose I am.
> Thou
> Whom I do not comprehend
> But Who has consecrated me
> To my fate
> Thou—[55]

4

The Mission

By confronting what is different from itself, religious life succeeds most easily in discovering its own identity. Religious life cannot remain indifferent in the face of the challenges that come to it from the poor and marginated, since the call of Christ, who wanted to be identified with the poor and humble, is what gives it impetus. Thus religious life has an inescapable mission of solidarity and commitment to the process of liberation and human progress.

In an undeniably classist society such as ours, toward which side does the institution of religious life lean? What is our testimony and to whom is it directed? Such questions, given the experience of religious life in Latin America, imply demands for radical conversion and a concomitant recapturing of a spirit more in keeping with the Gospel and more suited to the Beatitudes.

There is a time to talk about flowers. But there is also a time, such as the one in which we now live, in which it is necessary to speak of the exploited florist who looks for someone to join him in his attempt to begin a process of liberation. How can religious help him? It certainly should not be done haphazardly, but out of a sense of one's own identity. The chapters that follow try to orient a response in the light of the Gospels, heard and discerned in the yearning of our brothers and sisters for liberation.

9

Underdevelopment, Liberation, Evangelization, and Religious Life

Underdevelopment, liberation, evangelization, and religious life are four catchwords, each of which contains a host of theoretical and practical problems.[1] Our study is oriented in two directions.

First, we will try to relate the problems in all these areas in the light of one of them, religious life. The theme then sounds like this: How does religious life cooperate in the evangelization of a world which is aware of its underdeveloped state and which has already begun a process of true liberation? What should religious life be like and what form should its evangelization take?

Second, we will apply our initial observations to our concrete situation. In such a way we will avoid treating themes in idealistic and universal terms as though they are valid in all situations. We cannot theologize about a textbook reality divorced from the real world without ending in an ideological posture that no longer respects or regards history.[2]

Our first endeavor, to relate the problems, demands that we analyze and interpret the concrete situation of underdevelopment. This raises the question of the autonomy of a socio-analytical interpretation of phenomena and its proper method. Although faith may be part of the interpretive criteria used in the social analysis, it still is not the place where that analysis starts. One must rather respect the legitimate autonomy of the analysis. Faith, however, does enter into the choice of the type of analysis to be used. We should choose the one that has the greatest scientific validity, but that also best detects the inhuman and unjust structures operative in the system being analyzed, and that best expresses the aspirations to greater participation, justice, and freedom. Thus faith is better taken into account in light of the demands it makes, in its proper context, on society and the forms of social organization. Thus we must interpret theologically the sociological analysis.

Adopting a predetermined analysis of underdevelopment postulates a process of liberation as the solution to that problem. The process of liberation implies a revolutionary posture in the original sense of that word—it does not necessarily imply the use of violence—inasmuch as it pursues not the betterment of a system of underdevelopment—a reform—but the overcoming of that system.[3]

Our reflections on the process of liberation, which we propose as a remedy for underdevelopment, are not merely descriptive. They are action-oriented and appeal for a liberating program of action. This does not mean that liberation is already being carried out, or that awareness of liberation on the part of religious has made liberation the model that orients religious life's efforts toward evangelization. Nevertheless, we believe that it is through a process of liberation that one achieves the future desired by the most conscientious elements of our society. We also believe that the process of liberation best responds to the demands of both the Gospel and humanity for greater justice, participation, and freedom.

Religious life is called upon to incarnate itself in the underdeveloped world in which it lives.[4] Its incarnation must be like Christ's: it must not canonize the situation, but critically probe its roots and purify it. While we focus on the problem of evangelization within the concrete situation of underdevelopment, and while we focus on the need for liberation from the perspective of religious life, we must do so from one previously known and already defined factor: religious life. Religious life finds its identity only by confronting what is not itself; by being challenged and accepting the challenge, religious life arrives at its mission.

Religious life in Latin America, and particularly in Brazil, must define itself out of its missionary and prophetic commitment to the concrete situation in which it exists. We do not know a priori what religious life should be in that situation. The basic reference points of religious life (such as the experience of God in Jesus Christ through a functional charism, the total, public consecration to God and one's brothers and sisters, expressed historically by the three vows) will only be effective when incarnated in a life rooted in the concrete life of a people from whom it derives its vitality and to whom religious give the concrete witness they must give in the name of the Gospel.[5] The relationship between religious life and the situation is dialectical: religious life reflects the situation, takes it on and transforms it, while the situation is influenced by, and even determined by, the presence of religious life.

Methodologically our reflections are based on the liberation theology begun at Medellin, which represents a special way of constructing a theology and not a special theological theme.[6] The method begins with discovering a reality by using scientific research. It proceeds to interpret the data from the sociological analysis theologically. It then determines avenues to approach the practice of faith in ways responding to the problems that have been discovered. Its accent is not on the correct understanding of faith and of reality (orthodoxy), but on the needed transformation of reality and the practice of faith (orthopraxis). What leads one to modify a situation is not new convictions, nor simply a deeper and more real picture of reality, but new, effective attitudes born of a structural evaluation of the situation.

The Challenges of the Real Situation: The Socio-Analytical Interpretation

The Problem of Underdevelopment and Its Consequences

We are not trying here, even briefly, to make a sociological analysis of underdevelopment. We are accepting a type of interpretation which, despite its criticisms and its internal limitations, has proven to be more illuminating than any previous one: the theory of dependence.[7] According to this theory, underdevelopment cannot be adequately explained as a technological lag in a society with outmoded, premodern structures of production and consumption.

Underdevelopment is interpreted as a global, dialectical process that results from the capitalist system which has been established in the West over the past four centuries. In this system, a center arises which is highly developed in the areas of science, technology, and social well-being at the expense of peripheral areas from which cheap raw materials are extracted. The periphery takes on a dependent status in all areas of its life.

Development and underdevelopment are two sides of the same coin. And yet they are not interdependent relationships, but reflect the real dependence of the satellite or tributary nations on the great metropolitan centers.

From this point of view it seems evident that underdevelopment is not self-caused. Its cause lies in the development of the leading countries of the rich Northern Hemisphere. These countries and societies exist for their own sake; their dependencies are societies that exist for the sake of others.[8] The system of underdevelopment can be marked by a tremendous economic and social development, yet the structure of dependence is preserved. The countries in question thus remain underdeveloped. The structural relationships are those of oppressor and oppressed.

From their very beginnings Latin America and Brazil have lived in a state of dependence under successive centers of hegemony: first Spain and Portugal, then England, now the United States.[9] This dependence was embodied in every basic area of life: the political, economic, social, and labor systems. Among the many consequences of this system we will mention only the following four.

Dependence and Domination

The satellite nations enjoy a relative autonomy, since they find a place in the worldwide system. Yet they are not allowed to be self-determining or self-sufficient in responding to the aspirations of their people and their cultural values. Their principal values are imported.

Oppression

The oppressors succeed in inculcating into the oppressed their technique of domination, their economic policies, and their understanding of the human person. Their dependents, even before they know it, see in the oppressor the ideal of the person and of the society they aspire to. In this way oppression is internalized, keeping the oppressed submissive and "in their place" in the system. "To the oppressors, the others' self-awareness and humanization are not considered to be the search for human fulfillment, but to be subversion."[10] This explains the surprising serenity with which the central powers and their allies violently suppress those who question the system, believing them to be disturbing the established order, which they consider "just, natural, and human."

Margination

We must correctly understand that the satellite countries and their populations that are considered marginated are not on the fringes of the system. They are inside it. Yet they are being exploited and not being allowed to share in the benefits they are helping to produce. In Brazil, for example, the adopted model, publicly proclaimed by the official powers who are proud of their choice, is neocapitalism or free commerce. True, it allows great economic development, but at the expense of social justice, since only 5% of the nation's people reap the benefits. The result is margination, not in regard to the system (which would seem logical), but in regard to human values: dignity, participation, individual and social freedoms, honest labor. In terms of buying power, 56% of the people are on the verge of absolute margination, and 75% are considered relatively marginated. In the ten years between 1960 and 1970, the wealthy increased their wealth by 8% while the poverty of the poor increased 11%.[11] Behind these cold, hard facts there is a poorly concealed drama of hunger, misery, the breakdown of the family, hopelessness, and so on, which such a situation implies.

The Culture of Silence

The culture of silence originates in the different ways of being, thinking, expressing oneself, and organizing political and economic life within the dependent regime. "Being silent is not to have an authentic word to speak, but instead following the prescriptions of those who speak or impose their voices. . . . The voice of dependent societies is no more than the echo of the voice of the metropolitan centers."[12] The cultural ethos, such as that lived in Brazil, imposed in its schools and promoted by the communications media, is not a living font of life, but the pitiful reflection of one. It is not born, nurtured, and matured here, but in the imperial centers from which it is transplanted to the satellite nations.

Center and periphery, two aspects of the same reality or system, are not only a sociological reality, but are also a result of a particular way of understanding the human person and human life.[13] Since the dawn of the modern age in the sixteenth century, people have understood the task of life to be acquisition of knowledge and power in regard to reality—be it nature, humanity, or the life of God.

The overwhelming drive of acquisitiveness within the human person engendered the capitalistic tenet of private ownership of the means of production and an inordinate desire to amass wealth. The result was social inequalities and the concentration of power in the hands of the few to the detriment of the many, who became dependent on the minority. Such a way of living seems to have reached its peak today, or even to be going beyond the limits of its historical possibilities. Awareness of its limits and its imminent day of reckoning leads to a generalized crisis. Capitalism can only continue to impose itself and create the consciousness needed for collective consent through violence. There are foreshadowings that a new way of living is being conceived, probably one more oriented toward socialization and toward greater communication and harmony among people and between people and nature.

The Church in This Context

The Church is undoubtedly an important cog in the Western social order. It has had, and continues to have, undeniable merit and great value. It has always been embedded unwillingly in the imperial system of dependence and margination. It was the Church that planted the faith and kept it alive throughout South America.

Yet structurally the Church was the partner in domination and the accomplice in oppression. Remember that we are saying "structurally," and not "intentionally" or "consciously." Subjectively the Church was, and will always be, against all forms of violence between people or of one society toward another. Yet, in carrying out its historical function, and with the power and social prestige its strong institutions provided, the Church has been more on the side of the forces of domination than those of liberation. Faith and empire constituted a single concern.[14] Evangelization was carried out according to the models of the Post-Tridentine Church (opposed to reform and militant) of the Iberian peninsula, and was strongly affected by the struggles with the Moors. Missionary activity was a crusade; the Indian was an infidel to be subjugated and converted.[15] Helder Cámara could justly confess in Rome in 1974:

> Without judging the bishops and priests who have gone before us in both Latin America and the rich nations, we must recognize that, in general, we were, and to some extent still are, in some way concerned with upholding the governmental authority and the social order. Thus we could never discover that the so-called "social order" was, above all, a stratified disorder.[16]

The way power and the means of participation were distributed in the Church, totally centered in the hierarchy and virtually excluding the People of God from the creation and promotion of religious values, helped to augment the culture of silence even more. The never-criticized, but very criticizable way the Church lived and proclaimed such Gospel values as obedience, humility, law, and authority favored the established powers, rather than calling into question their human and religious quality. Respect, order, discipline, submission, and obedience were the great virtues Christians were told to practice. Freedom, personal growth, objective and critical evaluation, creativity, were considered Protestant values, suspected of being subversive to order and tradition. Structurally, the Church, instead of being the salt in society, was vinegar. It helped to operate the very machinery of power it found fault with.[17]

Religious life shared the fate of the Church. Controlled by the hierarchy, it could live out its prophetic and eschatological role only within predetermined limits. The history of Latin America and Brazil cannot be written without being, at the same time, the history of religious life on that continent.

Despite its great merit, past and present, the education religious life provided was in how to be integrated into the larger society rather than into a global process of reform or criticism of the prevailing social system. Structurally—not intentionally—religious life favored the privileged classes. It was supposedly nonpolitical; that very fact indicated real political pressure not to question the status quo. This attitude was, and is, very political, in favoring the prevailing system which permits social injustice. Religious life was compromised by its very activity of healing: dedication to the poor, the illiterate, the disinherited. The lack of effective criticism within religious life naively cooperated in the means used by society, and the Church itself, to maintain order.

The Project of Liberation

Confronted with the situation of underdevelopment, liberal or rebellious thought called for a process of liberation that would break the bondage of dependence and allow countries to determine their own destinies as autonomous entities and with their own, self-sustained national projects. Liberation is the opposite of dependence. It is the arduous process of setting free captive people. Through the process the nation is freed from oppressive dependence and for independent development that bears the imprint of that nation.

This liberation or emancipation is a project and a model. It says nothing about concrete strategy and tactics, but it has a normative and, to some degree, utopian nature. The goal must be worked toward, realizing that the objective conditions of history can still prevent the carrying out of such a project.

In order to be concretized, liberation, like any fundamental project, needs to take into account the historical viability and the scientific rationale of the project to see if it is possible. Liberation does not occur because of the act of will of a group or even of a whole nation. It presupposes objective conditions without which oppression would destroy it and be reinforced, retarding true liberation even further. "People cannot do more than the revolutions they have made."[18] Revolutions have objective laws and conditions that can be facilitated by groups but are not the result of acts of will demanded by a revolutionary ideology.

The concept of dependence clearly sees the goal of liberation, which must never be forgotten. In relation to the situation in Latin America and Brazil, liberation demands a utopian break with the imperial system, a break that, given the concrete situation, is totally nonviable. Yet this lack of historical viability must not make us give up or compromise the project of liberation. The project remains, and must always remain, since it objectively expresses destruction of the system of dependence. However, it must not be merely an ideal; steps must be taken to formulate a concrete plan of action involving tactics and strategy. Its remaining only as an ideal could be interpreted as a compromise with the system of dependence. But this is not so, as long as one maintains a liberating course of action.

In Latin America the imperialistic situation demands that changing the system be accomplished through changes in the system. This is the one viable way for liberation to be achieved. If the process does not continuously maintain a critical stance, or if it is not aware at each stage of its project of liberation (which demands the destruction of the system), it could become totally absorbed into the prevailing system of dependence.

The Church, on its part, has recognized the demand for liberation and has made it the center of its proclamation of the Gospel.[19] Medellin tried to interpret the condition of underdevelopment theologically. Liberation is not only a sociological category. The complete liberation Christianity has come to proclaim passes through partial, historical liberations, but is not the sum of these. These are rather historical forms of the presence of definitive and total liberation. As historical forms they are always incomplete, always open to something more that lies in God, who is complete and who completes—the Freedom which fulfills human freedom.

The Response of Faith: The Theological Interpretation of the Evidence

The socio-analytical data presented here with their own rationale must be interpreted theologically. Dependence, oppression, margination, and the culture of silence are phenomena detected by analysis, yet not merely that. They embody a structural injustice; they concretize the arrogant egoism of a small elite and imply great inhumanity. For Latin American theology it means, as the bishops saw at Medellin in 1968, that we live in a situation of social and structural evil, which offends God and his children.

In the widespread situation of underdevelopment, there is a theological meaning that intimately affects Christian faith, questions it, and causes it to act. The uncovering of dependence and oppression is not only a matter of analysis; it also demands denunciation. This situation contradicts the plan of God and his love, a plan of fraternal love and freedom, of justice and the participation of all.

Two questions are posed to the Church by this situation. First, how does it structurally participate in the origin of the situation, and go on participating in preserving such an evil system? By its way of being present in society, and by its way of proclaiming the Gospel message, as well as by its brand of Christian ethics, its preaching style, and the way it catechizes and administers the sacraments, to what extent is the Church upholding the status quo rather than questioning it and critically confronting it? The Church will probably pass through a phase of deep, purifying, and penitential self-criticism, which will bring about a conversion that means the search for a new identity and a new position in the social structure, one that no longer legitimates the powers of domination, but that identifies with the underprivileged classes.

The second question involves the search for a new Christian ethos, one that changes the practice of the faith so that it collaborates, out of its faith stance, with the process of liberation. The Church has undeniable social influence, and this is where the problem lies. Which side does this social influence favor? Does it favor the shaking off of all slavery and support those who want to do this, or does it work to improve the prevailing system of oppression from within? In Latin America, the Church has clearly chosen in favor of the poor and oppressed. Evangelization begins with them and their demands, and proceeds to other social classes in a loving way.[20]

The demand for a Christian faith practice that is more suited to the situation and more oriented toward its transformation has obliged theology to delve more deeply into the salvific aspect of political action. *Salvation* is a term that involves drawing everything together, and yet it cannot be realized without these partisan actions. Definitive, eschatological salvation comes about through historical liberations in all areas of human endeavor.[21] This allows Christian faith to identify the presence of the Gospel with those movements and activities that really bring about liberation, even when they are not explicitly Christian movements or are even inimical to Christianity.

The criterion of Christian authenticity is not that one has the word in the name of one's movement or party, but that the movement or party is really so. Thus it is clear that political theology deals not only with the political practices of Christians and the Church, but with all politics whether or not they have Christian characteristics. Theology can result in rationalizing—and turning into an ideology—the political activity of the Church, either that of the hierarchy or of lay movements. Political theology should be able to discover the Christian meaning even of a practice that calls itself "atheistic," since it is the reality and not the label that is important.

By its presence in the liberation process, faith should continue explicating the meaning that such categories as the Kingdom of God, eschatology, grace, sin, and redemption have for the people and for politics. For its part, religious life must continue to reexamine the basic values in its life-project, such as the experience of God in the following of Christ, consecration, vows, and asceticism, and try to discover the meaning these concepts have for people and politics. We will spell this out further later on.

Yet the Church is not master of the situation. Its commitment to the progressive liberation of society is lived out and concretized in circumstances that are not its free choice but that are imposed on it by the established powers. The empire keeps on balancing off its internal contradictions, achieving its chief objectives, and thus assuring that the system will go on. The Church, like the other liberation movements on the continent, must operate and incarnate itself in that society. Liberation does not occur with the wave of a magic wand, but emerges through a long process. The Church must take quiet steps to modify its own way of adapting to the dominant powers, always maintaining a living awareness of its conversion, based on the Gospel, to the poor and marginated.

Religious life also encounters tremendous obstacles in trying to find its place in the process of liberation. Both the Church and religious life, in order to ensure the effectiveness and value of their activity, must situate themselves critically in the oppressive situation. By the way they change the order, they will accomplish the transformation of the order. These changes will not come about without a keen sense of criticism and a firm understanding of the viability of the liberation project. It will often demand knowing how to wait, not passively, but actively, while continuing to work, like a person who acts cautiously and winds up realizing dreams which revolutionize everything.

The Evangelization Carried on by Religious Life

The condition of dependence that marks the real situation of Latin America and Brazil predetermines the direction evangelization must take.[22] It seeks to proclaim the Good News in a particular situation. To evangelize is not to proclaim a given set of responses to questions that must be answered, because evangelization is not mere indoctrination. It is basically an action, and every action in a given situation is an attempt to change the situation. Evangelization seeks to be a Christian response to questions posed by the real situation. Thus there is a close correlation between the nature of the reality and the nature of the Christian response.

Instead of trying to set up an abstract definition of what evangelization is and what the implications of the definition are, let us look at the evangelizing action of Jesus and the early Church.[23] Even today this remains a paradigm for the kind of evangelization religious life must carry on.

Evangelization: Living and Fighting for the Cause of Jesus

Jesus did not begin by preaching a doctrine about something. Nor did he begin his work of evangelization by proclaiming himself. He began by responding to the expectations of his people who lived "in eager longing" (Lk. 3:15). What was it they waited for in Jesus' time? They waited for the Kingdom, the in-breaking of a new heaven and a new earth, complete liberation, the saving intervention of God.[24] He responded to these expectations in the name of God. "The time is fulfilled and the Kingdom of God is near. Repent and believe the Good News" (Mk. 1:15).

The Gospel, the Good News, is not merely a proclamation. It is an intervention here and now, which changes the world and which can be proved: the blind see, the lame walk, the dead are raised, sins are forgiven, a new way of living is inaugurated, revealed in the actions of Jesus himself. Such events show that the Kingdom has come already (Lk. 7:22; Mt. 11:4) and thus is already in our midst (Lk. 17:21). With the coming of the Kingdom the power of the Evil One (in other words, whatever divides and creates enmity, whatever degrades the person and God) is being overcome.

Jesus' cause is the cause of the Kingdom. Jesus never spells out the meaning of the Kingdom. He assumes that people know what it means, not abstractly in clear-cut concepts, but as a complete reality that means something for them. The Kingdom is God's dominion over everything. When God manifests his power everything is changed: the world is transformed, people are freed, and the bonds of slavery become those of fraternal love. Justice, freedom, fellowship, love, mercy, reconciliation, peace, pardon, and intimacy with God are the causes Jesus fights for, and because of this he was persecuted, arrested, tortured, and sentenced to death. In order for the cause to continue, he rose from the dead and is always at the side of those who fight for the same things. Legalism in place of justice, discrimination in place of fraternity, laws instead of freedom, hatred instead of love for enemies, hardness of heart instead of mercy and compassion, vengeance instead of pardon, distance from God instead of intimacy make up a cause inimical to Jesus. Those who are for those things are against Jesus.

For this reason, all those, in any continent or nation, who work boldly for the triumph of justice are evangelizing, living the Gospel, and advancing the cause of Jesus Christ. It is not always where there is Christianity and explicit evangelization that true goodness, liberation, justice, and fellowship are to be found. But where fellowship, justice, and freedom are found, Christianity is truly incarnated and the Gospel is truly lived, even though anonymously or called by a different name. To evangelize is to live and fight for the cause of Christ.

The Gospel is not only a statement of fact: Salvation is already among you, the Kingdom has already come. It is also a command: Be converted. Without a conversion that affects our ways of thinking and living, the Kingdom does not come. The Kingdom does not come about by magic without human collaboration. If people do not want it, the Kingdom does not become present. God has chosen to rely on people's free cooperation. He prefers to postpone the in-breaking of the Kingdom rather than to impose it by force and coercion. Here is the hidden meaning of Christ's death: it was a consequence of human rejection.

Jesus did not want to use divine power to establish his Kingdom, violating human freedom. He preferred to die rather than do that.[25] In this way history failed to be open and to bring about the fulfillment of the project of the Kingdom. Even today we must take up the cause of Christ freely and carry it on willingly. Through such involvement the Kingdom will break into the world and renew the face of the earth. The transformation of the world in its awareness of God and of the demands of the Kingdom is not a theory, but a practice; that is, a process of conversion and liberation.

Evangelization: Living and Announcing Salvation and the Presence of Jesus the Liberator

With the rejection of Jesus, his cause remained unfinished, and thus became an ongoing task. Can we bring it about? Will the Kingdom come? Will it remain confined to a utopian realm? Are universal fellowship, freedom, justice and so on, not really values to be striven for, never to be fully realized or historified one day? Explicit evangelization (and therein lies the essence of Christianity) says: In Christ dead and risen the Kingdom has been completely fulfilled; in him true liberation even from death has been realized; in him the utopian has become the commonplace, the future present, the promise a reality.

The person does not live on ideas or abstract values. These ideas and values must be incarnated in a living experience of Jesus Christ, proclaimed by faith as the One who fulfilled human longings. Jesus is thus salvation made present. Not only is Jesus' cause proclaimed and fought for—the cause of all upright people in every age—but the realization of that cause is seen and lived in the person of the risen Christ. This is not proclaimed as a sublime ideology, which has more merit than the other ideologies that are put forth as interpretations of the human struggle. It is a sublime event that is proclaimed: through the resurrection of Jesus history was breached, and through it we can see complete, definitive liberation, the eschatological triumph of justice and freedom against all the mechanisms of injustice, vengeance, and oppression. The resurrection made it clear that the future belonged to the oppressed and to the victims of injustice, to the last of the world who will become the first. This can be seen because it was through One who was rejected and crucified that God chose to manifest the decisive action of history: the conquest of death, and, with it, of all the forces that allow or cause death—evil, disunity, sins against our brothers and sisters, injustice.[26]

The center of the Gospel is the positive picture inaugurated by the resurrection. The resurrection introduces a new conception of the world and makes it possible to live life and death, the meaning of the world and its realities, in a new way. As life is fostered, as interpersonal relationships become more and more fraternal, as every oppressive structure is being eliminated, the resurrection is progressing.

Thus the Gospel brings to all who accept it a commitment to the world, to the task of its transformation, to preparing for and advancing the resurrection. To live the Gospel and to make it live is to follow the path of Jesus, which culminates in his Passover. Following, and not merely theoretical contemplation, is what the Gospel commands. A liberating incarnation in the world, and not a denial or a flight from the world, is what the Gospel demands from us as a consequence of our following of Jesus.

From this perspective, the intimate connection between the liberation process and the work of evangelizing seems clear enough. The process of human liberation and progress, when it is carried out fully and in its proper way, is open to a transcendent, religious dimension. Evangelization makes that openness explicit, proclaiming God, Jesus, and his Kingdom as the ultimate meanings of all human activity and of the psychological and social process. On Mission Sunday, 1970, Paul VI reasoned this out very precisely:

> Between evangelization and progress there can be no relationship posed which excludes their coordination, complementarity and synthesis. . . . The basic problem simply amounts to the priority of their ends, as well as the priority of their intentions and responsibilities. It is undebatable that missionary activity is the primary end of evangelization, this priority being maintained both in the ideas that inspire it, and in the methods of organizing and carrying it out.[27]

Although distinct, the two are inseparable; both historical liberation and evangelization are grounded in the person, who must be saved not only at the end of time, but also along the path of his or her pilgrimage, anticipating the reality which will be realized in all its fullness at the end of time. Evangelization is a matter of converting eschatological truth into a meaning for all creation, and making it the center of its proclamation and hope. Salvation is not the result of historical liberations, but their fulfillment and transcendence.

The 1974 Synod of Bishops recognized this.

> We are in deep accord in reaffirming the intimate connection between the work of evangelization and the liberation spoken of. This accord has been reached not only from the close relationship between our faithful and the rest of humanity (whose life and destiny we share), but primarily from the Gospel which graciously has been entrusted to us and which is the Good News of salvation for everyone and every human society. This salvation must begin, and be manifested, here and now, in this world, even though it can only be fully realized beyond the bounds of time.[28]

Evangelization cannot be limited to the proclaiming of the Gospel. It must also be concerned with concretizing salvation in social and political areas. The resurrection is the sign par excellence, which prefigures and manifests true liberation. This is precisely why it constitutes the definitive salvific act according to Christian faith.

In light of this supreme fact of our faith—the resurrection—the other beliefs that make up the essence of our faith have been expounded: the divine sonship of Jesus, the Trinity as the transcendent ground for the Christ event and for all creation, the permanency of Christian hope in history through word and sacrament, lived in the Church as a united community of believers, and so on. Such beliefs, before becoming doctrinal formulas, were lived faith experiences that sprang from practice. In the context of being practiced, they took on meaning and came to shed light on our concrete existence.

The Church, express or explicit (but not exclusive) bearer of the Kingdom, did not always understand its mission as being eschatological salt within society. On occasion it gave legitimacy to historical situations, which were not always faithful to the Gospel. It was an organizing principle in society, and yet the fact of medieval society's being organized by the

Church did not ipso facto mean the triumph of the Gospel, or automatically create the beginning of a new type of relationship among people that was more just and fraternal.

Christianity, and the evangelization that expresses it, demand a conversion and the formation of new attitudes of all kinds toward reality. All orthodoxy and the formation of a Christian awareness are at the service of that ideal.

Evangelizing by Religious Life: Radicalization of the Way of Being Christian

Religious life does not arise from the hierarchical structure of the Church, but from the same soil as the Church does. Religious life extends and radicalizes the baptismal commitment. Religious are to be more radical Christians, in the sense of trying to live the life and holiness of the Church in all its radicalness. To the Church and the world, religious propose to be (in the words of Paul VI) specialists of God, but not specialists who have a lot of knowledge about God and can talk about him learnedly. They are specialists in the sense of experiencing God more vividly in the following of Christ and making that experience the basis for their life-project.[29]

The more transparent and radical this living religiously succeeds in being, the greater evangelizing effect it will have. It is not because religious do a certain number of things or aid different works; the religious' main work is himself or herself.[30] The conversion and the authenticity of religious speak for themselves, attesting to the truth of the Gospel. One's entire life becomes language, which proclaims and denounces to the extent that it is authentic and transparent. Thus, in order to evangelize, it is not necessary to use a catechetical approach, to be well-read in theology and the explanations of the mysteries of faith, nor to carry out a specific missionary work. The religious' own life is evangelizing by his or her special way of making God and Jesus the center of life. By evangelizing in this way, religious become signs or sacraments of the presence of God in the world around them.

It is not sufficient, however, just to say this. The real question is: In what sense does the religious become a sign to the surrounding world through his or her special way of being?

For that to truly happen, it is essential that one's participation in the situation be such that it can serve as a sign. Otherwise there is no evangelization by one's life. Thus, to evangelize in the context of Latin America and Brazil, religious must undergo a deep structural conversion in their lifestyle, in their apostolic work, and in their preaching. For the moment we will concentrate on lifestyle.

Faced with Political Oppression and Regimes of Dominance

Religious must avoid in their communities reflecting the social conventions and the distribution of power that occur in society. Traditionally religious life in community has been structured like a pyramid: the superior was the only one responsible for asking questions and for being creative. Obedience bound everyone to the superior.

In order to be a sign of freedom and not of domination, religious life must stress the responsibility of all members of the community. Being a superior is not a reality that can be exhausted by one's being a coordinator.[31] Each and every member must be able to consider himself or herself a superior to the extent that each is co-responsible for the common mission and project, which is truly a corporate project. The form of religious community should be transparent to the spirit of fraternal love, the participation of all, freedom in relationships instead of the subservience that is commonly found, mutual respect and not one member's using another. Religious life should be the testing ground for Christian freedom, for personal growth, for personal availability unhampered by a changeless, enslaving schedule. Such availability should not be for the greater convenience of the religious, but for the service of the brother or sister who seeks help or advice.

When viewed from the outside, religious life often appears strict, as stifling authentic living, bankrupt, and prey to numerous useless observances that are meant to occupy one's time rather than to nourish spiritual growth. Thus religious life has lost the effectiveness of its Gospel witness to liberation, its power to affirm a more radical life project of greater humanness in relation to other lifestyles.

Religious life cannot be a testing ground for Christian freedom unless religious first become aware of the real situation around them, of the actual mechanisms of injustice, of the existing forms of domination.[32] By their way of being free in word, action, and conscience, they are denouncing an unjust situation and living a more promising and efficacious alternative. Without a critical spirit, religious always run the risk of being swallowed up by the system and thus of becoming an unwitting cause of its legitimation.

In order to live this kind of witness, it is necessary to be constantly concerned about the Gospel motivation of religious life. The Gospel does not ask us to fit in nor for "conformity to this world" (Rm. 12:2), but for a critical spirit, quick to detect structural evil in society and able to discern the voice of God in the midst of human voices, which are more subtle today than before, masquerading as humanitarianism and religiously motivated goodness.

Faced with Misery, Injustice, and the Culture of Silence

Religious life will proclaim the Gospel by its lifestyle only when it succeeds in giving up its middle-class existence and converts itself to the poor, living like them, for them, and with them. Poverty should not be understood here as merely giving up material goods. This is basically a capitalistic concept (since it tends to define poverty in terms of material goods), and it hinders understanding the Gospel meaning of poverty, which is something deeper. Poverty is the ability to be in solidarity with the socially poor.[33]

Poverty is not a matter of simple asceticism, but of a real, interior and exterior self-emptying, of giving up certain thought categories that make it difficult to approach the poor, and giving up those goods that put us in the category of the secure and among the favored ones in the actual system of the distribution of goods. Giving up goods is not the first step. It must be the result of a change in attitude about solidarity with the poor and marginated. Giving up goods will also be in keeping with the extent of that solidarity: the less solidarity, the less the material poverty and the greater the obstacles that stand between these brothers and sisters and the sons and daughters of God. Such an attitude of solidarity and communion with the humiliated and exploited will denounce the injustice of the situation, making people alert to that fascination with power that the values of the system can arouse in people in whom the categories of domination, possession, and consumption of the dominant society have been inculcated.

Religious must root out all these middle-class thought categories that shaped their spirit through contact with school and society and that have succeeded in creating the real standard for evaluating reality. To appreciate the Gospel demands, which originate in the world of the oppressed and marginated, requires abandoning all those categories of interpretation. This can be achieved only by living with the poor and sharing their problems. More than ideas (which are generally secondary since they ordinarily originate from some experience), it is living that corrects life.

This solidarity with an oppressed people must make religious communities more open to the influence of popular culture, their forms of communication, of prayer, of piety, receiving from and contributing to its richness. By taking the position of the poor, religious are much better able to detect the real structure of the system that generates injustice and margination. The poor person is not poor, but impoverished. This is the consequence of unlawful gain; that is, it arises from a way of being related to goods that requires a whole social class to be impoverished so that some may be rich.

Only when one has plumbed the depths of this underworld spawned by the "world" will one be able to understand the anti-Gospel of our society and how contradictory is the pact made by the institutional Church and religious life with that society. The problem in overcoming this narcissistic and privatizing view is that we get caught up in considering the good will and good intentions of people, without ever getting to the deeper, structural level where the mechanisms of injustice originate. People, even those of good will, are at the mercy of the structure. To have a critical awareness is to put oneself in a position based on the Gospel in order to be able, from that position, to appreciate the difference between the level of structural injustice and the level of people who can be well-intentioned but naive.

In a widespread culture of silence, religious life is called upon to speak its words in holy freedom. The word is liberating within one's own community and liberating for those people who cannot speak without paying the consequences. Dialogue, dissemination of information, and constructive criticism are other ways of breaking with a regime that monopolizes words and authority.

The Gospel does not proclaim exaltation of the self, of wealth, power, sex, or buying power. An ideology favoring all these things is being constructed today by Western society, which has the impudence to consider itself the heir of the Christian faith experience. Religious life, bearing witness to the Gospel in its life project, must once more ground itself in the values of communion, participation, and freedom, of respect and fellowship, of the primacy of being over having. It is clear that religious life will thus live in a deep dialectical tension with contemporary society. Within this dialectic it must begin articulating a decisive negation, not with a reactionary spirit, but in order to make an act of love and freedom, which questions and criticizes, rejects and refuses all selfishness and all unbridled acquisitiveness, which is detrimental to the vast majority of people.[34]

Evangelizing by Religious Life: Reorienting Social Action

The evangelizing activity of religious life is not exhausted by the personal witness religious give through their special lifestyle. Religious life also makes itself present in the world through some kind of activity, embodied and sustained by institutions. The diverse charisms of founders are generally linked to certain apostolic works in society, such as schools, hospitals, or preaching. A problem appears here too, which we will now consider.

The Problem of Institutions

The problem of the kind of Gospel witness religious institutions give is a major one for evangelization. These institutions have been set up in order to make Christian love more effective and to give the Christian message a greater ability to transform society. We then must ask to what extent the institutions remain faithful to their original purpose, or to what extent they have been taken over by the established powers and converted, against the will of the religious involved, into devices for passing on the current ideology, which is very little, if at all, Gospel-oriented. How can we evangelize by means of these institutions today?

No one can deny that Catholic institutions in Latin America served as means of communicating the ideology of the ruling class, since, through them and thus in a Christian context, the leaders of society were educated. They were given a type of "Christian" formation that attempted the impossible task of reconciling a Gospel consciousness with the maintenance of slavery, subjugation of the Indians, and exploitation of the working class. Religion and evangelization were harmonized with an order that structurally maintained unjust and inhuman conditions.[35]

Such institutions persist today, but can they still carry out the same function? It is obvious that they must undergo a thorough reform, seriously asking themselves what kind of Gospel witness they give to the world.

Every institution has, to a lesser or greater degree, some kind of power. It must keep up with, and follow, the movement of history. This involves great sums of money, which basically depend on the graciousness of the government. Most religious institutions, especially Catholic colleges and universities, are no more than the fossil remains of a Catholic way of life. As models for faith in the world, such institutions are anachronistic and have definitely been superseded.[36] Thus their evangelizing witness is, in reality, irrelevant. By the very steps they must take to survive, they have become elitist, accessible only to the most privileged classes, and thus very submissive to the system and the ideological values it presents and encourages.

Such institutions generally cannot pass through the sieve of the Gospel. The criterion Jesus established for real service (service of other people, which is, at the same time, service of

God) is concern for the poor and abandoned. The rich man is not only asked to fulfill the Law—every Jew and every individual is asked to do that. He is also asked for a complete availability and openness, a total renouncement, in order to be united to the poor (Lk. 19:18–21). The Lord tells the Pharisee who asks who his neighbor is, the parable of the Good Samaritan, the Gentile who was the only one who took care of the injured man abandoned on the road. The neighbor is the one I am near, especially the poor and the oppressed, with whom the eternal judge identified himself (Mt. 25:45).

> If Church institutions are at the service of the liberation of the common people, fallen by the side of the road, beaten and robbed, it is a sign they are responding to the proclamation of the Gospel. If, however, they prefer the ruling classes, the power of the oppressor over the oppressed, of the rich over the poor, passing by indifferently like the priest and the Levite to the plight of the poor, it is a sign their light has been hidden under a table or a bushel basket so as not to blind the greedy vision of the rich, or that their leaven has been removed from the dough so as not to lessen the profits of the rich, or that their salt has become tasteless so as not to make bitter the tongues of those who cry "Lord, Lord" but do not fulfill the will of God. Such institutions have fallen into a phariseeism which, in its hypocrisy, does not incarnate the witness it preaches, and which is able "to cross land and sea to gain a single convert, and, once gotten, you make him fit for hell" (Mt. 23:15).[37]

It is not enough to point to the personal psychological and economic sacrifices great institutions demand. No one can deny that these institutions take a great deal of energy and imply constant abnegation on the part of their members. No one questions this. The question is whether these institutions structurally, and given the great power and authority they have, proclaim the Gospel or suppress it. In dealing with this question we cannot quiet our consciences by appealing to subjective factors, no matter how valid they might be. Let us repeat that we must ask about the nature of their *institutional* witness. Structurally, against the will of their members, are these institutions really more of a countersign than a sign of the Gospel?

Many religious have begun to see this contradiction. They have begun to appreciate that the poor must be evangelized through means accessible to the poor and that any means that becomes divorced from, and independent of, the good of people quickly becomes an end in itself. Such institutions need to be defended for their own sake; they need people to care for them; they enter into power and interest struggles. Power never relinquishes power of its own accord; it rather tries to maintain and extend its power and influence more and more. How difficult it is to encounter the Gospel in this, and how easy it is to discover in this the selfishness of human beings and their instinct for security. The Gospel becomes transparent only when there are no special interests, when the power, self-sufficiency, and wealth of the institutional means are not the primary concern.

From this viewpoint the good will of religious is absolutely not enough. The problem is not with their good will or sincerity, but with the place of religious life and its institutions in the social structure. Are they on the side of the privileged or on the side of the poor and marginated? The Lord had a choice and he chose the poor and humble. Religious, with a life project that follows Jesus Christ, cannot choose otherwise.

Institutional Reform

Confronted with reflections like these, many may experience qualms of conscience—this is not a bad sign. It is a good thing, placing the person in an attitude of obedience, of truly hearing the Gospel, of regarding the demands of the Gospel. Such an attitude is already initiating some reforms in institutions.

Yet genuine reform does not start by destroying everything the past has built. The Gospel does not dispense us from good sense or propose angelic ideals. It commands us to accept the contradictions of life responsibly, without adapting ourselves to them. It calls us back to a process through which we liberate ourselves and our activities from all darkness opposed to the Gospel in order to let the light born of the Gospel shine more and more. This is the real meaning of conversion.

We can be even more concrete. We have inherited from the past many outstanding institutions. We are not going to tear them down, since, if we do, we will have to answer to God and to other people. We will rather make ourselves aware of the contradiction to the Gospel which they embody and because of which we cannot blindly defend them. Nevertheless we will oblige ourselves to live with them with deep humility, with sacrifice, and even with a bad conscience, doing everything possible to purify them and make them recover their original Gospel meaning, since they were born of the desire to make Christian love more effective. Thus we must simplify them as much as possible, making them more and more functional. We must speak with complete clarity so we can eliminate the ambiguities that they have because they are institutions. We must always allow their Christian character to shine through by putting them in their proper context, not allowing any kind of power or special interest, symbolized by money, to be emphasized. We must understand how they constitute a way of being present in the world that we have inherited from the past, and for that reason they may not be models for the future. We must realize that, in initiating other works, we must never repeat that experience, which, even though it may have had a meaning for the Christian way of life in another time, would definitely be opposed to the Gospel today. Finally, we must see if we can pass the responsibilities discharged by these institutions on to the state, which has the right to provide for the public welfare. Within state-run institutions religious can bear much more visible witness to the truth of the Gospel without institutional ambiguities.

To a greater or lesser degree, and in all respects, we must try new forms of religious life that will suitably respond to changes in society and to the demands of the Christian conscience and of the mission of religious life toward new developments, always seeking to play a greater role in the lives of the humble. We live in a time of change, which does not yet allow us to see clearly what the form of institutional Gospel presence will ultimately be in the midst of the world. In any case we must make sure it will not be some kind of romantic return to the grand undertakings that sought to set up a Christian domain and a staunch Gospel presence, in a now-secularized world that is ideologically non-Christian.

Everything seems to indicate that such works would be taken over by the state or, by dint of having to maintain themselves, would become more and more elitist (which would compromise the Gospel witness) or give rise to a kind of Christian moral education, personal and private, akin to the ideology of the ruling class.

In conclusion we can affirm that religious life, in regard to its works, is called to live for the poor, with the poor, and like the poor. These are really three aspects of the same process of renunciation and following Christ.

It may well happen that, as heirs of a concept of religious life oriented toward the construction of great institutions, we cannot succeed right now in doing more than living for the poor. This would not be a small accomplishment. It amounts to reorienting the works to the advancement of the poor, works which up to now especially served the class that was more privileged and less committed to the Gospel.

Yet we cannot be content to remain there. It is urgent that we live with the poor, learning their worthiness to go forward; that we live marginated in order to detect the unjust structures and the anti-Christianity of the larger society. This will lead religious life to a commitment to liberation and poverty, not for the sake of wealth that would once more become oppressive, but for the sake of moderation in material goods and a way of possessing things that no longer discriminates or creates barriers between people, but that instead makes possible a dignified sharing in the benefits of culture and technology. This solidarity and this voluntary assuming of poverty according to the Gospel more convincingly evangelizes than any activity carried on by great institutions. It is a new practice. It is this that convinces and converts, not sophisticated and useless discourses of great theological precision about what evangelization is and how it should be carried on.

The result of this movement, by its process of radicalization, is to live like the poor. This identification is not, in our opinion, a simple act of will, but a charism from God. To give up not only the advantages of technological culture, but also those of study, of access to greater understanding of the world and the human person, sharing all the intellectual, social, and religious limitations of the poor, is a divine gift given to many in Latin America. Inspired simply by a deep love of God, they begin to live among the poor, like the poor, and for the poor, not only to take them out of poverty and better their lot, but also to learn from them how to take up the cross of life together with them, and thus to live the mystery of Christ's passion and save their own souls.

This experience, without any rationale to justify it and without any motive except God as encountered in the poor, may give us a perspective on wealth that only poverty can reveal. There is no social ill or structural injustice that can destroy any of the human, spiritual, religious, and mystical riches that are revealed among the poor and the humble of the world. These are the triumph of God's grace over the subtle forms of human sinfulness. The ability to appreciate riches like those hidden in poverty, to become poor so as to experience these riches, is a gift of God.

Commitment like this should not degenerate into a rationale that justifies poverty and social wretchedness; these things incarnate sinfulness and degrade God. Yet it is clear that, despite their being manifestations of sinfulness, they hide the presence of God, a presence it has been given to some to see, making them, as a result, sharers in that situation. This phenomenon, occurring to a greater or lesser degree throughout all Latin America, is beyond any ideology or concept of liberation; it is a manifestation of God's perfect freedom within the world, freedom that liberates our freedoms. It does not belittle our freedoms, but gives us what we are looking for and pursuing through our historical freedoms: freedom beyond poverty and wealth.

Evangelizing by Religious Life: Recovering the Gospel Freedom of the Word

The specific charism of religious life is prophetical and eschatological. Religious live out the Absolute they have encountered and to which they have consecrated themselves.

The experience of an Absolute allows us to put things in their proper perspective. It is not that things have no value, but that their values are controlled by the Absolute within history. Thus authentic religious who profoundly live their experience of God embrace the world as the place where they encounter God and where their encounter is shown to be real and efficacious.

Nevertheless, religious life is free in relation to the world, since it is not God. The eschatological does not cause a flight from the world, but a way of living within it that is characterized by the experience of an Absolute to which everything is related and in relation to which all is relative. Religious are situated in a dialectical position within the Church, committed to it, yet at the same time realizing that the Church itself is relative, a pilgrim on the way to God.

The Prophetic and Liberating Word

From its eschatological perspective it is easy to understand the prophetic mission of religious: to proclaim, by what they are and how they live in the world, the definitive reality of God and his Kingdom, and to denounce all fixed and absolute forms, especially those that oppose the plan of God through injustice and oppression. In their prophetic role, religious are not an extension of the institutional Church. Vatican II emphasized in *Lumen gentium* that religious life does not arise out of the hierarchical structure of the Church, but from its charismatic structure, or from its life and holiness.

By being situated in the charismatic dimension, religious life must not be locked into overly institutionalized structures. The institutional is based on a different logic than the charismatic. The institution needs security, certainty, and power. The charismatic, in order to be such, lives out of the truth, risks new roads, and presents its daring and valiant witness as its only power or value. Thus religious life is not called upon to give a predetermined type of organized and official pastoral aid. It enters into the pastoral effort, but with a sovereign freedom. It is called in its own way to make faith and the Good News present, usually in areas where the organized pastoral effort does not reach: in margination, in the secularized areas of our society, in the professions, for instance. This is how it works with the local Church, opening itself in a permanent way to the inescapable mission of that Church, the immense task that is never fulfilled in its entirety from within.[38]

Confronted with a culture of silence within society, and even within the Church itself, religious life should pledge itself to ransoming the imprisoned word. The word is held captive because it is not permitted to be communicated or to fulfill its communicative function, being used instead to transmit the myths of the power elite, myths that survive more or less consciously in the minds of religious who received the classical formation from orders and congregations. This formation defended the superiority of religious life over any other state in life—its special calling, its special virtues, its unique duty to represent people before God and to save their souls, its certain and orthodox knowledge. Yet all these things did not make religious life closer to the people, but only made it seem above and beyond them. The result was the myth of the inferiority of the lay vocation, of the ignorance of the laity, of their superstitions, of their bodily and intellectual impurity. It created a mind-set of a caste or an elite, full of good will, pitying the unhappiness of people, and thus coming to their aid—without any critical or structural insight that allowed religious to see the root of the problem. In this way they found themselves unwittingly buttressing and solidifying the existing system.

For the word to be free again, and for the Gospel message to continue to be the Gospel and not degenerate into an agent to pacify those who rebel against the injustices they suffer, or to silence the words spoken by their lives, religious must pass through a true Paschal experience.[39] They must die to their present mind-set and rise to letting themselves be, and speak for, people without a voice. This does not mean being ignorant but, at the most, untaught. It is not being uncultured; it is merely not having a middle-class culture. Those who know life, who create culture through their endeavors, are those who find meaning in life, perhaps through religiousness embodied in a mythical universe, which is as valid (as a mode of experience) as the scientific. Through their religiousness, often belittled by the official, elitist, clerical orthodoxy, these people have found the power and the strength to survive, to struggle, to keep on believing, working, and sacrificing themselves for their families. They have become strong in suffering in order to live a freedom that eludes the manipulations of their oppressors. This passage—or Passover—is a form of poverty that religious publicly profess to live.

People who involve themselves in the world of the common people begin to change; they become committed and converted. There are so many human and Gospel values a suffering people teaches through its own life. Thus the Greek fathers could aver: the poor are our teachers, the humble our sages. This sympathy with the poor and the oppressed, this love with which one loves others no matter how different they may be, that which one learns from them, letting them be without condemning them, brings religious to liberating action, making them attentive to the voices of the oppressed to whom religious have adapted themselves in order to speak their transforming word.

Religious life is already closely tied to the world by its work of evangelization, by the part it plays in the educational system with its great Catholic colleges and universities. Its choice in these situations is either to proclaim the Gospel of liberation or to reinforce the status quo. To proclaim the Gospel of liberation, it must critically articulate the content of the Christian faith in such a way that it reveals its power to point out the existence of an unjust situation in language that cannot be taken and used by those in power. If evangelization seeks to maintain some kind of neutrality, speaking a language that does not criticize, it will eventually be absorbed by the system; by not taking any critical positions, and thus legitimating the situation, it will fortify the existing order. Neutrality is not possible here. Either the person is naive and does not know what is really happening, or the person is very clever, hiding his or her option for the system under the cloak of neutrality.

A Critical Stance

In light of what has been said, it is urgent for religious life to take a critical position.[40] Encouraging that critical position is the need to overcome the conformity and passive acceptance found in the situation. This means to take a conscious position within the situation, accepting the challenges that call for a transforming action. Criticism is not carried on from a point outside the situation; rather it penetrates to the roots of the situation, accepts it for what it is, and transforms it from within. The critic is a radical, that is, one who attempts to get to the root of a problem. To go to the roots of a problem is to be a humble, objective critic.

Opposed to the critic is the sectarian or fanatic who is moved by uncritical emotions. Thus the fanatic is arrogant, reactionary, closed to dialogue, an activist imposing his or her own views, a person who deals in half-truths proclaimed as absolutes. The fanatic is not free and is thus incapable of helping to liberate. Only the person who is free helps in liberation. The only free person is one who is critical, who is aware of manipulative, partisan mechanisms, who reacts against these mechanisms not out of fanaticism, but out of a choice that seeks viable pathways to a world where fellowship is less difficult.

The critic, the free person, is not a mere spectator of history, but a responsible participant who knows how to participate without trying to advance a process he or she recognizes as unviable, and who also does not hold onto what exists while knowing that its transformation can be accelerated by one's action and the reasons for that action.[41]

Education is either liberating, or else a way of integrating people uncritically into the established order.[42] Religious life, with all the means it employs on behalf of the word, should continually pose for itself the question of its liberating or oppressing function. Without this vigilance it can run the risk—with the Gospel of liberation and of the new humanity in Christ—of being a force that preserves the old humanity with all its bondage of self-centeredness and oppression.

Pablo Freire, one of the most distinguished Brazilians of this century, elaborated an entire pedagogy oriented toward the complete liberation of both oppressor and oppressed without an explicit Gospel inspiration.[43] For him, liberation is an act of love "as opposed to the lack of love which is hidden in the heart of the oppressor's violence, a lack which also exists in cases in which bogus generosity masquerades as love."[44]

Freire's method of becoming aware of, and driving out, the oppressor in each oppressive situation is not merely juggling positions within the structure of oppression; it is destroying the very structure that permits oppressors and oppressed to exist. This destruction is not achieved by magic, but through a process of liberation that frees the oppressed, who then free the oppressor. Yet the oppressed will free the oppressor only when they are free of oppression carried out with an attitude of vengeance, hatred, reprisal, excessive fear, and the selfish possession and retention of goods. The goal of the oppressed must not be to become like the oppressors, but to become more human, and thus better able to love and more capable of dialogue, creativity, and fellowship.

These values are profoundly Gospel-oriented and make up the central concerns of the cause of Christ. The psychological and sociological approach of Freire aids in using Gospel ideas in a pedagogical method. Whoever works for the transformation of society because he or she knows and believes this is not the best society, or the one humanity most deserves, sees how this great Brazilian teacher has made an invaluable contribution to the working of the Gospel message. A religious life attentive to its prophetical, critical mission in the world cannot ignore this contribution to its evangelizing and educational endeavor.

The Charismatic Emphasis

It is also necessary to emphasize that religious life by its very nature is situated more in a charismatic context than in an institutional one. Thus evangelization through the word must more fully recapture its charismatic character. Evangelization by religious life should not purely and simply be the preaching of a doctrine already established or the spreading of an ecclesiastical structure. It should rather be a much more creative, prophetic work of being attuned to the signs of the times and of more adequately translating the Gospel into the contemporary idiom.

Doing this involves many risks and is impossible without

imagination and without autonomy from the institutional and the repetitious. Evangelization must bring about a contemplative vision of life. Religious do not bring the Gospel to people who do not know it, rather, they discover the Gospel already present in their brothers and sisters, who are always being visited by the Holy Spirit and the risen Christ. Thus they must adopt an attitude of listening and of obedience, learning from people what God wants to teach them. The explicit word of evangelization does no more than awaken and articulate the Gospel already present in people.

Thus evangelization is not simply indoctrination or the imposition of a religious system. It is transformed into an encounter, a giving and receiving, a progressive unveiling of Christ in the world. J. Comblin said "Mission is not the path of growth of the Church, but the path of its discovery."[45] We must ask: When will evangelization become seriously concerned with the revelation of God in Brazilian history? In the Bible there were prophets who discerned God's plan in the history of the people of Israel and who proclaimed it to everyone. It is the duty of religious, by virtue of their prophetical and eschatological charism, to live with the same outlook.

Only religious who are aware of their place among the People of God can fulfill that mission. Their place is not in the institutional or hierarchical but in the charismatic, which always lives in a certain tension with the institutional and on its fringes. This is creative. This position is very important since it determines the kind of language and procedure it develops for evangelization. If religious life comes to be absorbed into institutional and hierarchical ways of thinking, it will be no more than indoctrinating and spreading a system. But if it maintains its specifically charismatic identity, it will look for and find new paths for the Gospel and will be present wherever official means cannot or do not reach.

Starting from this point, perhaps religious will come to understand that evangelizing the poor and entering into a real process of liberation is possible only if religious place themselves in the position of the poor and abandon the position of the rich. One cannot evangelize the poor if one is rich or uses discourses composed by the rich.[46] One must be poor. From such a position, according to the Gospel, it is possible to reach everyone, poor or rich, since then the rich are questioned about the human and Gospel consequences of their wealth.

Religious life thus feels itself called to meet an unexpected challenge that comes from its mission of evangelization: to make real in the world and in the Church the meaning of the permanent conversion demanded by the Good News of Christ. Conversion makes us itinerant, always going forth from our native land like Abraham, to seek the other land where the other is and where we are to proclaim the presence of God and his liberating grace.

Is It Possible to Evangelize in a Rich World with the Tools of the Poor?

The preceding reflection perhaps raises two questions in the reader's mind: Must we not also evangelize the rich, the ruling class? Is it not also possible to evangelize using the means of the rich?

Such questions strongly indicate the position in the social structure occupied by the person who asks them, namely, the privileged position of the rich. Such questions can even be formulated to legitimize the rich means they use.

Obviously we must also evangelize the rich. The problem is, nevertheless, how to do it. Over the centuries the Church, especially in Latin America, fell into the fallacy (which many bishops supporting pontifical universities never abandoned) of thinking that, by educating and influencing the ruling classes, fundamentally Christian people could be formed who would then transform society. Yet the desired effect never came to pass. Why? The mechanisms of excuse and justification enabled the institution to rationalize this way: society did not change because the Christians leaving Catholic schools did not follow up with their own conversions. Being converted leads immediately to social transformation. Since the transformation did not occur, the blame should be placed on the Christians' lack of conversion.

The problem remains: Why were the Christian alumni of our Catholic schools not converted? The answer cannot lie in their bad will. It undoubtedly lies in the very structure of the Catholic school.

The structure of the Catholic school is strongly shaped by the structure of the dominant society. It is a school to which, largely if not exclusively, only the privileged classes have access. Consider the pontifical universities, for example. They participate in the world of the rich and powerful. Wealth and poverty, class distinctions, and the margination of the majority are not the result of individual failings such as prejudice, ill will, or climate. Such factors are real, but are not the explicit, structural cause of the condition.

The cause lies in the cultural ethos, in the form of ownership of human goods, both material and cultural, with their easy accumulation in the hands of only a few, as opposed to the vast majority who remain excluded from them. This fact reveals the structural injustice. The rich are not rich, but enriched at the expense of the poor. The poor are not poor, but are impoverished by the boundless greed of the rich and powerful.

Christianity can accept a society based on oppression, violence, and injustice only through what historian Eduardo Hoornaert calls the *transculturation* of the Gospel.[47] The Christian message comes to be transformed, transculturated, and ideologized, ending up adapting itself to the system without challenging the system in the least. A kind of Christianity arises that gives its own meaning to love, faith, freedom, obedience, conversion, and other Christian themes, different from the meanings they have in the Gospel. This kind of Christianity blithely speaks of "our brother slave" without noticing the contradiction to the Gospel that is involved.

This Christianity resists being questioned by the Gospel. The ecclesiastical institution always accepts an interpretation of the Gospel that favors the system and crowns its successes. By identifying faith with an institution, the triumphs of the institution are the triumphs of faith—a transculturation of the Gospel faith into a Christian rationale of the ruling elite.

In a similar way, the experience of authentic, Gospel Christianity is only possible on an internal, personal level, or through persecution and martyrdom. Anyone who, in the name of the Gospel, dares to criticize such a Christian institution or the transculturation of Christian themes is persecuted, exiled, denounced, even ending up in the courts of the Inquisition.[48] Since being a prophet is very demanding, most people take refuge in an interior Christianity.

This contradiction is still embodied in great Catholic institutions. They are controlled by the ideology of the larger society. They either adapt to it, transculturating Christianity and robbing it of its critical force, or become suspect, persecuted, marginated, and eliminated. The institutions see themselves as forced to get along with the system that discriminates and grants privileges. Learned Christians come forth from that kind of Christianity, but not reformers. Moreover, history shows that generally such Christians are great defenders of institutions, but socially and personally indifferent to faith and the Gospel.[49]

We cannot evangelize the rich when we are involved in the same social structures that they are. Power contaminates and even corrupts the salt the Gospel speaks of. The Gospel undergoes a transculturation, with the result that authentic Christianity is damaged.

The Church will only evangelize in the sense Christ intended when it changes its social position and class and becomes really poor. This is especially true for religious life. The means of the rich ill accord with Gospel poverty. The means of the rich need power in order to be maintained. They compromise people and turn them into objects; instead of remaining means, they become ends in themselves to the people who have committed themselves to these things and need them to live. The Gospel then becomes the platform for special interests, a means of control and power. Power never unites people, nor does it promote salvation or fellowship. Rather it separates and divides, for the sake of the special interests to which it is tied. The Gospel becomes transculturated into a rationale that justifies rich and powerful institutions, no longer the Gospel of Christ calling always for the renunciation of all ambition to control.

The document of the 1971 Synod of Bishops, *Justice in the Modern World,* keenly recognized this.

> Concern for material goods, no matter what use they are put to, must never become so critical an issue that it makes the Gospel witness the Church must give the world ambiguous. The retention of a privileged position must constantly be submitted to that criterion established by that principle. And generally even when it becomes difficult to determine the line between what is needed for good operation and what is demanded by prophetic witness, this principle should undoubtedly be firmly maintained: our faith imposes on us a certain moderation in the use of material things, and the Church must live, and administer its own goods, in such a way that the Gospel is proclaimed to the poor. If, on the other hand, the Church appears as one of the rich and powerful things of this world, its credibility will be greatly diminished.[50]

Placing itself in the position of the poor, living for the poor, with the poor, and, as far as possible, like the poor, the Church can address the rich. It will speak with authenticity, constantly remembering the function of all wealth, which is legitimate only when it brings about fellowship. The poor will, in turn, feel themselves to be members of the Church because they share in it and its life. Religious life, making this qualitative leap into poverty, will be doing no more than living out the consequences of its vow of poverty. Poverty lived capitalistically, or always in reference to goods (how much one can have, for example) is not Gospel poverty, the object of the vow. Gospel poverty is poverty that creates solidarity with the poor, in whom one discovers the privileged locus of the Lord's presence, poverty that renounces and liberates and can thus proclaim conversion and the message of Christian hope with no danger of being contaminated with power or the special interests of individuals, which are not the interests of God.

Being poor, religious can evangelize within the rich institutions of society and those not their own without obscuring the visibility of the Gospel with all its demands for the complete transformation of all people and society.

Conclusion: The Mystique of Commitment and Perseverance

The tasks of religious life in relation to evangelization in a context of awareness of underdevelopment and in relation to a process of liberation, are of the utmost urgency. We cannot allow subterfuges or an evasive tranquilizing of conscience in order to remain in the same situation we find ourselves in now and to have no doubts about our fidelity to the Gospel. The situation of general margination denounces us as causing such a condition to the extent that we actually benefit from the status quo.

Paying attention to the cry for justice, dignity, humanity, and fellowship from those who suffer, we can and must hear the inescapable call to conversion that comes to us from them. To evangelize is to take up the cause of Christ and to make his liberating person present in what we are and what we do, through a concrete practice that involves total liberation. To evangelize is to be converted, not through intellectual attempts to justify everything in order to leave the situation as it is, but through an urgent change of attitude, and even a change of position within the social structure. Evangelizing will thus be an action that liberates people and the situation in which they live in order to help others, to the full extent of our freedom, to enter into the same process of advancement. In the Latin American context, the Gospel is oriented to nothing other than liberation and the demand for commitment. Christ Jesus finds, in our commitment, his second coming as liberator.

The power of the imperial system, promoting perpetual bondage, may make us feel impotent. We can do nothing. We are so few. Faced with this feeling, which undermines the hopes of Christians, a mystique of perseverance becomes essential. It is a mystique that makes us believe, even in the face of our feeling of ineffectiveness, and makes us fight for a world we do not yet see appearing over the horizon but which we believe is the future of humanity, a world in which "love may be less difficult."[51] It is a mystique that takes up the sorrowful experience of the Pasch (Passover) in expectation of a long wait and a long vigil for the coming of the new humanity. It is a mystique that provides meaning so that one acts when one must and waits when one must. In short, it is a mystique that makes us attentive to the demands of the Holy Spirit, manifested in the signs of the times.

Religious life, in a world where so many people and so many Gospel values remain in bondage, can be a sign of joy, of hope, and of true liberation, so that no one need be depressed or disheartened by the power of social evil or by the ability of the prevailing system to balance its contradictions.

Even within that captivity religious life can be free, bearing witness to the unutterable and unsuspected hope revealed in the risen Christ: the future does not belong to those who oppress, marginate, and accumulate wealth, but rather to those who share, liberate, give of themselves, and join together as brothers and sisters. It is in the weak, the poor, the crucified that the new humanity and the new power which transfigures everything is revealed. In them is the Gospel wherein all liberation is contained.

10

Religious Life and the Process of Liberation

This last, brief chapter, as one can easily appreciate, tries to synthesize all the previous ones. It must be understood in light of the spiritual orientation proposed by the CLAR (*Conferencia Latino-Americana de Religiosos,* the Latin-American Conference of Religious) in various official documents, especially the following: "Poverty and Religious Life in Latin America," "Formation for Religious Life in Latin America," "Religious Life According to the Spirit in Latin America," "The Political Dimension of Religious Life and Its Latin American Perspectives," and "Prophetic Thrusts of Religious Life in Latin America." In these documents there is an attempt to consider responsibly, and to promote, religious life in the concrete situation in which the entire continent lives and waits.

Religious Life Incarnated and Seen in a Concrete Situation

Religious life, like any other type of life, is situated in a definite, historical context. It is challenged, and it points out and foreshadows new horizons for that concrete world in which it exists. The human situation, in its political, economic, social, and religious dimensions, is marked by a dependence of the periphery on the great centers of decision-making and leadership, which dependence gives rise to structural poverty, social injustices, and lives shaped by violence and oppression.

Religious life wants to share in, and really does share in, the sorrows and anxieties of the people of Latin America, as well as in their joys and hopes for liberation. It views the situation as one of tremendous challenge. How far can religious life help people to be liberated without compromising its essential identity? How much does it see in this situation a real opportunity, a true *kairos,* to be converted, to reexamine its forms of presence in the world, and to obey the voice of God it hears in this concrete situation? Does it play a critical role, or is it reinforcing the system that causes margination and misery? Does the social influence religious life possesses (and it does) lean in favor of those with whom Jesus allied himself in such a special way: the poor, the socially marginated, and those considered public sinners by the religious establishment of his time?

A socio-analytical study of the real situation gives rise to a religious and theological reflection: poverty is not a guiltless reality, but the result of social sin; the dependence of some people on other people in an oppressive regime is not something neutral, but the result of a bitter, collective selfishness. What does it mean to bear witness to God and to Christ, to his grace and love, in a world of hunger, margination, and the violation of basic human rights? What new possibilities are opened up for the experience of God in a religious life that attempts to take seriously the problems of the world around it, considered all together?

In all Latin America a deep longing for liberation is felt. It has arisen within a general system of bondage, embodying itself in a process that begins with a radical increase in awareness of the structures that cause oppression, and takes concrete steps toward liberation in relation to education, commitment to the poor, creation of greater fellowship. For a believer, such progress is not only human progress; it is the concrete way in which God's grace and Christ's liberation are being realized in history. This situation is calling on religious life to define itself and understand itself in light of the challenges the situation poses. Every day religious grow more and more aware of their social responsibility.

Religious life possesses in itself inestimable values that, when viewed in their Gospel and liberation dimensions, can motivate and shape commitment by religious to a process of real liberation. We have already seen that this is not a matter of working haphazardly or without taking into consideration the specific character of religious life itself. It is a matter of playing a real role in society that accords with the way of life of religious and their own identity as religious. It is not merely external adaptations, but a concrete, living response, dynamic and effective, in the name of faith and the religious vocation, to the burning challenges of a world that experiences margination, that seeks help and solidarity in the process of its liberation.

Religious Life in the Process of Liberation

The identity of religious life basically consists in the incarnation of the experience of God through the following of Christ by means of total consecration to God through the three vows, lived in community as a prophetic sign of a future promised by God and incarnated in the world.

Yet, without further explanation, these basic concepts are too abstract. These concepts take on reality only by starting with the concrete situation in which religious exist. It is in this situation that religious life can exercise a liberating function, making itself effectively present, and putting itself on the side of people in its historical journey, just as God has intended.

The Meaning of the Experience of God in Our Situation

Even though there are varied social and economic conditions on the Latin American continent, there are, as we have seen, common denominators, called "underdevelopment," "dependence," and a longing for progress and "liberation." In this experience God appears essentially as the God of justice for the poor, the God of liberation for the oppressed, the God of the future for those with no horizon, and the God of consolation for those violently repressed. The dependence and misery of millions is thus forcing faith to see God as the One opposed to what we find in the social structures. God demands that we destroy this inhuman situation, which he does not want to exist. Thus a real experience of God takes place in the commitment to securing the rights of the oppressed, in combatting poverty, illiteracy, and margination. Fr. De Lubac reminds us that "to lack love or justice is to be separated from God, making the worship of God idolatry."[1]

God is only real and valuable for human life when he reveals himself as he does in Scripture: as the radical meaning of life, as hope for people in the midst of their abandonment, as the promise of freedom and justice for the oppressed, and as the ultimate, definitive future for each person.

In Latin America, the holy name of God has been manipulated. The image offered is one of a supreme being who created a world where social class, rich and poor, must always exist. He is a God who demands observance of natural law; competition, domination by the strongest, and free enterprise are consequences of this natural law. The image of God thus does nothing but rationalize the status quo. An experience of the living and true God begins with questioning this manipulation of God in order to serve special interests created by human beings.

Catholicism is the predominant religion of our continent. But faith in the God of Jesus has not attained its full Christian explication. We are not going to repeat what we have said at length in previous chapters.[2] Here we will add only that religious life, attempting to discover the living God manifested in the situations of human history, is called to bear witness to a God who questions an effective situation of inhumanity that contradicts his salvific plan of love, solidarity, fellowship, and justice among people. For religious to make that God whom they experience in contrast to the world their life-project is to place religious life at the center of a conflict. In that conflict religious life must be a sign of a world, or of an ideal of the world, where exploitation of one person by another no longer exists and where total reconciliation (the Kingdom of God) takes place.

The Following of Christ for Religious in Latin America

Religious propose to live for God by following Christ. The *sequela Christi* (the following of Christ) is an essential trait of authentic religious life. Nevertheless, a certain interpretation has been given to the following of Christ, which made it a personal thing and deprived it of its historical, theological, and evangelical content of the characteristics of denunciation and liberation that were found in the life and message of Jesus.

The themes of the cross, sacrifice, humility, obedience, and poverty were presented in a way that exalted the cross for the sake of the cross, suffering for the sake of suffering, instead of orienting people toward battling against, and overcoming, the cause of particular sufferings and crosses imposed by other people. The death of Christ was an historical fact, not as the result of an a priori decree of God, but of the way Christ lived in response to a situation, the result of a conflict his message and his demands caused within Judaism.

Christ proclaims an absolute meaning for his world and for that of any age, a meaning defined and made explicit as the Kingdom of God, which he proclaimed and wanted to establish among people. This meaning, this Kingdom, was not restricted to certain areas of life, but to all its dimensions, to life as a whole. He does not preach a tradition or law, but truth and love. His God is the God of love and pardon, who loves everyone indiscriminately (Lk. 6:35) and offers salvation to everyone.

If there is something to be emphasized, it is that Jesus incarnates the universal offer of salvation, especially to the afflicted, the sick, the poor and weak (Mt. 2:17; Lk. 19:10), since he himself prefers to be close to these kinds of people, and to be their friend.

Salvation or damnation of the individual is decided by the person's acceptance or rejection of people, especially of the poor and insignificant in whom God himself is hidden (Lk. 6:20–21; Mt. 25:40).

Christ did not shrink from the consequences of his solidarity with the poorest and most marginated. He was accused of insanity, heresy, subversion, gluttony, and drunkenness. He discriminated against no one, not even his detractors: he accepted their dinner invitations, seeking and trusting in their conversion. "Anyone who comes to me I will not cast out" (Jn. 6:37). Thus St. John describes Christ in his being-for-others. He accepted his own death, not fatalistically or in a stoical way, but as the supreme act of love and sacrifice for the liberation of all people.

Christ died for the same motives that the prophet-martyrs died: as a witness to the truth, faithful to the message of justice, the rights of the oppressed, universal fellowship, divine sonship, and the Father's limitless goodness. Abandoned by everyone, even his Father, on the cross (Mk. 15:34), Jesus did not despair, but trusted, thought of others, and gave himself totally and unconditionally to the Mystery of God. The resurrection confirmed that God was on his side and that a utopian future for the whole world had been assured beforehand by God.

To follow Christ, then, is to live his choices and in accordance with them. We know what they were and whom he preferred. Religious must then seek to be identified with the weakest just as the Son of God did. To follow Christ is to choose this path, considering as normal and logical the real possibility of persecution, slander, imprisonment, and even death for the sake of people. Religious life, if it concretely commits itself as Christ did, not only makes itself an outcast, but chooses sacrifice and martyrdom, which take many varied forms in Latin America today.

Consecration as Mission Before the World

All Christians, by virtue of their baptismal consecration, are called to live their experience of God by imitating and following Christ. Religious commit themselves publicly within the Church to live such a life in a radical way, becoming a prophetic and eschatological sign of God and of transcendent realities. This is their task received from their consecration; they are "set aside for God."

Consecration, being set aside for God, implies a renunciation of the world. But it is very important to understand the meaning of this renunciation correctly. Consecration as renunciation is also a mission. We are not going to dwell on this idea any further, since it has already been fully explained in previous chapters. Consecration is thus "not isolation from the world, but insertion into it in the name of God."[3] Religious are sent by God with a special mission.

This concept of religious consecration forms the theological basis of the religious commitment to society. The very fact of being consecrated, with a "more intimate" or "special consecration,"[4] is also a new and "special" commission to serve the cause of God, Christ, and the Church, whose aim in the world is to live according to the demands of the Kingdom in all its radicalness and all its fullness. Religious are thus also related to the world in a "special" way with the responsibility, in the name of God, Christ, and the Church, of creating a society more in keeping with the Kingdom of God. This is clear.[5]

Concretely the Kingdom of God is love, justice, peace, and truth. To build, or help build, peace, truth, justice, and love, is to build the Kingdom of God already present in the world and continually growing toward the Parousia of Christ. Put in another way, it is building the earthly city in accordance with the demands of the Kingdom of God.[6]

The Social Dimensions of the Vows

The three vows (poverty, chastity, and obedience) concretize and explicate the one, basic consecration of religious to God, interpreting what religious life means by its being set aside and by its mission.

In what the vows say about being set aside, they indicate a complete, generous giving of self to the divine love, so that the religious becomes an eschatological sign of how we will be in the Kingdom. As to what the vows imply about mission:

> Poverty does not demand that the religious sever relationships with the world, chastity that the religious break off relationships with people of the opposite sex, nor does obedience mean a break with society. Such relationships, on the contrary, take on a different quality by virtue of

> one's total dedication to God. The vows consecrate, dedicate, free people, making them available for the cause of God and Christ in the world.[7]

Without detracting from the values of reservation and of personal sanctification, the Latin American situation calls for emphasizing the aspect of mission and of the social implications of the vows.

Poverty truly implies a giving up of earthly goods and a longing for God. Yet this is not enough. Such a concept does not offer sufficient grounds for answering the challenge of today, which demands our deeper commitment to solidarity with the poor and wretched. Religious, in their practice of poverty, must simultaneously combine the free divestment of earthly goods with commitment to those who lack such goods, since

> It is this simultaneity which, based on true communion with the hopes and endeavors of people, makes it possible for religious to speak that critical, unsettling word which ends up, one day, opening people to Jesus Christ. This word has nothing in common with that of the dreamer or idealist . . . nor that of the pharisee living in his ivory tower, but with that of a person who fights alongside others in battle.[8]

Sharing in the poverty of the poor and taking seriously their most urgent and legitimate demands are ways in which religious give an answer to the system that causes this kind of structural poverty.

Chastity means a superabundance of love for God and, we must add, flows out of that. There are ways of living chastity that may not be very Gospel-oriented. For our time, chastity means much more than purity (with which it has often been identified). Chastity constitutes transcendent availability.

> The availability which springs from the vow of chastity frees us from certain commitments in order for us to take greater risks in choices and activities which become prophetic in society. . . . Through chastity the religious offers a prophetic response to the problems of the relationship which exists between the world of riches and the sexual exploitation of a large part of humanity. . . . Through chastity we permit the possibility of taking a critical stance toward a new form of oppression, not in a moralizing and puritanical way, nor simply as a public censor, but getting to the root of the commercial exploitation of sex:

> distortion of the concept of the human person, the radical deterioration of love, and a self-centered, hedonistic, and selfish view of life.[9]

The ideal of chastity for the Kingdom of Heaven may once again find its original inspiration.

Obedience means communion with the will of God, which is discovered in community and in concert with authority. But it is not enough to practice obedience within the community; religious obedience also has a social thrust. The social dimension of this vow implies taking up the apostolate of the community as a concrete response to the will of God within a given situation. We must listen to the plan of God here and now, in this concrete, existential situation. Centering ourselves on this concept of obedience, we can work together for the establishment of justice with respect to the human person.[10] All this can mean, and may even demand, working as marginated or among the marginated, a critical attitude, an eagerness and openness to listen to the will of God in the signs of the times and accepting the implications of these factors for our own position.

Fellowship Open to the People Around Us

In the history of religious life, members of institutes have always been centered in their own communities, their own brotherhood or sisterhood. The experience of God, though, is also an experience of our sister or brother in the faith community.

The theological horizon here must be widened. Religious life often becomes the be-all and end-all, centered entirely in itself or in a particular congregation and community, dedicating almost all its time and attention to domestic problems. In Latin America, solidarity and coming together, collaboration in and commitment to the process and advancement toward greater humanization and liberation, all call upon the community to be open to the people around it. We are called upon to assume the culture of our people, their way of life, their human and religious values, their sense of fellowship, justice and hospitality, their prayer forms, their Marian devotions, their joviality, and their festive nature.

Our continent expects this Gospel witness of love and fellowship from religious. About this it has been forcefully said:

> If religious community is the matrix which gives birth to, and brings to fulfillment, people freed from themselves, their private emotions, their selfishness, people familiar with what keeps people enslaved, unified and serene, joyful in their hope for the future, brothers and sisters of all, what hope is opened for all the world! People will then see that the dream of a better world, in which each person will be brother or sister to the other, is not an unattainable utopia, but in the process of being born. And this is all because they have allowed themselves to believe in Jesus Christ and in his promise, because they have allowed themselves to be led by the Spirit and to be embraced by the purifying flame.[11]

All this, together with the commitment it implies, demands a true conversion, since we are generally in the habit of expressing our faith and spirituality in theological categories that are imported or official, that have no basis in, or contact with, dialogue with people.

This conversion or turning toward people creates a favorable climate in religious for a commitment more in keeping with the Gospel, which prefers the less privileged members of society. There are many religious who have discovered the real meaning of their vocation through their contact with people and in sharing those people's struggles and dreams. Participating in community groups frees religious life from its social dependence on its traditional areas of support. The challenges presented to religious by the situation force them to foster their creative imagination in order to incarnate the spirit of the Gospel in more suitable forms. Thus religious receive a new freedom and establish a new kind of relationship between their religious experience and their expression of that experience.

The Critical and Prophetic Presence of Religious in the World

Solidarity with the poor for the sake of the Gospel makes religious break with a style of life and relationship proper to the privileged sectors of society. Its presence in the world becomes a critical sign, a prophetic sign. The poor we are united with are not simply the poor; they are the impoverished ones from whom the means and possibility of being a member of society were taken away, leaving them marginated.

A clear love for the poor makes us understand the basic social structure that causes poverty, generally no more than the by-product of the wealthiness of rich and powerful minorities. Thus religious need to be critical, not naive. They must be endlessly attentive to their constant manipulation by the state, which uses religious life to still consciences by appearing to be a real servant in the world of the poor. The critical presence of religious implies, on the one hand, denunciation of a structural situation that contradicts the plan of God and the Gospel message, and on the other the proclamation of true fellowship and sharing in the goods and the duties that all should share.

This sign

> will be more visible the more it is humble and simple. In fact, the encounter with Christ in the least of his brothers and sisters, far from being expressed in an attitude of scorn and pharisaical self-affirmation, is expressed in a humble attitude which recognizes the sin in each of us and in the organization of society. This recognition engenders an endlessly renewed intention of conversion, personal as well as communal and social.[12]

This critical, prophetic attitude, confronted with the dominant powers in Latin America, may involve sacrifices, and even conflicts, for religious communities. The knowledge that they will be calumniated, denounced as subversive, contradicted, and legislated against should not surprise them, since Christ and his apostles were defamed and accused of all of this. This is the price of liberating freedom, so high that it sometimes is paid for by blood and death. But this sacrifice is not in vain. It is a perpetual accusation leveled at a world closed in on itself. It arouses the consciences of those who violently and unjustly try to suppress those who, risking their reputations and their lives, take up the defense of the oppressed, the exploited, the humble of the earth.

The Role of Religious in the World of the Poor

In the previous chapter we said that religious congregations have begun to ask seriously about the Gospel character of their presence, through their educational and charitable works and institutions, in Latin American society. Such works have actually been linked to the established regime and order in society. But we cannot allow our mission to buttress this structure and its value system or, to put it better, to accept the presupposed values of the contemporary social system.

It is no small beginning to notice everywhere the precarious position religious find themselves in when they assume a social role different from that proper to them, from that for which their institutes were founded: the role of being sent to bring the Good News to the poor and marginated. We repeat once more that it is evidently not a matter of abandoning what religious congregations have built up or established in Latin American history. It is only a matter of using these works and institutions with a different spirit: a spirit of solidarity and liberation of the poorest and most helpless.

A wise and determined role in our world restores the ability of religious to criticize and keep watch, restores their historical sense and their awareness of the viability of the projects of liberation that must be undertaken. Religious can be politically uninvolved. They must be able to criticize the prevailing ideologies, knowing how to discover the hidden interests in them, which they support, and to detect their vision of the human person, which is not always anthropologically or theologically admissible. Vigilance is necessary in regard to created interests that protect themselves and never give up the prerogatives.

Religious also cannot escape proclaiming other values that support and make possible the participation of all, a new sense of fellowship, a more equitable distribution of cultural and economic goods. Thus religious need to be attentive to the events occurring in the country and throughout the continent, in order to know how to interpret them from a contemplative vision of reality, either as bringing salvation (in order to promote it) or as denying the human in its relation to God and the sons and daughters of God (in order to combat it).

Through this contemplative vision, the poor become a christophany, the key to social transcendence, showing that society is not perfect, not even in a fundamental way, since, in order to maintain the wealth of a few, it is necessary to marginate other brothers and sisters. The poor, by their very presence, are making a utopian (and not always realizable) call for a way of living together in which poverty and every structure that allows one person to exploit another are destroyed. The poor denounce the weakness of this world and reveal that, without the spirit of the Beatitudes, society cannot be transfigured or offered to God, and that, without radical conversion, the world cannot be the locus of the Kingdom of God.[13] The poor are a theophany and a christophany insofar as they are a permanent reminder of concrete transcendence, which calls into question all our actions, attitudes, and endeavors.

Sharing in the situation of the poor causes religious life to situate itself precisely where God-with-us chose to pitch his tent.

> Only by rejecting poverty and becoming poor in order to protest against it can the Church, and even moreso religious life, preach something which is their own: spiritual poverty, that is, the openness of people and of history to the future promised by God. Only thus can it fulfill, with the prospect of being heard, the prophetic function of denouncing all injustice which wars against people and of liberatingly proclaiming a true human fellowship. . . . For the Latin-American Church and for religious life, this witness is today the inescapable and urgent test of the authenticity of its mission.[14]

The Spirituality of Hope within Captivity

After we have said all this, someone may think that such traditional aspects of religious life as prayer and meditation, spirituality, and mysticism are completely absorbed into a commitment to secular tasks that aim at merely human progress and liberation.

This is not true and it cannot be true. Nor must this ever happen, since such activities deal with things that are today more urgent than ever. To retain their specific religious identity, to thrive and grow in their experience of God in the following of Christ, to make the special contribution of religious as religious, religious must constantly foster the spirit of prayer and prayer itself,[15] meditation, and the interior life with its process—however painful it may be—of introspection.

Prayer and meditation should spring from a contemplative attitude even in the midst of action. The commitment mentioned before is only true and evangelizing when it is born of a Gospel dynamism lived in one's own interiority and from a deep interior experience of God and Jesus Christ, nourished by, and expressed in, personal and community prayer. In accordance with the classical maxim *contemplata aliis tradere* (contemplate in order to give yourselves to others), we must not separate action and prayer. Action, to be authentic, must remain pervaded and inspired by contemplation, and must spring from the fullness of the contemplative life.[16] Even at their peak, activity and commitment must seek and situate their formal and efficient causes in contemplation. It would be a disastrous error to think that the interior life could live only off its own resources and not frequently seek God in solitude and in prayer life.

All real contemplation, if it wants to be Christian and Gospel-oriented to the imitation and following of Christ, must have times to be practiced (although not in the same way by all religious) and must lead to prophetic witness and to commitment. Vatican II reminds all religious that

> they must consider contemplation along with apostolic love. By the former they adhere to God in mind and heart; by the latter they strive to join themselves to the work of redemption and of spreading the Kingdom of God.[17]

Moreover, only the fostering of prayer and contemplation, of the interior life, will give religious the indispensable power for real, deep commitment in the situation we have discussed on several occasions.

Only from that permanently contemplative and mystical attitude can religious give solid support, transcendence, and power to their hope, proclaiming and bringing about the advent of the new future, which Christ makes possible in the world through his work of redemption and liberation.

> The traveller who climbs his mountain under the guidance of a star, if he is too much absorbed with the difficulties of the climb, risks forgetting the star which is guiding him. If he does not journey by more than the path, he never gets anywhere. . . . Whatever may be the need for action, one must not forget—under pain of condemning that activity to ineffectiveness—the call which must give it direction.[18]

On the other hand, as called upon to be a living, acting prophecy of that hope, only a contemplative attitude on the part of religious life, and its openness to the transcendent, changes that hope into denunciation, protest, and challenge against a whole world without hope, against all who live with false hopes and for the sake of false hopes—challenge and denunciation which mercilessly destroy all idols and all idolatries, without substituting other, new idols and idolatries for them.[19]

Finally, only a deep introspection of the experience of God changes hope into a hope against hope, since religious perhaps will never in their lifetime see that new society and that new human being for which they work, spend themselves, and commit themselves. This is the deepest call that comes to us and the deepest demand that that hope imposes on us:

> We must love even the one we will never see. This is the secret of persevering and hope-filled action: it does not allow creativity to waste itself only on what can be immediately seen or felt, but keeps on working determinedly for the beginning or the birth of that new future which will come after us. A love of this kind is what gave the prophets, the saints, the revolutionaries the strength to die for the future they caught glimpses of. They made their life a seed of great hope, knowing that the grain which does not die in the earth produces no fruit (Jn. 12:24). Watch and listen, you solitary one. The winds of future are blowing, fanning hope. The Good News is whispered in attentive ears. You, the solitary ones of today, will one day be a great people: the earth will truly become the place of salvation. Around it will waft a new fragrance bringing salvation and new hope.[20]

Even in this situation religious must imitate Christ who also had to pass this test—one of the other ways in which the cross presents itself: the impossibility of transforming his people and his world, and yet continuing to preach, to call people to conversion, never losing hope in the future triumph of justice over injustice, of love over hate, of fellowship over division and schism. Such a sacrifice is radically liberating and purifying, since it obliges us to transcend our own achievements and makes us live a life of pure faith, where our only hope lies in a dimension that surpasses the results of our own plans and endeavors that can be immediately verified.

Living with such an attitude, religious life also becomes, for the people with whom it lives and to whom it is committed, a source of hope and faith in the meaning of life, despite its apparent meaninglessness and despite the shadows that continually obscure that meaning. To find, despite all this, joy in living and strength for commitment to something that ordinarily has no immediate prospect of success is to bear witness, in the midst of the poor, to true Christian hope and the presence of the peace the world cannot give.

Conclusion

We end this book fully aware of not having treated, even briefly, certain problems that are, nonetheless, important within religious life. Perhaps we should have treated other, even more urgent ones. Yet we have chosen to limit ourselves to the preceding reflections, which come from a concrete experience, from vital questions that religious groups everywhere have posed and keep on posing in search of a clear answer.

We have not tried to demonstrate to our readers any claim to greater wisdom. Nothing is further from our intention, knowing how much more valuable is knowledge that can always be increased. In this enduring school of history, of living together and mutually listening with our brothers and sisters, the author has done no more here than to express the fruit of dialogue with his companions. It is presented to our readers as a fraternal dialogue. It is a dialogue not about theological theories, but about our religious life in regard to its need to be more realistic and more committed in its internal and external goals.

Perhaps we have not achieved greater certainty. But surely we have succeeded in arousing greater fidelity to the Truth which liberates. The most decisive thing is not the theology of religious life but religious life itself. Theology exists in relation to life. It is life that will judge the value of all theology. Perhaps today there are too many theologians and too few mystics. Mystics are the ones who do more to make history advance. Having them among us and traveling in their company is the way, despite all historical contradictions, we can go on singing, dancing, and uttering praise to meet the Lord who will come and is always coming.

Notes

Chapter 1

1. Cf. Ranke-Heinemann, Uta, "Die Gottesliebe als ein Motiv fuer die Entstehung des Moenchtums," *MThZ,* 8 (1957a), 289-294; Leloir, L., "Témoignage monastique et présence au monde," *NRTh,* 89 (1966), 673-692.

2. Kloppenburg, "A doutrina do Vaticano II sobre a naturaleza de vida religiosa," *REB,* 30 (1967), 59–70 (especially 68).

3. Comblin, J., "A vida religiosa como consagração," *Grande Sinal* (1970), 21–30 (especially 29–30).

4. Cf. *Irenikon,* 34 (1961), 217-231; 346–392.

5. Izarn, P., "Monachisme en Ethiopie," *Bulletin S. Jean Baptiste,* 8 (1967), 20–30; Meinardus, Ofa, "Récent développement in egyptien monastichisme," *Oriens Christianus,* 49 (1965), 79–89.

6. Cf. Morán, A., "Congregaciones religiosas en el anglicanismo," *Manresa,* 32 (1960), 139–160; Hunt, L., "Ecumenismo in San Francisco: I francescani anglicani," *Vita Minorum,* Nov.-Dec. 1965, 49–58.

7. Cf. Mooy, S., "Taizé," *Convergência,* 3 (1970), 14–18; Malhei, M., "Redescubrimiento de la vida religiosa comunitaria en el protestantismo," *Teología y Vida,* 4 (1963), 105–112.

8. Cf. Estal, J. M., "Monaquismo en el Islam," *Ciudad de Dios,* 173 (1960), 560–583; Lechevalier, L., "Le monachisme et l'Islam," *Col-*

lectanea Cisterciensia, 29 (1967); Lindblom, J., *Prophecy in Ancient Israel,* Oxford, 1963, 66.

9. Cf. Müller, K., "Qumrán," *Sacramentum Mundi,* Barcelona, 1974, 5: 718–738, and its large bibliography.

10. Cf. Leclercq, J., "Impressions sur le monachisme en Inde," *Le défi de la vie contemplative,* Paris, 1970, 257–277; Lassier, S., "Le renoncement en Inde," *Christus,* 66 (1970), 249–258.

11. Cf. Leclercq, "Les leçons du monachisme bouddhiste," *Le défi de la vie contemplative,* 278–350; Masson, J., "Réalités sur-humaines et suprèmes dans le bouddhisme," *Studia Missionalia,* 17 (1968), 201–202; Enomiya Hugo, M., *Zen-Buddhismus,* Koeln, 1966; De Lubac, H., *Aspects du bouddhisme,* I; *Amida,* II, Paris, 1955.

12. Cf. Cornelius, E., "Phénomène universel de la vie religieuse," *Lumière et Vie,* 96 (1970), 4–24; "A vida religiosa na historia," *Convergência,* 3 (1970), the complete issue.

13. Reflections of Thomas Merton, *A via de Chuang Tzu,* Petrópolis, 1969, 13.

14. Cf. the classical works of Wach, J., *Das Wessen der religiösen Erfahrung,* Stuttgart, 1962, 53–79; Van der Leeuw, *Phaenomenologie der Religion,* Tübingen, 1956, 67, 522–527; Vergotte, A., *Psicología religiosa,* Madrid, 1973, 37–102; *L'homme et la religion,* Rome, 1968.

15. Cf. Hostie, R., *C. G. Jung und die Religion,* Freiburg-Munich, 1957, 135–201; C. G. Jung, *Z. Psycologie westlicher und oestlicher Religion, Complete Works,* vol. 11, Zurich-Stuttgart, 1963.

16. Cf. *Paulo VI e as religiosas,* Sao Paulo, 1968, 87.

17. Cf. Comblin, "Os fundamentos teologicos da vida religiosa," *REB,* 29 (1969), 308–352 (especially 338, note 62, where he makes critical reflections on other currents of thought different from ours, from a Thomistic point of view).

18. Cf. Boff, L., "Die Kirche als universale sacramentum salutis und die Religionen der Erde," *Die Kirche als Sakrament im Horizont des Welterfahrung,* Paderborn, 1972, 426–441.

19. Cf. Rahner, K., "Para la teología de la Encarnación," *Escritos de Teología,* Madrid, 1964, 4: 139–157; Kern, W., "La realidad—Cristo en el horizonte de nuestro mundo," *Mysterium Salutis,* Madrid, 1969, vol. 3, part 2, pp. 563–597; Pannenberg, W., *Fundamentos de Crostología,* Salamanca, 1974, 233–263; Boff, L., *Jesús Cristo Libertador,* Petrópolis, 1972, 193–222.

20. Cf. Boff, *O Evangelho do Cristo cosmico,* Petrópolis, 1971, 67–68.

21. Cf. the famous work of Bloch, E., *Das Prinzip Hoffnung,* 2 vols., Frankfurt, 1959; Moltmann, J., *Teología de la esperanza,* Salamanca, 1972; various authors, *Diskussion ueber die Theologie der Hoffnung,* Munich, 1967; Boff, *Vida para alèm da morte,* Petrópolis, 1972.

22. In regard to this contention, cf. Rahner in his important study, "Sobre la unidad del amor a Dios y el amor al prójimo," *Escritos in Teología,* 6: 271–292; Warnach, V., *Agape: Die Liebe als Grundmotiv der nt. Theologie,* Düsseldorf, 1951.

23. Benoit, P., "Corps, tête et plérôme dans les épîtres de la captivité, *Revue Biblique,* 63 (1956), 5–44; Robinson, J. A. T., *Le Corps: Étude sur la théologie de Saint Paul,* Lyon, 1966, 85–130; Veja Mensching, G., "Glaube und Nachfolge: Religions geschichtliche Gedanken ueber die Religion Jesu," *Gott Mensch,* Vieweg Verlag, 1948, 171–175.

24. Hengel, M., *Nachfolge und Charisma,* Berlin, 1968; Betz, H. D., *Nachfolge und Nachahmung Jesu Cristi im NT,* Tübingen, 1967; Schulz, A., *Nachfolgen und Nachahmen: Studien ueber das Verhaltnis der nt. Juengerschaft zur urchristlichen Vorbildethik,* Munich, 1962.

25. Van der Leeuw, G., *Phaenomenologie der Religion,* p. 554.

26. Cf. Dinkler, E., *Jesuworte vom Kreuztragen,* Berlin, 1954, 110–129.

Chapter 2

1. Augustine, *Sermo* 52. 6 (PL 38, 360). In *De Trinitate* (8. 8. 12), he says, "Do you think about what God is? Do you consider how he is God? Whatever you decide, he is not; whatever your mind comprehends, he is not. But no matter what it please you to accept, God is love. Love is what we can be sure of."

2. De Lubac, H., *Sur les chemins de Dieu,* Paris, 1956, 203.

3. Ibid., pp. 124–125.

4. In regard to the philosophical problems with the categories of immanence, transcendence, and transparency, cf. Boff, L., "Das Sakramentale denken: Legitimitat und Grenzen einer Sakralen Denkweise," in *Die Kirche als Sakrament im Horizont der Welterfahrung,* Paderborn, 1972, 123–181.

5. Chardin, T., *Le milieu divin,* Paris, 1957, 162. [English translation: *The Divine Milieu,* New York, 1965, 131—ed.]

6. Rehm, M., *Das Bild Gottes im Laten Testaments,* Würzburg, 1951; Eichrodt, W., *Das Gottesbild des Alten Testaments,* Stuttgart, 1956.

7. Among the most important texts: Rahner, K., "Gottererfahrungheute," *Schritten zur Theologie,* Zurich, 1970, 9: 161–176; Kasper, W., "Möglichkeiten der Gotteserfahrung heute," *Glaube und Geschichte,* Mainz, 1970, 120–158; Schupp, F., "Gotteserfahrung in der Säkularität: Diagnosen der Studien von Glauben und Theologie," *ZKTh,* 91 (1969), 493–500;

Ebeling, G., *Gott und Wort,* Tübingen, 1966; various authors, *Wer ist eigentlich Gott?,* Munich, 1969; Gadavsky, V., *Gott ist nicht ganz tot,* Munich, 1970; Schillebeeckx, E., *Interpretación de la fe,* Salamanca, 1973; Mouroux, J., *L'Expérience chrétienne: Introduction à une théologie,* Paris, 1954 (especially pp. 13–36); Morel, G., *Problèmes actuels de Religion,* Paris, 1968; Légaut, M., *L'homme à la recherche de son humanité,* Paris, 1971, 145–210; Ladrière, J., *L'articulation du sens,* Paris, 1970, 191–242; Dewart, L., *O futuro da fé,* Sao Paulo, 1970, 229–241; Schutz, C., "Experience of God Today?" *Monastic Studies,* 9 (1972), 7–22; Zellers, U., "Experiência de Deus em Tereza de Avila hoje," *Estudios,* 31 (1971), 53–63; Puntel, B. L., "Deus na Teología hoje," *Perspectiva Teológica,* 1 (1969), 15–24 (one of the best studies among those cited here); Almeida, L. M., "A experiência fundamental de Deus," *Cadernos Beneditinos,* 11 (1973), 5–26; Gomes, C. F., "Experiência de Deus e monaquismo hoje," ibid., 27–49; Vaz, H. de L., "A experiência de Deus," *Grande Sinal,* 27 (1973), 483–498; Roqueplo, P., *Expérience du monde: expérience de Dieu?* Paris, 1968; Roqueplo, P., *L'énérgie de la foi,* Paris, 1973; Ladrière, J., *La science, le monde et la foi,* Casterman, 1972; Döring, H., "Gotteser kenntnis oder Gotteserfahrung," *Theologie und Glaube,* 64 (1974), 89–114; Riesenhuber, K., *Experiência existecial e religiao,* Sao Paulo, 1972.

8. Cf. Foulquié, P., *Dictionnaire de la lengue philosophique,* Paris, 1962, 255–260; Kessler, A. S.; Schöpf, A.; Wild, C., "Erfahrung," in *Handbuch philosophischer Grundbegriffe,* Munich, 1973, 2: 373–386; Kasper, op. cit., 124–133.

9. Rombach, H., *Substanz, System, Struktur,* Freiburg-Munich, 1966; Chevalier, *Historia del pensamiento,* Madrid, 1969, vol. 3.

10. Wittgenstein, L., *Tractatus logico-philosophicus* (Schriften I), Frankfurt, 1969, 52.

11. Merton, *A via de Chuang-tzu,* p. 193.

12. Vaz, op. cit., especially note 30.

13. Cf. the studies of Arroyo, G., "Pensamiento latinoamericano sobre subdesarrollo y dependencia externa," and "Consideraciones sobre el subdesarrollo de América Latina," in *Fe cristiano y cambio social en América Latina,* Salamanca, 1973, 305–322 and 323–334, where he summarizes, with a large bibliography, the principal theories and authors that have offered interpretations of the Latin American situation.

14. Cf. *REB,* 34 (1974), 197.

15. Loc. cit.

16. Ibge, *Pesquisa Nacional por Amostra de Domicilios,* 1972, books 2 and 3.

17. Langoni, C. G., *Distribuiçao da Renda e Desenvolvimento Econŏmico do Brasil,* Rio de Janeiro, 1973, table 3.5, p. 64.

18. Jaguaribe, H., *Brasil: crise e alternativas,* Rio de Janeiro, 1974, pp. 55, 62.

19. *Análise de "modelo" brasileiro,* Rio de Janeiro, 1972, 77.

20. Marcuse, H., *Eros y civilización,* Mexico City, 1965, 83.

21. Segundo, J. L., *Nuestra idea de Dios* (*Teología abierta para el laicado adulto,* 3), Buenos Aires-Mexico City, 1970, 50.

22. De Lubac, *Sur les chemins de Dieu,* p. 125.

23. Remember the beautiful phrase of St. Augustine, "When He is thought to be absent, He is seen; when He is present, He is not seen," *De videndo Deo* (Letter 147 to Paulinus), 6. 18 (PL 33, 604).

24. Puntel, op. cit., pp. 22–23.

25. The idea of the diaphany and transparency of God in the world is strongly grounded in the theological and mystical tradition: "God completely within and completely without, exalted and intimate, flowing into us and around us. God above whom there is nothing, outside of whom there is nothing, without whom there is nothing. God under whom everything is, in whom everything is, with whom everything is" (Hilary, *De trinitate,* 1. 6). "Within God is spiritual height and depth; nor can the soul ever reach him unless it goes forth from itself" (Augustine, *In Ps. 130,* 12; PL 37, 1712). "God is within everything, outside everything, above everything, below everything. He is above through his power, below through his sustenance, outside through his greatness, inside through his intimacy. Ruling on high, upholding from below, surrounding from outside, penetrating within. In some ways above, in some ways beneath; in some ways outside, in some ways within, and yet completely one and the same everywhere—by sustaining, ruling; by ruling, sustaining; penetrating by surrounding and surrounding by penetrating" (Gregory the Great, *Moralia in Iob,* 11. 12.20). "Alpha and Omega, O Great God, . . . above all, below all, outside all; within all and yet not shut in; outside all and yet not shut out; above all and yet not exalted; beneath all and yet not in thrall. Above all, ruling; beneath all, sustaining; outside all, embracing; within all, filling; within, never compressed; outside, never attenuated; above, never held up; below, never worn down." (Hilderbert de Lavardin, *Carmina miscellanea,* 71; PL 171, 1411).

26. Rahner, op. cit., 166–167.

27. Boff, L., "El destino del hombre y del mundo, CLAR (25), Bogota, 1975, 22–23.

28. Cf. Grant, R. M., *Le Dieu des premiers chrétiens,* Paris, 1955; Pezeril, D., "Le Dieu de Jésus-Christ," in *N'avons-nous pas le même Père?,* Paris, 1972, 111–129; Schierse, F. J., "Der Gott Jesu—ein neuer Gott?," *Wort und Wahrheit,* 26 (1971), 191–203; Blank, J., *Jesus von Nazareth,* Herder, 1972, 58–68; Guillet, J., *Jésus devant sa vie et sa morte,* Paris, 1971, 221–242.

29. Cf. Boff, "Foi Jesus um revolucionário?," *REB,* 31 (1971), 97–118, where he cites bibliography from the end of the nineteenth century through 1971; Gonçalves, O. L., "Jesus e a contestaçao politica," *Vozes,* Petrópolis, 1974;

Hengel, M., *Eigentum und Reichtum in der frühen Kirche,* Stuttgart, 1973, 31–39. For all practical purposes, Palestine found itself living on the periphery from 587 B.C. on, dependent on the great Empires: Babylonia, until 538; Persia, until 331; Macedonia and Alexander, until 323; Ptolemaic Egypt, until 197; Seleucid Syria, until 166. It came under Roman power in the year 64. In the year 40 B.C., by a decree of the Senate, Herod, the son of Antipater, was proclaimed king of the Jews. He was a pagan, supported by Rome.

30. Cf. Jeremias, J., *Les paraboles de Jésus,* Paris, 1964, 194–199.

31. Cf. Mesters, C., "Jesus e o povo," in *Palavra de Deus na história dos homens,* Petrópolis, 1971, 2: 135–181; Boff, *Jesus Cristo Libertador,* pp. 76–112.

32. Samain, E., "O discurso-programa de Nazaret (Lc 4, 6–19)," *REB,* 34 (1974) 261–287.

33. Cf. Niederwimmer, K., *Jesus,* Göttingen, 1968, 53–70; Ernst, J., *Anfänge der Christologie, Stuttgart Bibel-Studien* 57, Stuttgart, 1972, 145–158.

34. Jeremias, *Teología del Nuevo Testamento,* Salamanca, 1974, 1: 87; Jeremias, "Abba," in *Abba: Studien zur neutestamentlichen Theologie und Zeitgeschichte,* Göttingen, 1966, 15–82.

35. Mesters, op. cit., p. 157.

36. Jeremias, *Teología del Nuevo Testamento,* p. 138.

37. Romer, K., *Esperar contra toda a esperanza,* Rio de Janeiro, 1973, 20.

38. Schierse, F. J., "La revelación de la Trinidad en el Nuevo Testamento," *Mysterium Salutis,* part 2, section 1, pp. 117–165; Duquoc, C., "Le dessein salvifique de la revélation de la Trinité en Saint Paul," *Lumière et Vie,* 29 (1956), 67–94; Lavalette, H. de, "Dreifaltgkeit," *LThK,* 3 (1959), 543–548.

39. Schierse very pertinently observes that "we must always avoid the false interpretation that Jesus' offered weak and cloudy views on the teachings of Christian faith and that the real, complete truth was defined by the Church later on. In reality quite the reverse happened: Jesus revealed, in his words and actions, the full, definitive truth, and all later explanations are merely tentative statements to explain conceptually this or that aspect of the content of revelation." (*La revelación de la Trinidad,* p. 126).

40. Ibid., p. 146 ff.

41. Rahner, "El Dios Trino como principio y fundamento transcendente de la historia de la salvación," *Mysterium Salutis,* part 2, section 1, p. 438. Rahner further explains, "Evidently we cannot ignore that, in the case of the Trinity, 'distinct form of subsistence' must not be understood to mean that this form is something later, a 'modality' without which something substantially real could also exist. The real divinity necessarily exists in three forms of subsistence, and one cannot conceive of a divinity which would be a real, prior basis for these forms (except as a merely rational abstraction).

Thus the one God is Father, Son, and Spirit'' (ibid., pp. 438–439).

42. Ibid., p. 383.

43. Van der Berg, A., ''A SS Trinidade e a existência humana,'' *REB*, 33 (1973), 629–644.

44. *Passio Sanctorum Sclitanorum, Lateinische, Märtyrerakten*, Munich, 1960, 25: ''Si tranquilas praebueris aures tuas, dico Mysterium Simplicitatis.''

45. *Paulo VI e as religiosas*, p. 87.

46. *A vida segundo o Espirito nas comunidades religiosas da America Latina*, CLAR, Rio de Janeiro, 1973, 17–23.

47. Cf. Tillard, *El proyecto de vida de los religiosos*, Madrid, 1974, 471.

48. Cf. Boff, ''A naturaleza espiritual do religioso,'' *Grande Sinal*, 26 (1972), 257–263.

49. Merton, T., ''La reconquista del Paraíso,'' in *Zen e as aves de rapina*, Rio de Janeiro, 173, 121.

50. Cf. chapter 3 of this same work.

51. Gutiérrez, *Teología de la liberación*, pp. 371–372.

52. Cf. Boff, *O Evangelho do Cristo cósmico*, pp. 57–63.

53. Cf. Merton, op. cit., p. 74.

54. Cf. the basic work of Kuiter, H. M., *Gott in Menschengestalt: Eine Dogmatisch-hermeneutische Studie über die Anthropomorphismen der Bibel*, Kaiser Verlag, Munich, 1967.

55. Cited by D. T. Suzuki in *Zen e as aves de rapina*, p. 124.

Chapter 3

1. Pomenius, *De vita contemplativa*, 3. 24 (PL 59, 470).

2. Augustine, *De civitate Dei*, 10. 6 (PL 41, 283).

3. Cf. *La pobreza e la religiosa hoje*, Sao Paulo, 1968, 35.

4. Cf. Séjourné, P., ''Voeux de religion,'' *DThC*, 15 (1950), col. 3.271 ff.

5. Ibid.

Chapter 4

1. There are a great number of books and articles about the problem of poverty, although they are not oriented to the true perspective nor do they orient one toward the true perspective. We mention only those we deem most suitable: González Ruíz, J. M., *Pobreza evangélica y promoción humana*, Barcelona, 1968; Hauck, F., and

Brammel, E., "Ptochós," in *ThWNT,* 6: 885–915; Jeremias, J., "¿Quienes son los pobres?" in *Teología del Nuevo Testamento,* 1: 134–138; Boff, "A pobreza no mistério do homen e de Cristo," *Grande Sinal,* 28 (1974), 163–183; Gutiérrez, G., "Pobreza, solidaridad y protesta," *Teología de la liberación,* Lima, 1971, 351–372; CLAR, *La pobreza evangélica hoy,* Bogota, 1971; CLAR, *Pobreza y Vida Religiosa na America Latina,* Rio de Janeiro, 1969.

2. Ruiz, p. 31.

3. *Contra gentiles,* 3. 134.

4. CLAR, "Los pobres y la pobreza en los Evangelios y en los Hechos," in *La pobreza evangélica hoy,* pp. 27–44.

5. *Los pobres de Yavé,* Barcelona, 1965, 145.

6. *Teología del Nuevo Testamento,* 1: 138.

7. *Los pobres de Yavé,* p. 37.

8. Jeremias, op. cit., pp. 134 ff.

9. Op. cit., p. 37.

10. *Teología de la liberación,* p. 370.

Chapter 5

1. Carrel, A., *La incógnita del hombre,* Barcelona, 1941.

2. This is a deep mystery before which St. Augustine, both with amazement and inquiry, asked himself, "Who am I and how do I exist. . . ? Therefore, what am I, my God?" (*Confessions,* 9. 1 and 10. 17). The person is the mystery and the answer, the problem and the solution; he is both the sphinx and Oedipus. One's entire being is marked by this.

3. Beauvoir, Simone de, *El Segundo Sexo* (2 vols.), Buenos Aires, 1970.

4. Ricoeur, P., *Finitude et culpabilité,* Paris, 1960, 2: 13, 220, etc. As Ricoeur rightly said, "Eve is not woman in the sense of a second sex; every woman and every man is Adam, and every man and every woman is Eve. Every woman sins in Adam, and every man is seduced in Eve" (p. 239). As bibliography on this theme let us cite the following: Dumas, F. A., *A dialética do homen-mulher no mundo atual,* Petrópolis, 1967; Devaux, A., *Teilhard e a vocaçao da mulher,* Petrópolis, 1967; Jeannière, A., *Antropología sexual,* Sao Paulo, 1965, especially pp. 104–117; Bieliauskas, J., "Aspects psycologiques de la masculinité et de la femininité," in *Mariage et célibat,* Paris, 1965, pp. 117–134; Braunschweig, D., and Fain, M., *Éros et Antéros,* Paris, 1971; Buytendijk, F., *La femme: Ses modes d'être, de paraître, d'exister,* Desclée de Brouwer, 1967; Deutsch, H., *La psycologie des femmes,* Paris, 1949; Mead, M., *Macho e Fémea,* Petrópolis, 1973; Mead, M., *Sexo y temperamento,* Buenos Aires, 1955, pp. 149–156; Rouge-

mont, D., *L'amour et L'Occident,* Paris, 1939; Muraro, R. M., *A mulher na construçao do mundo futuro,* Petrópolis, 1973; Muraro, R. M., *Libertaçao sexual da mulher,* Petrópolis, 1971; Lersch, T., *Von Wesen des Geschlechter,* Munich, 1947; Neumann, E., *Die Grosse Mutter: Der Archetyp des grossen Weiblichen,* Zurich, 1956; Valabregue, C., *La condition masculine,* Paris, 1968; Weininger, *Sesso e carattere,* Milan, 1912; Scherer, G., *Nueva comprensión de la sexualidad,* Salamanca, 1968; Hegel, G., *Phaenomenologie des Geistes,* Hamburg, 1952, especially pp. 318–330; Neumann, E., *Ein Beitrag zur seelischen Entwicklung des Weiblichen,* Zurich, 1952; Neumann, E., *Ursprungsgeschichte des Bewustseins,* Munich, 1968; Bachofen, J., *Mutterrecht und Urreligion,* Stuttgart, 1954; Jung, C. G., *Tipos psicológicos,* Rio de Janeiro, 1974, especially pp. 476–481; Jung, C. G., *Symbole der Wandlung,* Zurich, 1952; Jung, C. G., *Mysterium conjunctionis,* Zurich, 1968; Marañón, G., *Los estados intersexuales en la especie humana, Complete Works,* vol. 3, Madrid, 1967, 155–185; Marañón, G., *Intersexualidad histológica e intersexualidad química, Complete Works,* vol. 3, pp. 225–228; Marañón, G., *Revisión del concepto de la evolución de la sexualidad humana, Complete Works,* vol. 3, pp. 445–460; Marañón, G., *Los estados intersexuales en la pubertad, Complete Works,* vol. 3, pp. 511–523; Marañón, G., *Asimetía de los caracteres sexuales, Complete Works,* vol. 2, pp. 267–269; Lestapis, E., *La pareja humana,* Barcelona, 1971; Vela, L., "La relación varón-mujer," *Misión abierta,* 3 (1976), 30–34; Amezua, E., "Sexualidad y pareja," *Misión abierta,* 3 (1976), 35–41; Cencillo, L., "Alienación, frustración y liberación de la mujer," *Misión abierta,* 3 (1976), 22–29; Forcano, B., "Sentido y contenido cristiano de la sexualidad," *Misión abierta,* 3 (1976), 47–60.

5. Cf. the reflections of Larrain, H., "El celibato: punto de vista psicológico," *Mensaje,* 15 (1966), 367–377.

6. Cf. Boff, L., *El destino del hombre y del mundo,* especially "Hombre y mujer: uno bajo la mirada del otro," pp. 65–66; Díez Presa, M., "Virginidad y madurez humana," *Vida religiosa,* 303 (1976), 53–66.

Chapter 6

1. Aristotle, *De anima,* 3. 8. 431 b 21; Thomas, *De anima,* 3. 13, n. 787 ff.

2. On these perspectives on obedience one can profitably consult: "Obéissance religieuse et exercise de l'autorité, by various authors, in *Donum Dei* (Cahiers de la Conférence Religieuse Canadienne, 3), Ottawa, 1961; Muller, A., *El problema de la obediencia en la Iglesia,* Madrid, 1970; Rahner, K., *Marginales sobre la autoridad y la obediencia,* Madrid, 1962; Ranquet,

J., "La obediencia," in *Consejos evangélicos y madurez humana,* Madrid, 1969, 99–156; various authors, *L'obéissance et la religieuse d'aujour d'hui,* Paris, 1951; Rueda, B., *Redescubrir la obediencia,* Madrid, 1975; Gutiérrez-Vega, L., *Autoridad y obediencia en la vida religiosa,* Madrid, 1974; various authors, *¿Nuevo estilo de obediencia?* Santander, 1971; Hausherr, I., *La obediencia religiosa,* Bilbao, 1968; "Las virtudes humanas en la formación sacerdotal," *Seminarium,* 21 (1969), 369–572.

Chapter 7

1. The bibliography on this is abundant, but of varying value. Among the best we cite: Bejer, S., "Sécularité et consecration del la vie dans les Institutes séculiers," *Gregorianum,* 51 (1970), 433–484; Gutiérrez, A., "Consecratio et saecularitas in Institutis saecularibus," *Commentarium pro religiosis et missionariis,* 51 (1970), 193–207; Granero, J., "La sociedad moderna y la vida religiosa," and Guerrero, J., "La vida religiosa frente a la secularización," both in *Manresa,* 42 (1970), 243–252 and 115–124; Fernández, D., "La renovación de la vida religiosa en un mundo secularizado," *Pastoral misionera,* 5 (1970), 490–502; Sebastián Aguilar, F., *Secularización en la vida religiosa,* PPC, Madrid, 1970; Gutiérrez, L., "La secularización en la vida religiosa," *Confer,* 15 (1970), 41–56; Bovis, A., "Vie religieuse et sécularisation," *La vie consacrée,* 41 (1969); De Bont, W., "La sécularisation de la pensée" and "La sécularisation de l'eschaton," *La vie spirituelle,* suppl. 32 (1969), 5–28 and 462–482; Ruiz, J., "Vida espiritual y secularización," *Manresa,* 41 (1969), 341–352; García, J., and Isusi, B., *El reto de la sociedad moderna a la vida religiosa,* Bilbao, 1970; Guerrero, J., and Rondet, M., *El porvenir del la vida religiosa en el mundo secularizado,* Bilbao, 1970; Comblin, J., "Os religiosos e o mundo," *REB,* 29 (1969), 550–579—this is one of the most enlightening studies that has been done; Perani, P., "Vida religiosa e secularizaçao," *Convergencia,* 4 (1971), 61–64; Hortal, J., "Estado de vida consagrada—estado secular," *Perspectiva teológica,* 3 (1971), 197–212.

2. Comblin, op. cit., p. 555.

3. In the theology of St. John consecration always implies mission. Christ is consecrated and sent into the world (Jn. 10:36). In his high priestly prayer, Jesus prays to the Father to sanctify and consecrate the disciples and send them, as the Father has sent him (Jn. 17:17–19). Cf. Thusing, W., *Herrilchkeit und Einheit: Eine Auslegung des hohen-*

priesterlichen Gebets Johannes, Dusseldorf, 1962, 91–97; Bultmann, R., *Das Evangelium des Johannes,* Gottingen, 1964, 389–392.

4. Comblin, "A vida religiosa como consecraçao," *Grande Sinal,* 24 (1970), 21–30.

5. The literature on this theme abounds in almost all languages. Cf. Koppenburg, B., *O cristao secularizado,* Petrópolis, 1970; Lepargneur, H., *A secularizaçao,* Sao Paulo, 1971; Koch, D., *Fundamento secular cristao do desenvolvimento,* Petrópolis; Comblin, *Secularización: mitos, realidades y problemas, Concilium,* vol. 47 (1969), 115–126; various authors, *Les deux visages de la theologié de la sécularisation,* Castermann, 1970.

6. Von Rad, G., *Theologie des Alten Testamentes,* pp. 160–162; Scheffczyk, L., *Der Mensch als Bild Gottes: Wege der Forschung,* vol. 124, Darmstadt, 1969. This work brings together all the efforts of the last decades under one heading.

7. Cf. Boff, "Cristianismo, fator de um humanismo secular planetário," *Vozes,* 64 (1970), 461–468.

8. *GS,* 36, where is added: "The person who with perseverance and humility is able to penetrate the secrets of reality is raised up, even without knowing it, as by the hand of God, who assures that all things have consistency and that they may be what they are."

9. *AA,* 7. There is added how "it is necessary that secular people take on the responsibility which is specifically theirs to restore the temporal order, and, guided by the light of the Gospel and the mind of the Church and motivated by Christian charity, that they take part in this order directly and in a concrete way."

10. *GS,* 43.

11. Cf. Bauer, A., *Freiheit zur Welt Versandnis und Weltverhaeltnis des Christen nach der Theologie Friedrich Gogartens,* Paderborn, 1967, especially pp. 51–55.

12. Cf. Moltmann, J., *Sobre la libertad, la alegria y el juego,* Salamanca, 1972; *El lenguaje de la liberación,* Salamanca, 1974; "Dios reconcilia y hace libres," *Selecciones de teologia,* 1971, 214–222; Cox, H., *La fiesta de los locos,* Madrid, 1972.

13. *PC,* 2; *LG,* 44.

14. Sebastián Aguilar, op. cit., p. 160; Fernández, op. cit., note 1, pp. 21–22.

15. Comblin, "Os religiosos e o mundo," p. 562.

16. *GS,* 39.

17. Cf. Cardinal Alfrink, "E preciso anunciar as riquezas do Senhor," *Grande Sinal,* 25 (1970), 25–28.

18. Boff, "Elementos para una teologia da fossa," *Vozes,* 65 (1971), 64–66; and "A funçao do humor na teologia e na Igreja," *Vozes,* 64 (1970), 571–572.

19. *LG,* 46; cf. Pius XII, alocution *Annus sacer, AAS,* 43 (1951), 30.

Chapter 8

1. Rahner, *Trevas e luz na ordçao,* Sao Paulo, 1961, foreword.

2. Kung, H., *Veracidad: El futuro de la Iglesia,* Barcelona, 1970.

3. Ibid., p. 25.

4. Burgalassi, S., "O drama dos "ex" una soluççao ilusória?," in *Padres amanha,* IDO-C 2, Petrópolis, 1970, 153.

5. Bishop, H., *Os teólogos da morte de Deus,* Sao Paulo, 1969; see also the October, 1969, issue of *Times.*

6. Cf. Rahner and Greinacher, H., *Handbuch der Pastoraltheologie,* vol. 2, part 1, Freiburg, 1966, 208–214.

7. Cf. *GS,* 36 and 43; *AA,* 7.

8. Cf. *GS,* 36; Kloppenburg, B., *O cristao secularizado,* Petrópolis, 1970, 27–28.

9. Leist, F., *Der Mensch im Bann der Bilder,* Munich, 1966.

10. Cox, *The Secular City,* London, 1965, 49–58.

11. Horney, K., *Der neurotische Mensch unserer Zeit,* Munich, 1968.

12. Bro, B., *Aprendendo a rezar,* Sao Paulo, 1970, preface.

13. Cf. various authors, *La prière,* Paris, 1958; Jacquemont, P., *Oser prier ou l'originalité du chrêtien,* Paris, 1960, Cognet, L., *La prière du chrêtien,* Paris, 1966; Rhyner, D., *Prayer in the Secular City,* London, 1967; Hinnebusch, P., *La oración, búsqueda de autenticidad,* Santander, 1970; Bloom, A., *Oración viva,* Bilbao, 1969; Galot, J., *La oración, intimidad filial,* Bilbao, 1969; Leclercq, J., "Prière et Vitesse," in *Le défi de la vie contemplative,* Paris, 1970; D'Hoogh, F., "La oración en una sociedad secularizada," in *Concilium,* 49 (1969), 359–375; Guerra, A., "Crisis de la oración personal en un mondo secularizado," *Revista de espiritualidad* (1970), 7–48; Bethge, E., "Le culte dans un monde séculier," *Communio* (1970), 42–60.

14. Cf. the principal bibliography: Hamman, A., *La prière,* vol. 1: *The New Testament,* Paris, 1958; Nielen, J., *Gebet und Gottesdienst im Neuen Testament,* Freiburg, 1937; Jeremias, J., "Das tägliche im Leben Jesu und in der ältesten Kirche," in *Abba,* Gittingen, 1966, 67–80; Kerkhoff, R., *Das unablässige Gebet,* Munich, 1954.

15. Cf. Norden, E., *Agnostos Theos,* Leipzig, 1923, 280–308.

16. Strahtmann, H., *Das Evangelium nach Johannes,* Gottingen, 1963, 23.

17. Ott, W., *Gebet und Heil,* Munich, 1965; Hamman, op. cit., 144–158.

18. Kerkhoff, op. cit., 58–60.

19. Jeremias, op. cit., 152–171.

20. Leclercq, op. cit., 118.

21. Cf. D. T., "Was macht uns heute das Beten schwer?," *Der Grosse Entschluss,* 19 (1964), 337 ff.

22. *Escritos completos de San Francisco de Asís* (BAC, 4), Madrid, 1949, 576; cf. Koper, R., *Das*

Weltverständnis des Hl. Franziskus von Assisi, Werl, 1959, 83–93.

23. Cf. Benedetto, L., *Il cantico di Fratre Sole,* Firenze, 1941; Scheffczyk, L., "Der 'Sonnengesang' des Hl. Franziskus von Assisi und die 'Hymne an die Materie' des Th. de Chardin," *Geist und Leben,* 35 (1962), 219–233.

24. Sauer, E., *Die religiöse Wertung der Welt in Bonaventuras Itinerarium mentis in Deum,* Werl, 1937, 58–60; Bougerol, G., "Structuration des trois voies de la vie spirituelle dans la pensée de Saint Bonaventure," *Études Franciscaines,* 19 (1969), 397–410.

25. Chardin, T., "Genèse d'une pensée," *Lettres 1914–1919,* Paris, 1964.

26. Cf. Boff, *O Evangelho do Cristo cósmico,* 46–49.

27. *Monumenta Ignatiana,* 1. 3, p. 502.

28. Ibid., p. 510.

29. Cf. Libanio, J., "Pecado e Opçao fundamental," *Atualizaçao,* 12 (1970), 31–42, and 13–14 (1971), 27–36; Flick-Alzeghy, "L'opzione fundamentale della vita morale e la grazia," *Gregorianum,* 41 (1960), 593–619; Reiners, H., *Grundintention und sittliches Tun,* Freiburg, 1966.

30. Cf. Gibbard, M., "La oración en tiempo de duda," *Concilium* 52 (1970), 169–185.

31. *AA,* 7.

32. Cf. Danielou, J., *Oraçao problema politico,* Petrópolis, 1966, 17–31.

33. Cf. Chomsky, N., *Linguajem e pensamiento,* Petrópolis, 1971; Pesch, O., *Sprechender Glaube,* Mainz, 1970, 45–68; Ebeling, G., *Der dialogische Personalismus in der evangelischen und katolischen Theologie,* Paderborn, 1963, 266–271.

34. Cf. Callois, R., "Théorie de la Fête," *Nouvelle Revue Française,* 53 (1939), later collected in his book, *L'homme et le sacré,* Paris, 1950, 121–162. One of the best analyses has been done by J. Pieper, *Zustimmung zur Welt: Eine Theorie des Festes,* Munich, 1963; Aubry, A., *"Liturgia, Fiesta e Imaginacion,"* *Concilium* 49 (1969), 376–389; the complete number 58 of *Lumière et Vie* (1962); Cox, H., *La fiesta de los locos;* Moltmann, J., *Sobre la libertad, la alegría y el juego,* Salamanca, 1972; Rizzi, A., "La fiesta verità dell'uomo," *Rivista Liturgica,* 57 (1970), 236–247.

35. Cited by Pieper, op. cit., p. 81.

36. Cf. *Nachgelassene Aufzeichnungen aus den Jahren 1882 bis 1888, Complete Works,* vol. 16, p. 37.

37. Nietzsche, F., *Der Wille zur Macht,* book 4, n. 1032.

38. Cf. Pesch, O., op. cit., pp. 75–76 (n. 30); Rahner, "Thesen zum Thema 'Glaube und Gebet'," in *Geist und Leben,* 1969, 177–184.

39. Cf. *Fröhliche Wissenschaft* 3, sayings 343 and 125, Darmstadt, 1960, 205 and 126–127; Cox, *La fiesta de los locos,* in the chapter, "La fiesta y la muerte de Dios."

40. Cf. Jolif, J., "L'homme a

besoin de la fête, *Lumière et Vie,* 58 (1962), 15.

41. Saint-Exupêry, A., *El Principito, Complete Works,* vol. 1, Barcelona, 1967, p. 556; cf. Bouyer, L., *L'homme et le rite,* Paris, 1964; Langer, S., *Das Symbol im Denken, im Ritus und in der Kunst,* Berlin, 1957, 146–171.

42. Saint-Exupêry, op. cit., pp. 555–556.

43. Ibid., p. 555.

44. Guardini, R., *El espíritu de la liturgia,* Barcelona, 1946, 137–157.

45. Thomas, 2–2, q. 168, aa. 2–4.

46. Cf. Rahner, H., *Der spielende Mensch,* Einseldeln, 1960.

47. Moltmann, op. cit.

48. Gregory Nazianzus, *Carmina,* 1. 2.2, verse 589; PG 37, 624.

49. Plato, *Laws,* 644 D.

50. Rahner, H., op. cit., p. 26 (n. 40).

51. Cf. Boff, "A funçao do humor na teologia en na Igreja," *Vozes,* 64 (1970), 571–572; Leclercq, "Actualité de l'humour," in op. cit., pp. 359–368; Trueblood, E., *The humor of Christ,* London, 1965; Carreteio, J., "Sobre el humor y la ascética," *Manresa,* 38 (1966), 13–32.

52. Lersch, T., *Philosophe des humors,* Munich, 1953, 26.

53. Leclercq, op. cit., p. 137.

54. Bossis, G., *Lui e io,* Turin, 1963.

55. Hammarskjöld, Dag, *Pensamientos,* Rio de Janeiro, 1967, 218. [Eng. trans. *Markings,* New York, 1964, 214–215—ed.]

Chapter 9

1. Cf. the bibliography on underdevelopment collected in *In Search of a Theology of Development: A Sodepax Report* (Cartigny, Switzerland), 1969; *Towards a Theology of Development: An Annotated Bibliography Prepared for Sodepax,* 1969; cf. Boff, "Evangelizaçao e promoçao humana," *Atualizaçao,* 25–26 (1972), 58–78. There are a great many books on the theology of liberation: cf. Vekemans, R., *Desarollo y revolución, Iglesia y liberación,* Bogota, 1972, Barcelona, 1972; various authors, *Bibliografía de la teología de la liberación,* OCSHA, Madrid, 1972; *Encuentro de El Escorial,* 1972; *Fe cristiana y cambio social en América Latina,* Salamanca, 1973, 391–415; Monte, F., *Teología de la liberación,* revised bibliography in *Mensaje* (1973), 277–283. A representative book published under the auspices of CELAM is *Liberación: Diálogos en el CELAM,* Bogota, 1974.

2. Cf. Assmann, H., "Evangelización y liberación," in *Teología desde la praxis de la liberación,* Salamanca, 1973, 141–156; Scannone, J., "Teología, cultura popular y discernimiento," *Revista del Centro de Investigación y Acción Social,* 23 (1974), 3–24.

3. Cf. Gutiérrez, *Teología de la liberación,* 35–59.

4. Cf. the significant documents of CLAR: *La dimensión política de la vida religiosa* and *Tendencias proféticas de la vida religiosa en América Latina,* SEDOC, 1975.

5. Cf. Boff, *Atulaidade da experiência de Deus,* Rio de Janeiro, 1974, 33–41.

6. Cf. Vidales, C., *Cuestiones en torno al método de la teología de la liberación,* Lima, 1972; Dussel, E., *Método de una filosofía de la liberación,* Salamanca, 1974, 50–87.

7. The bibliography on this theme is large. The Brazilian viewpoint is expressed principally by C. Furtado, F. Cardoso, F. Fernandes, O. Ianni, T. do Santos, and others. There is a good approach in Comblin, J., *Théologie de la pratique révolutionnaire,* Paris, 1974, 118–127; also excellent are the studies cited earlier: Arroyo, G., "Pensamiento latinoamericano sobre el subdesarollo y dependencia externa" and "Consideraciones sobre el desarollo de América Latina," in *Fe cristiana y cambio social en América Latina,* Salamanca, 1973, 305–322 and 323–334.

8. This terminology is used by Paulo Freire, *Concretización,* Buenos Aires, 1974, 67.

9. Cf. Sunkel, O., and Paz, P., *El subdesarollo latinoamericano y la teoría del desarollo,* Mexico City, 1970; Amin, Samir, *Le développement inégal,* Paris, 1972.

10. Freire, op. cit., p. 65.

11. Cf. Langoni, C., *Distribuçao da renda econômica do Brasil,* Rio de Janeiro, 1973, 64; Jaguaribe, H., *Brasil: Crise e alternativas,* Rio de Janeiro, 1974, 55; Sodrè, N., *O modelo politico brasileiro,* Petrópolis, 1974.

12. Freire, op. cit., pp. 68–70.

13. Cf. Scannone, "La liberación latinoamericana, ontología del proceso auténticamente liberador," *Stromata,* 18 (1972), 107–150 and 150–160; Boff, "Teologia da captividade, A anti-historia dos humilhados e ofendidos" and "Ainda a teologia da captividade," in *Grande Sinal,* 28 (1974), 355–368, 426–441.

14. Cf. Dussel, *Hipótesis para una historia de la Iglesia en América Latina,* Barcelona, 1967.

15. Cf. Hoonaert, E., *Formaçao do catolicismo brasileiro: 1500–1800,* Petrópolis, 1974, 31–65.

16. Helder Cámara, "Libertaçao humana e evangelizaçao," *REB,* 34 (1974), 976.

17. A history of the Church in Brazil that analyzes its presence in society from the perspective of those oppressed and marginated by the power structure is still lacking. The CEHILA called for a two-volume work written from this perspective. Cf. Bruneau, T., *O catolicismo brasileiro en época de transiçao,* Sao Paulo, 1974.

18. Comblin, op. cit., p. 65.

19. Cf. the important work for understanding the new consciousness of the Church by R. Muñoz, *Nueva conciencia de la Iglesia en América Latina,* Salamanca, 1974.

20. Alonso, A., *Iglesia y praxis de liberación,* Salamanca, 1974; Gera, L., "Aspectos eclesiológicos de la

teología de la liberación," in *Liberación: Diálogos en el CELAM,* 381–400.

21. Cf. Arias, M., *Salvaçao hoje,* Petrópolis, 1974, 23–32.

22. Cf. Avila, R., *Teología, evangelización y liberación,* Bogota, 1973; Gutiérrez, G., "Praxis de la liberación, teología y liberación," in *Liberación: Diálogos en el CELAM,* 68–100; Seminario de estudios IPLA, *Pastoral popular y liberación en América Latina,* Quito, 1972; AA, *Hombre nuevo: nueva educación,* Santo Domingo, 1972; Alonso, op. cit., pp. 197–247; various authors, *O Sinodo de 1974: A evangelizaçao no mundo de hoje,* Sao Paulo, 1974.

23. Cf. Schurmann, H., "Das hermeneutische Hauptproblem der Verkündigung Jesu," in *Traditionsgeschichtliche Untersuchungen zu den synoptischen Evangelien,* Düsseldorf, 1968, 13–25; Gnilka, I., *Jesus Christus nach frühen Zeugnissen des Glaubens,* Munich, 1970; Dodd, C. H., *The Apostolic Preaching and Its Development,* London, 1935, 1951.

24. Cf. Boff, Jesús Cristo Libertador, pp. 77–79.

25. Cf. González Laus, J., *La nueva humanidad,* Madrid, 1974, 1: 124–145; Boff, "Libertaçao de Jesús Cristo pelo caminho da opressao," *Grande Sinal,* 28 (1974), 589–615.

26. Cf. Duquoc, C., *Christologie,* Paris, 1972, 2: 224–226.

27. Cf. SEDOC, 3 (1970), 158–162; cf. the opening speech to the 1974 Synod of Bishops by Paul VI in *REB,* 34 (1974), 932–933; Boff, "Evangelizaçao e promoçao humana: sus implicaçoes teologicas e politicas," *Atualizaçao,* 25 (1972), 58–78.

28. *REB,* 34 (1974), 940.

29. Cf. CLAR, *Vida segundo o Espirito nas comunidades religiosas da America Latina* (RB, 9), Rio de Janeiro, 1974, 21–23.

30. Azevedo, M., "Evangelizaçao e vida religiosa," *Convergencia,* 8 (1975), 71–86.

31. Cf. Figueiredo, F., "Autoridade e obediência na Igreja," *REB,* 34 (1974), 586–599; Boff, "Tensao entre a busca de realizaçao pessoal e a obediência religiosa," *REB,* 34 (1974), 329–342; Gutiérrez-Vega, L., *Autoridad y obediencia en la vida religiosa,* Madrid, 1974.

32. Cf. CLAR, "Dimensao politica da vida religiosa," in SEDOC, 1975; "Tendencias profeticas da vida religiosa na America Latina," in SEDOC, 1975.

33. Cf. CLAR, *Pobreza e vida religiosa na América Latina* (CRB, 4), Rio de Janeiro, 1970; Gutiérrez, *Teología de la liberación,* pp. 351 ff.

34. Cf. Alves, R., *Il figlio del domani,* Brescia, 1972, 188.

35. Cf. Guzmán, J., "La negación de lo 'cristiano' como afirmación de la fe," in *Pueblo oprimido, señor de la historia,* Montevideo, 1972, 35–48.

36. From this statement we cannot generalize the idea of the impossibility of the Catholic school. The Church can and must maintain its centers of formation and education

imbued with Gospel values and the Catholic world view. And yet, we believe this does not require adopting the entrepreneurial form we find in existing Catholic schools. This entrepreneurial form, by placing the school within the prevailing socio-economic system, obscures its Gospel witness. We believe a school or center of formation imbued with a Catholic world view can, through foundations or other means external to the school, perfectly witness to the Gospel.

37. Frei Betto, "Exigências da conversao cristá," *Grande Sinal,* 29 (1975), 178–179.

38. Cf. *A vida religiosa na Igreja particular,* Sao Paulo, 1974; CLAR, *Significado de las comunidades religiosas en las Iglesias locales de América Latina,* Bogota, 1975.

39. Cf. Freire, P., "Educación, liberación, Iglesia," in *Teología negra, teología de la liberacíon,* Salamanca, 1974, 13–48.

40. Cf. Libano, J., *A consciência critica do religioso,* Rio de Janeiro, 1974.

41. Freire, *Educaçao como prática da liberdade,* Rio de Janeiro, 1974, 50–55.

42. Cf. the three volumes: *Educación liberadora* (*Dimensiones politica, sociológica, metodológica,* Bogota, 1973; CLAR, *El religioso educator,* Bogota, 1975.

43. In addition to the works of Freire cited, cf. *Pedagogía do oprimido,* Rio de Janeiro, 1974; *Conscientisation et révolution,* Paris, 1973.

44. Freire, op. cit., p. 63.

45. Comblin, "Atualidade da teologia da missao (III)," *REB,* 33 (1973), 584.

46. Cf. Hoonaert, "A evangelizaçao segundo a tradiçao guadalupana," *REB,* 34 (1975), 543.

47. Cf. Hoonaert, "Para una história da Igreja no Brasil," *REB,* 35 (1975), 129–131.

48. Cf. Hoonaert, "A tradiçao lascasiana no Brasil," *REB,* 70 (1970), 850–870.

49. Cf. Mendes, C., "Memento dos vivos," op. cit., 77–115; Bruneau, T., *O catolicismo brasileiro em época de transiçao,* Sao Paulo, 1974, 137.

50. Documentos Pontificios, 184, Petrópolis, 1972, 16 (n. 47).

51. Freire, *Pedagogía do oprimido,* Rio de Janeiro, 1974, 218.

Chapter 10

1. De Lubac, *Sur les chemins de Dieu,* p. 125.

2. Cf. chapter 2, "How God appears in the Oppressed World of Latin America."

3. "Vida según el Espíritu," nn. 96–97.

4. Cf. *LG* 44, *PC,* 5.

5. Cf. *LG* 44, *PC,* 2, 5, 8.

6. Cf. *LG,* 46, and *GS,* 39.

7. "Vida según el Espíritu," n. 101.

8. Tillard, J., *Religiosos: una presencia en el mundo,* Madrid, 1976, 53–54.

9. "Dimensión política de la vida religiosa," p. C, c.

10. Tillard, op. cit., p. 64.

11. Matura, T., "Crear una comunidad religiosa hoy," in *La comunidad religiosa,* Madrid, 1972, 301.

12. "Dimensión política de la vida religiosa," III, B.

13. Cf. *LG,* 31.

14. Gutiérrez, G., *Teologia de la liberación,* 371–372.

15. Cf. *PC,* 6.

16. Thomas, 2–2, q. 188, a. 6.

17. *PC,* 5.

18. Saint-Exupéry, *Carta a un rehén,* Complete Works, 1: 495.

19. Gutiérrez-Vega, L., "Reflexión teológica sobre la especificidad evangelizadora de la vida religiosa," in *Los religiosos y la evangelización de mundo contemporáneo,* Madrid, 1975, 147.

20. Alves, R., *Fihos de amamhà,* 1974, 206–207.

List of Abbreviations

AA	Apostolicam actuositatem
AAS	Acta apostolicae sedis
BAC	Biblioteca de Autores Cristianos
CEHILA	Bishops Conference on the History of the Church in Latin America
CELAM	Latin American Conference of Bishops
CLAR	Latin American Conference of Religious
DThC	Dictionary of Catholic Theology
GS	Gaudium et spes
IPLA	Pastoral Institute of Latin America
LG	Lumen gentium
LThK	Lexicon for Theology and Church
MThZ	Munich Theological Journal
NRTh	New Theological Review
PC	Perfectae caritatis
PG	Patrologia Graeca (Migne)
PL	Patrologia Latina (Migne)
REB	Brazilian Ecclesiastical Review
ThWNT	Theological Dictionary of the New Testament
ZKTh	Journal for Catholic Theology